Anonymous

The Works of Ossian, the Son of Fingal

Vol. 1 containing, Fingal, an ancient epic Poem. Third Edition

Anonymous

The Works of Ossian, the Son of Fingal
Vol. 1 containing, Fingal, an ancient epic Poem. Third Edition

ISBN/EAN: 9783337297756

Printed in Europe, USA, Canada, Australia, Japan

Cover: Foto ©Suzi / pixelio.de

More available books at **www.hansebooks.com**

THE
WORKS
OF
OSSIAN,
THE
SON of FINGAL.

IN TWO VOLUMES.

Tranflated from the GALIC LANGUAGE

By JAMES MACPHERSON.

VOL. I. containing,

FINGAL, an Ancient EPIC POEM,

IN SIX BOOKS;

AND

SEVERAL OTHER POEMS.

Fortia faƈtu patrum.   VIRG.

THE THIRD EDITION.

LONDON:
Printed for T. BECKET and P. A. DEHONDT,
at Tully's Head, near Surry Street, in the Strand.
MDCCLXV.

EARL of BUTE,

Knight of the moſt Noble Order of the Garter, &c. &c.

MY LORD,

I Preſume to preſent to your lordſhip a com‑ pleat edition of the Works of Oſſian. They have already been honored with your approbation, and have been received with applauſe by men of taſte throughout Eu‑ rope. This addreſs therefore is not an en‑ deavor to ſecure the continuance of the pub‑ lic favor through the ſanction of your name. Little ſolicitous myſelf about the reputation of an author, I permit, with no concern, the Old Bard to take his chance with the world : It proceeds, my Lord, from another cauſe ; the ambition of being hereafter known to have met with your favor and protection in the execution of this work ; an honor which will be envied me, perhaps, more ſome time

hence

DEDICATION.

hence than at prefent. I throw no reflexions on this age, but there is a great debt of fame ówing to the EARL of BUTE, which hereafter will be amply paid : there is alfo fome fhare of reputation with-held from Offian, which lefs prejudiced times may beftow. This fimilarity between the Statefman and the Poet, gives propriety to this dedication ; though your Lordfhip's avowed patronage of literature requires no adventitious aid to direct to you the addreffes of authors. It is with pleafure I embrace this opportunity of teftifying in public with what perfect attachment,

    I am,

       my Lord,

          your Lordfhip's moft humble,

          moft obliged,

          and moft obedient fervant,

          JAMES MACPHERSON.

CONTENTS.

CAR-

CONTENTS.

A

DISSERTATION

CONCERNING THE

ANTIQUITY, &c. of the POEMS

O F

OSSIAN the Son of FINGAL.

INQUIRIES into the antiquities of nations
afford more pleasure than any real advantage
to mankind. The ingenious may form fyftems
of hiftory on probabilities and a few facts; but
at a great diftance of time, their accounts muft
be vague and uncertain. The infancy of ftates
and kingdoms is as deftitute of great events, as of
the means of tranfmitting them to pofterity.
The arts of polifhed life, by which alone facts
can be preferved with certainty, are the production of a well-formed community. It is then hiftorians begin to write, and public tranfactions to
be worthy remembrance. The actions of former
times are left in obfcurity, or magnified by uncertain traditions. Hence it is that we find fo

2   much

much of the marvellous in the origin of every
nation; pofterity being always ready to believe
any thing, however fabulous, that reflects honour on their anceftors. The Greeks and Romans were remarkable for this weaknefs. They
fwallowed the moft abfurd fables concerning the
high antiquities of their refpective nations.
Good hiftorians, however, rofe very early
amongft them, and tranfmitted, with luftre, their
great actions to pofterity. It is to them that
they owe that unrivalled fame they now enjoy,
while the great actions of other nations are in-
volved in fables, or loft in obfcurity. The Celtic nations afford a ftriking inftance of this kind.
They, though once the mafters of Europe from
the mouth of the river Oby *, in Ruflia, to
Cape Finifterre, the weftern point of Gallicia in
Spain, are very little mentioned in hiftory.
They trufted their fame to tradition and the
fongs of their bards, which, by the viciffitude
of human affairs, are long fince loft. Their ancient language is the only monument that remains of them ; and the traces of it being found
in places fo widely diftant from each other,
ferves only to fhew the extent of their ancient
power, but throws very little light on their
hiftory.

* Plin. l. 6.

Of

OF all the Celtic nations, that which poffeffed old Gaul is the moft renowned; not perhaps on account of worth fuperior to the reft, but for their wars with a people who had hiftorians to tranfmit the fame of their enemies, as well as their own, to pofterity. Britain was firft peopled by them, according to the teftimony of the beft authors [*]; its fituation in refpect to Gaul makes the opinion probable; but what puts it beyond all difpute, is that the fame cuftoms and language prevailed among the inhabitants of both in the days of Julius Cæfar [†].

THE colony from Gaul poffeffed themfelves, at firft, of that part of Britain which was next to their own country; and fpreading northward, by degrees, as they increafed in numbers, peopled the whole ifland. Some adventurers paffing over from thofe parts of Britain that are within fight of Ireland, were the founders of the Irifh nation: which is a more probable ftory than the idle fables of Milefian and Gallician colonies. Diodorus Siculus [‡] mentions it as a thing well known in his time, that the inhabitants of Ireland were originally Britons; and his teftimony is unqueftionable, when we confider

---

[*] Cæf. l. 5. Tac. Agric. l. 1. c. 2.   [†] Cæfar.
Pomp. Mel. Tacitus.   [‡] Diod. Sic. l. 5.

that,

iv   A DISSERTATION concerning the

that, for many ages, the language and cuftoms of both nations were the fame.

TACITUS was of opinion that the ancient Caledonians were of German extract. By the language and cuftoms which always prevailed in the North of Scotland, and which are undoubtedly Celtic, one would be tempted to differ in opinion from that celebrated writer. The Germans, properly fo called, were not the fame with the ancient Celtæ. The manners and cuftoms of the two nations were fimilar; but their language different. The Germans * are the genuine defcendants of the ancient Daæ, afterwards well known by the name of Daci, and paffed originally into Europe by the way of the northern countries, and fettled beyond the Danube, towards the vaft regions of Tranfilvania, Wallachia, and Moldavia; and from thence advanced by degrees into Germany. The Celtæ †, it is certain, fent many colonies into that country, all of whom retained their own laws, language, and cuftoms; and it is of them, if any colonies came from Germany into Scotland, that the ancient Caledonians were defcended.

BUT whether the Caledonians were a colony of the Celtic Germans, or the fame with the Gauls

* Strabo, l. 7.   † Cæf. l. 6. Liv. l. 5. Tac. de mor. Germ.

tha
t

that firft poffeffed themfelves of Britain, is a matter of no moment at this diftance of time. Whatever their origin was, we find them very numerous in the time of Julius Agricola, which is a prefumption that they were long before fettled in the country. The form of their government was a mixture of ariftocracy and monarchy, as it was in all the countries where the Druids bore the chief fway. This order of men feems to have been formed on the fame fyftem with the Dactyli Idæi and Curetes of the ancients. Their pretended intercourfe with heaven, their magic and divination were the fame. The knowledge of the Druids in natural caufes, and the properties of certain things, the fruit of the experiments of ages, gained them a mighty reputation among the people. The efteem of the populace foon increafed into a veneration for the order; which a cunning and ambitious tribe of men took care to improve, to fuch a degree, that they, in a manner, ingroffed the management of civil, as well as religious, matters. It is generally allowed that they did not abufe this extraordinary power; the preferving their character of fanctity was fo effential to their influence, that they never broke out into violence or oppreffion. The chiefs were allowed to execute the laws, but the legiflative power was en-

tirely

vi A DISSERTATION concerning the

tirely in the hands of the Druids *. It was by their authority that the tribes were united, in times of the greateſt danger, under one head. This temporary king, or Vergobretus †, was choſen by them, and generally laid down his office at the end of the war. Theſe prieſts enjoyed long this extraordinary privilege among the Celtic nations who lay beyond the pale of the Roman empire. It was in the beginning of the ſecond century that their power among the Caledonians begun to decline. The poems that celebrate Trathal and Cormac, anceſtors to Fingal, are full of particulars concerning the fall of the Druids, which account for the total ſilence concerning their religion in the poems that are now given to the public.

THE continual wars of the Caledonians againſt the Romans hindered the nobility from initiating themſelves, as the cuſtom formerly was, into the order of the Druids. The precepts of their religion were confined to a few, and were not much attended to by a people inured to war. The Vergobretus, or chief magiſtrate, was choſen without the concurrence of the hierarchy, or continued in his office againſt their will. Continual power ſtrengthened his intereſt among

* Ceſ. l. 6.   † Fer-gubreth, *the man to judge.*

the

the tribes, and enabled him to fend down, as hereditary to his pofterity, the office he had only received himfelf by election.

ON occafion of a new war againft the *King of the World,* as the poems emphatically call the Roman emperor, the Druids, to vindicate the honour of the order, began to refume their ancient privilege of chufing the Vergobretus. Garmal, the fon of Tarno, being deputed by them, came to the grandfather of the celebrated Fingal, who was then Vergobretus, and commanded him, in the name of the whole order, to lay down his office. Upon his refufal, a civil war commenced, which foon ended in almoft the total extinction of the religious order of the Druids. A few that remained, retired to the dark receffes of their groves, and the caves they had formerly ufed for their meditations. It is then we find them in *the circle of ftones,* and unheeded by the world. A total difregard for the order, and utter abhorrence of the Druidical rites enfued. Under this cloud of public hate, all that had any knowledge of the religion of the Druids became extinct, and the nation fell into the laft degree of ignorance of their rites and ceremonies.

IT is no matter of wonder then, that Fingal and his fon Offian make fo little, if any, mention

tion of the Druids, who were the declared enemies to their fucceffion in the fupreme ma-
giftracy. It is a fingular cafe, it muft be allowed, that there are no traces of religion in the
poems afcribed to Offian ; as the poetical compofitions of other nations are fo clofely connected
with their mythology. It is hard to account for
it to thofe who are not made acquainted with
the manner of the old Scottifh bards. That race
of men carried their notions of martial honour
to an extravagant pitch. Any aid given their
heroes in battle, was thought to derogate from
their fame; and the bards immediately tranf-
ferred the glory of the action to him who had
given that aid.

HAD Offian brought down gods, as often as
Homer hath done, to affift his heroes, this poem
had not confifted of eulogiums on his friends, but
of hymns to thefe fuperior beings. To this day,
thofe that write in the Galic language feldom
mention religion in their profane poetry ; and
when they profeffedly write of religion, they never interlard with their compofitions, the actions of their heroes. This cuftom alone, even
though the religion of the Druids had not been
previoufly extinguifhed, may, in fome meafure, account for Offian's filence concerning the
religion of his own times.

To

To fay, that a nation is void of all religion, is the fame thing as to fay, that it does not confift of people endued with reafon. The traditions of their fathers, and their own obfervations on the works of nature, together with that fuperftition which is inherent in the human frame, have, in all ages, raifed in the minds of men fome idea of a fuperior being.---Hence it is, that in the darkeft times, and amongft the moft barbarous nations, the very populace themfelves had fome faint notion, at leaft, of a divinity. It would be doing injuftice to Offian, who, upon no occafion, fhews a narrow mind, to think, that he had not opened his conceptions to that primitive and greateft of all truths. But let Offian's religion be what it will, it is certain he had no knowledge of Chriftianity, as there is not the leaft allufion to it, or any of its rites, in his poems ; which abfolutely fixes him to an æra prior to the introduction of that religion. The perfecution begun by Dioclefian, in the year 303, is the moft probable time in which the firft dawning of Chriftianity in the north of Britain can be fixed.---The humane and mild character of Conftantius Chlorus, who commanded then in Britain, induced the perfecuted Chriftians to take refuge under him. Some of them, through a zeal to propagate their tenets, or through fear,

went beyond the pale of the Roman empire, and
fettled among the Caledonians; who were the
more ready to hearken to their doctrines, as the
religion of the Druids had been exploded fo long
before.

THESE miffionaries, either through choice,
or to give more weight to the doctrine they advanced, took poffeffion of the cells and groves
of the Druids; and it was from this retired life
they had the name of *Culdees* *, which in the language of the country fignified *fequeftered perfons.*
It was with one of the *Culdees* that Offian, in his
extreme old age, is faid to have difputed concerning the Chriftian religion. This difpute is
ftill extant, and is couched in verfe according
to the cuftom of the times. The extreme ignorance on the part of Offian, of the Chriftian tenets, fhews, that that religion had only been
lately introduced, as it is not eafy to conceive,
how one of the firft rank could be totally unacquainted with a religion that had been known
for any time in the country. The difpute bears
the genuine marks of antiquity. The obfolete
phrafes and expreffions peculiar to the times,
prove it to be no forgery. If Offian then lived
at the introduction of Chriftianity, as by all ap-

* Culdich.

pearance

pearance he did, his epoch will be the latter end of the third, and beginning of the fourth century. What puts this point beyond difpute, is the allufion in his poems to the hiftory of the times.

THE exploits of Fingal againft Caracul *, the fon of the *King of the World*, are among the firft brave actions of his youth. A complete poem, which relates to this fubject, is printed in this collection.

IN the year 210 the emperor Severus, after returning from his expeditions againft the Caledonians, at York fell into the tedious illnefs of which he afterwards died. The Caledonians and Maiatæ, refuming courage from his indifpofition, took arms in order to recover the poffeffions they had loft. The enraged emperor commanded his army to march into their country, and to deftroy it with fire and fword. His orders were but ill executed, for his fon, Caracalla, was at the head of the army, and his thoughts were entirely taken up with the hopes of his father's death, and with fchemes to fupplant his brother Geta.---He fcarcely had entered the enemy's country, when news was

---

* Carac'huil, *terrible eye*. Carac-'healia, *terrible look*. Caracchallamh, *a fort of upper garment*.

brought

brought him that Severus was dead.---A fudden peace is patched up with the Caledonians, and, as it appears from Dion Caffius, the country they had loft to Severus was reftered to 'them.

THE Caracul of Fingal is no other than Cara-calla, who, as the fon of Severus, the Emperor of Rome, whofe dominions were extended al-moft over the known world, was not without reafon called in the poems of Offian, *the Son of the King of the World.* The fpace of time be-tween 211, the year Severus died, and the be-ginning of the fourth century, is not fo great, but Offian the fon of Fingal, might have feen the Chriftians whom the perfecution under Dio-clefian had driven beyond the pale of the Roman empire.

OSSIAN, in one of his many lamentations on the death of his beloved fon Ofcar, mentions among his great actions, a battle which he fought againft Caros, king of fhips, on the banks of the winding Carun *. It is more than proba-ble, that the Caros mentioned here, is the fame with the noted ufurper Caraufius, who affumed the purple in the year 287, and feizing on Bri-tain, defeated the emperor Maximian Herculius, in feveral naval engagements, which gives pro·

---

* Car-avon, *Winding river.*

priety

priety to his being called in Offian's poems, *the King of Ships*. The *winding Carun* is that fmall river retaining ftill the name of Carron, and runs in the neighbourhood of Agricola's wall, which Caraufius repaired to obftruct the incurfions of the Caledonians. Several other paflages in the poems allude to the wars of the Romans; but the two juft mentioned clearly fix the epoch of Fingal to the third century; and this account agrees exactly with the Irifh hiftories, which place the death of Fingal, the fon of Comhal, in the year 283, and that of Ofcar and their own celebrated Cairbre, in the year 296.

SOME people may imagine, that the allufions to the Roman hiftory might have been induftrioufly inferted into the poems, to give them the appearance of antiquity. This fraud muft then have been committed at leaft three ages ago, as the paffages in which the allufions are made, are alluded to often in the compofitions of thofe times.

EVERY one knows what a cloud of ignorance and barbarifm overfpread the north of Europe three hundred years ago. The minds of men, addicted to fuperftition, contracted a narrownefs that deftroyed genius. Accordingly we find the compofitions of thofe times trivial and puerile to the laft degree. But let it be allowed, that,

4   amidft

amidft all the untoward circumftances of the
age, a genius might arife, it is not eafy to determine what could induce him to give the honour of his compofitions to an age fo remote.
We find no fact that he has advanced, to favour
any defigns which could be entertained by any
man who lived in the fifteenth century. But
fhould we fuppofe a poet, through humour, or
for reafons which cannot be feen at this diftance
of time, would afcribe his own compofitions to
Offian, it is next to impoffible, that he could
impofe upon his countrymen, when all of them
were fo well acquainted with the traditional
poems of their anceftors.

THE ftrongeft objection to the authenticity of
the poems now given to the public under the
name of Offian, is the improbability of their being handed down by tradition through fo many
centuries. Ages of barbarifm fome will fay,
could not produce poems abounding with the
difinterefted and generous fentiments fo confpicuous in the compofitions of Offian; and could
thefe ages produce them, it is impoffible but they
muft be loft, or altogether corrupted in a long
fucceffion of barbarous generations.

THESE objections naturally fuggeft themfelves
to men unacquainted with the ancient ftate of
the northern parts of Britain. The bards, who
were

were an inferior order of the Druids, did not
fhare their bad fortune. They were fpared by
the victorious king, as it was through their
means only he could hope for immortality to his
fame. They attended him in the camp, and
contributed to eftablifh his power by their fongs.
His great actions were magnified, and the populace, who had no ability to examine into his
character narrowly, were dazzled with his fame
in the rhimes of the bards. In the mean time,
men affumed fentiments that are rarely to be
met with in an age of barbarifm. The bards
who were originally the difciples of the Druids,
had their minds opened, and their ideas enlarged,
by being initiated in the learning of that celebrated order. They could form a perfect hero
in their own minds, and afcribe that character to
their prince. The inferior chiefs made this ideal
character the model of their conduct, and by
degrees brought their minds to that generous
fpirit which breathes in all the poetry of the
times. The prince, flattered by his bards, and
rivalled by his own heroes, who imitated his
character as defcribed in the eulogies of his
poets, endeavoured to excel his people in merit,
as he was above them in ftation. This emula-
tion continuing, formed at laft the general character of the nation, happily compounded of

what

what is noble in barbarity, and virtuous and generous in a polilhed people.

WHEN virtue in peace, and bravery in war, are the characteriſtics of a nation, their actions become intereſting, and their fame worthy of immortality. A generous ſpirit is warmed with noble actions, and becomes ambitious of perpetuating them. This is the true ſource of that divine inſpiration, to which the poets of all ages pretended. When they found their themes inadequate to the warmth of their imaginations, they varniſhed them over with fables, ſupplied by their own fancy, or furniſhed by abſurd traditions. Theſe fables, however ridiculous, had their abettors; poſterity either implicitly believed them, or through a vanity natural to mankind, pretended that they did. They loved to place the founders of their families in the days of fable, when poetry, without the fear of contradiction, could give what characters ſhe pleaſed of her heroes. It is to this vanity that we owe the preſervation of what remain of the works of Oſſian. His poetical merit made his heroes famous in a country where heroiſm was much eſteemed and admired. The poſterity of theſe heroes, or thoſe who pretended to be deſcended from them, heard with pleaſure the eulogiums of their anceſtors; bards were employed to repeat

peat .

peat the poems, and to record the connection of
their patrons with chiefs fo renowned. Every
chief in procefs of time had a bard in his family,
and the office became at laft hereditary. By the
fucceffion of thefe bards, the poems concerning
the anceftors of the family were handed down
from generation to generation ; they were repeated to the whole clan on folemn occafions,
and always alluded to in the new compofitions of
the bards. This cuftom came down near to
our own times ; and after the bards were difcon-
tinued, a great number in a clan retained by
memory, or committed to writing, their compofitions, and founded the antiquity of their
families on the authority of their poems.

THE ufe of letters was not known in the north
of Europe till long after the inftitution of the
bards : the records of the families of their patrons, their own, and more ancient poems were
handed down by tradition. Their poetical compofitions were admirably contrived for that pur-
pofe. They were adapted to mufic; and the
moft perfect harmony was obferved. Each
verfe was fo connected with thofe which preceded
or followed it, that if one line had been remembered in a ftanza, it was almoft impoffible to
forget the reft. The cadences followed in fo natural a gradation, and the words were fo adapted

to the common turn of the voice, after it is
raifed to a certain key, that it was almoft impoffible, from a fimilarity of found, to fubftitute
one word for another. This excellence is peculiar to the Celtic tongue, and is perhaps to be
met with in no other language. Nor does this
choice of words clog the fenfe or weaken the expreffion. The numerous flections of confonants,
and variation in declenfion, make the language
very copious.

THE defcendants of the Celtæ, who inhabited
Britain and its ifles, were not fingular in this
method of preferving the moft precious monuments of their nation. The ancient laws of the
Greeks were couched in verfe, and handed down
by tradition. The Spartans, through a long
habit, became fo fond of this cuftom, that they
would never allow their laws to be committed to
writing. The actions of great men, and the
eulogiums of kings and heroes, were preferved in
the fame manner. All the hiftorical monuments
of the old Germans were comprehended in their
ancient fongs *; which were either hymns to
their gods, or elegies in praife of their heroes,
and were intended to perpetuate the great events in
their nation which were carefully interwoven with

* Tacitus de mor. Germ.

them

them. This fpecies of compofition was not committed to writing, but delivered by oral tradition *. The care they took to have the poems taught to their children, the uninterrupted cuftom of repeating them upon certain occafions, and the happy meafure of the verfe, ferved to preferve them for a long time uncorrupted. This oral chronicle of the Germans was not forgot in the eighth century, and it probably would have remained to this day, had not learning, which thinks every thing, that is not committed to writing, fabulous, been introduced. It was from poetical traditions that Garcillaffo compofed his account of the Yncas of Peru. The Peruvians had loft all other monuments of their hiftory, and it was from ancient poems which his mother, a princefs of the blood of the Yncas, taught him in his youth, that he collected the materials of his hiftory. If other nations then, that had been often overun by enemies, and had fent abroad and received colonies, could, for many ages, preferve, by oral tradition, their laws and hiftories uncorrupted, it is much more probable that the ancient Scots, a people fo free of intermixture with foreigners, and fo ftrongly attached to the

---

* *Abb: de la Bleterie Remarques fur la Germanie.*

memory

memory of their anceftors, had the works of their bards handed down with great purity.

It will feem ftrange to fome, that poems admired for many centuries in one part of this kingdom fhould be hitherto unknown in the other; and that the Britifh, who have carefully traced out the works of genius in other nations, fhould fo long remain ftrangers to their own. This, in a great meafure, is to be imputed to thofe who underftood both languages and never attempted a tranflation. They, from being acquainted but with detached pieces, or from a modefty, which perhaps the prefent tranflator ought, in prudence, to have followed, defpaired of making the compofitions of their bards agreeable to an Englifh reader. The manner of thofe compofitions is fo different from other poems, and the ideas fo confined to the moft early ftate of fociety, that it was thought they had not enough of variety to pleafe a polifhed age.

This was long the opinion of the tranflator of the following collection; and though he admired the poems, in the original, very early, and gathered part of them from tradition for his own amufement, yet he never had the fmalleft hopes of feeing them in an Englifh drefs. He was fenfible that the ftrength and manner of both languages were very different, and that it

was

was next to impoffible to tranflate the Galic poetry into any thing of tolerable Englifh verfe; a profe tranflation he could never think of, as it muft neceffarily fall fhort of the majefty of an original.

It is therefore highly probable, that the compofitions of Offian would have ftill remained in the obfcurity of a loft language, had not a gentleman, who has himfelf made a figure in the poetical world, infifted with the prefent editor for a literal profe tranflation of fome detached piece. He approved of the fpecimen, and, through him, copies came to the hands of feveral people of tafte in Scotland.

Frequent tranfcription and the corrections of thofe, who thought they mended the poems by modernizing the ideas, corrupted them to fuch a degree, that the tranflator was induced to hearken to the folicitations of a gentleman defervedly efteemed in Scotland, for his tafte and knowledge in polite literature, and publifhed the genuine copies under the title of *Fragments of Ancient Poetry.* The fragments, upon their firft appearance, were fo much approved of, that feveral people of rank, as well as tafte, prevailed with the tranflator to make a journey to the Highlands and weftern ifles, in order to recover what remained of the works of

Offian

Offian he fon of Fingal, the beft, as well as moft ancient of thofe who are celebrated in tradition for their poetical genius. A detail of this journey would be both tedious and unentertaining; let it fuffice therefore that, after a peregrination of fix months, the tranflator collected from tradition, and fome manufcripts, all the poems in the following collection, and fome more ftill in his hands, though rendered lefs complete by the ravages of time.

THE action of the poem that ftands the firft, was not the greateft or moft celebrated of the exploits of Fingal. His wars were very numerous, and each of them afforded a theme which employed the genius of his fon. But, excepting the prefent poem, thofe pieces are in a great meafure loft, and there only remain a few fragments of them in the hands of the tranflator. Tradition has ftill preferved, in many places, the ftory of the poems, and many now living have heard them, in their youth, repeated.

THE complete work, now printed, would, in a fhort time, have fhared the fate of the reft. The genius of the highlanders has fuffered a great change within thefe few years. The communication with the reft of the ifland is open, and the introduction of trade and manufactures has deftroyed that leifure which was formerly

dedicated

dedicated to hearing and repeating the poems of ancient times. Many have now learned to leave their mountains, and feek their fortunes in a milder climate; and though a certain *amor patriæ* may fometimes bring them back, they have, during their abfence, imbibed enough of foreign manners to defpife the cuftoms of their anceftors. Bards have been long difufed, and the fpirit of genealogy has greatly fubfided. Men begin to be lefs devoted to their chiefs, and confanguinity is not fo much regarded. When property is eftablifhed, the human mind confines its views to the pleafure it procures. It does not go back to antiquity, or look forward to fucceeding ages. The cares of life increafe, and the actions of other times no longer amufe. Hence it is, that the tafte for their ancient poetry is at a low ebb among the highlanders. They have not, however, thrown off the good qualities of their anceftors. Hofpitality ftill fubfifts, and an uncommon civility to ftrangers. Friendfhip is inviolable, and revenge lefs blindly followed than formerly. '

To fpeak of the poetical merit of the poems, would be an anticipation on the judgment of the public: And all that can be faid of the tranfla-tion, is, that it is literal, and that fimplicity is ftudied. The arrangement of the words in the
original

original is imitated, and the inverfions of the
ftyle obferved.   As the tranflator claims no merit from his verfion, he hopes for the indulgence
of the public where he fails.   He wifhes that the
imperfect femblance he draws, may not preju-
dice the world againft an original, which contains what is beautiful in fimplicity, and grand
in the fublime.

FINGAL,

AN ANCIENT

EPIC POEM.

In SIX BOOKS.

B

ARGUMENT to Book I.

Cuchullin, (general of the Irish tribes, in the minority of Cormac, king of Ireland) sitting alone beneath a tree, at the gate of Tura, a castle of Ulster, (the other chiefs having gone on a hunting party to Cromla, a neighbouring hill) is informed of the landing of Swaran, king of Lochlin, by Moran, the son of Fithil, one of his scouts. He convenes the chiefs; a council is held, and disputes run high about giving battle to the enemy. Connal, the petty king of Togorma, and an intimate friend of Cuchullin, was for retreating till Fingal, king of those Caledonians who inhabited the north-west coast of Scotland, whose aid had been previously sollicited, should arrive; but Calmar, the son of Matha, lord of Lara, a country in Connaught, was for engaging the enemy immediately.—Cuchullin, of himself willing to fight, went into the opinion of Calmar. Marching towards the enemy, he missed three of his bravest heroes, Fergus, Duchomar, and Caithbat. Fergus arriving, tells Cuchullin of the death of the two other chiefs; which introduces the affecting episode of Morna, the daughter of Cormac—The army of Cuchullin is descried at a distance by Swaran, who sent the son of Arno to observe the motions of the enemy, while he himself ranged his forces in order of battle.——— The son of Arno returning to Swaran, describes to him Cuchullin's chariot, and the terrible appearance of that hero. The armies engage, but night coming on, leaves the victory undecided. Cuchullin, according to the hospitality of the times, sends to Swaran a formal invitation to a feast, by his bard Carril, the son of Kinfena.—Swaran refuses to come. Carril relates to Cuchullin the story of Grudar and Brassolis. A party, by Connal's advice, is sent to observe the enemy; which closes the action of the first day.

F I N G A L,

AN ANCIENT

E P I C   P O E M.

In S I X B O O K S.

❀❀❀❀❀❀❀❀❀❀❀❀❀❀❀❀❀❀❀❀❀❀❀❀❀❀❀❀❀
B O O K I.
❀❀❀❀❀❀❀❀❀❀❀❀❀❀❀❀❀❀❀❀❀❀❀❀❀❀❀❀❀

CUCHULLIN * fat by Tura's wall; by
the tree of the ruftling leaf.-----His fpear
leaned againft the moffy rock. His fhield lay

* Cuchullin, or rather Cuth-Ullin, *the voice of Ullin*, a poetical name given the fon of Semo by the bards, from his com-
manding the forces of the Province of Ulfter againft the Fer-
bolg or Belgæ, who were in poffeffion of Connaught. Cuchullin when very young married Bragela the daughter of Sorglan, and paffing over into Ireland, lived for fome time with
Connal, grandfon by a daughter to Congal the petty king of
Ulfter. His wifdom and valour in a fhort time gained him fuch
reputation, that in the minority of Cormac the fupreme king of
Ireland, he was chofen guardian to the young king, and fole
manager of the war againft Swaran king of Lochlin. After a
feries of great actions he was killed in battle fomewhere in Connaught, in the twenty-feventh year of his age. He was fo remarkable for his ftrength, that to defcribe a ftrong man it has
paffed into a proverb, " He has the ftrength of Cuchullin."
They fhew the remains of his palace at Dunfcaich in the Ifle of
Skye ; and a ftone to which he bound his dog Luath, goes ftill
by his name.

by

by him on the grafs. As he thought of mighty
Carbar †, a hero whom he flew in war; the
fcout § of the ocean came, Moran ‡ the fon of
Fithil.

R I S E, faid the youth, Cuchullin, rife; I fee
the fhips of Swaran. Cuchullin, many are the
foe: many the heroes of the dark-rolling fea.

M O R A N! replied the blue-eyed chief, thou
ever trembleft, fon of Fithil: Thy fears have
much increafed the foe. Perhaps it is the
king || of the lonely hills coming to aid me on
green Ullin's plains.

---

† Cairbar or Cairbre fignifies a ftrong man.

§ We may conclude from Cuchullin's applying fo early for foreign aid, that the Irifh were not then fo numerous as they have
fince been ; which is a great prefumption againft the high antiquities of that people. We have the teftimony of Tacitus that
one legion only was thought fufficient, in the time of Agricola,
to reduce the whole ifland under the Roman yoke ; which would
not probably have been the cafe had the ifland been inhabited for
any number of centuries before.

‡ Moran fignifies many ; and Fithil, or rather Fili, an inferior bard.

|| Fingal the fon of Comhal, and Morna the daughter of
Thaddu. His grandfather was Trathal, and great grandfather
Trenmor, both of whom are often mentioned in the poem.—
Trenmor, according to tradition, had two fons ; Trathal, who
fucceeded him in the Kingdom of Morven, and Conar, called by
the bards *Conar the great*, who was elected king of all Ireland,
and was the anceftor of that Cormac who fat on the Irifh throne
when the invafion of Swaran happened. It may not be improper here to obferve, that the accent ought always to be placed
on the laft fyllable of Fingal.

I S A W

I saw their chief, fays Moran, tall as a rock of ice. His fpear is like that blafted fir. His fhield like the rifing moon. He fat on a rock on the fhore : his dark hoft rolled, like clouds, around him.----Many, chief of men! I, faid, many are our hands of war.---Well art thou named, the Mighty Man, but many mighty men are feen from Tura's windy walls.----He anfwered, like a wave on a rock, who in this land appears like me? Heroes ftand not in my prefence : they fall to earth beneath my hand. None can meet Swaran in the fight but Fingal, king of ftormy hills. Once we wreftled on the heath of Malmor *, and our heels overturned the wood. Rocks fell from their place; and rivulets, changing their courfe, fled murmuring from our ftrife. Three days we renewed our ftrife, and heroes ftood at a diftance and trembled. On the fourth, Fingal fays, that the king of the ocean fell; but Swaran fays, he ftood. Let dark Cuchullin yield to him that is ftrong as the ftorms of Malmor.

No: replied the blue-eyed chief, I will never yield to man. Dark Cuchullin will be great or dead. Go, Fithil's fon, and take my fpear :

* Meal-mór—*a great hill.*

ftrike

ftrike the founding fhield of Cabait ||. It hangs at Tura's ruftling gate; the found of peace is not its voice. My heroes fhall hear on the hill.

HE went and ftruck the boffy fhield. The hills and their rocks replied. The found fpread along the wood : deer ftart by the lake of roes. Curach * leapt from the founding rock ; and Connal of the bloody fpear. Crugal's † breaft of fnow beats high. The fon of Favi leaves the dark-brown hind. It is the fhield of war, faid Ronnar, the fpear of Cuchullin, faid Lu-gar.------Son of the fea, put on thy arms ! Calmar lift thy founding fteel ! Puno ! horrid hero, rife : Cairbar from thy red tree of Cromla. Bend thy white knee, O Eth ; and defcend from the ftreams of Lena.------Ca-olt ftretch thy white fide as thou moveft along the whiftling heath of Mora : thy fide that is white as the foam of the troubled fea, when the dark winds pour it on the murmuring rocks of Cuthon ‡.

|| Cabait, or rather Cathbait, grandfather to the hero, was fo remarkable for his valour, that his fhield was made ufe of to alarm his pofterity to the battles of the family. We find Fingal making the fame ufe of his own fhield in the 4th book.------A horn was the moft common inftrument to call the army together before the invention of bagpipes.

* Cu-raoch fignifies *the m..dnefs of battle.*

† Cruth-geal------*fair-complexioned.*

‡ Cu-thón—*the mournful found of waves.*

Now

Now I behold the chiefs in the pride of their
former deeds; their fouls are kindled at the
battles of old, and the actions of other times.
Their eyes are like flames of fire, and roll in
fearch of the foes of the land.——Their mighty
hands are on their fwords; and lightning pours
from their fides of fteel.——They came like
ftreams from the mountains; each rufhed roaring from his hill.   Bright are the chiefs of
battle in the armour of their fathers.——
Gloomy and dark their heroes followed, like
the gathering of the rainy clouds behind the
red meteors of heaven.——The founds of crafh-
ing arms afcend.   The grey dogs howl between.
Unequally burfts the fong of battle; and rocking Cromla * echoes round.   On Lena's dufky
heath they ftood, like mift † that fhades the hills
of autumn: when broken and dark it fettles
high, and lifts its head to heaven.

---

* Crom-leach fignified a place of worfhip among the Druids.
It is here the proper name of a hill on the coaft of Ullin or
Ulfter.

    † ———νεφέλησιν ἐοικότες ἅς τε Κρονίων
Νηνεμίης, ἕςησεν ἐπ᾽ ἀκροπολοισινόρεσσιν
Ατρέμας.   Hom. Il. 5. v. 522.
    So when th' embattled clouds in dark array,
    Along the fkies their gloomy lines difplay;
    The low-hung vapours motionlefs and ftill
    Reft on the fummits of the fhaded hill.   Pope.

HAIL, faid Cuchullin, fons of the narrow vales, hail ye hunters of the deer. Another fport is drawing near: it is like the dark rolling of that wave on the coaft. Shall we fight, ye fons of war! or yield green Innisfail ‡ to Lochlin?——O Connal ‖ fpeak, thou firft of men! thou breaker of the fhields! thou haft often fought with Lochlin; wilt thou lift thy father's fpear?

CUCHULLIN! calm the chief replied, the fpear of Connal is keen. It delights to fhine in battle, and to mix with the blood of thoufands. But tho' my hand is bent on war, my heart is for the peace of Erin *. Behold, thou firft in Cormac's war, the fable fleet of Swaran. His mafts are as numerous on our coaft as reeds in

‡ Ireland fo called from a colony that fettled there called Falans.—Innis-fail, *i. e.* the ifland of the Fa-il or Falans.

‖ Connal, the friend of. Cuchullin, was the fon of Cathbait prince of Tongorma or the *ifland of blue waves*, probably one of the Hebrides. His mother was Fioncoma the daughter of Congal. He had a fon by Foba of Conachar-neffar, who was afterwards king of Ulfter. For his fervices in the war againft Swaran he had lands conferred on him, which, from his name, were called Tir-chonnuil or Tir-connel, *i. e.* the land of Connal.

* Erin, a name of Ireland; from *car* or *iar* Weft, and *in* an ifland. This name was not always confined to Ireland for there is the higheft probability that the *Ierne* of the ancients was Britain to the North of the Forth.—For Ierne is faid to be to the North of Britain, which could not be meant of Ireland.

STRABO, l. 2. & 4. CASAUB. l. 1.

the

the lake of Lego. His fhips are like forefts cloathed with mift, when the trees yield by turns to the fqually wind. Many are his chiefs in battle. Connal is for peace.——Fingal would fhun his arm the firft of mortal men : Fingal that fcatters the mighty, as ftormy winds the heath ; when the ftreams roar thro' echoing Cona : and night fettles with all her clouds on the hill.

FLY, thou chief of peace, faid Calmar † the fon of Matha ; fly, Connal, to thy filent hills, where the fpear of battle never fhone ; purfue the dark-brown deer of Cromla : and ftop with thine arrows the bounding roes of Lena. But, blue-eyed fon of Semo, Cuchullin, ruler of the war, fcatter thou the fons of Loch- lin ‡, and roar thro' the ranks of their pride. Let no veffel of the kingdom of Snow bound on the dark-rolling waves of Inis-tore ||.   O ye dark winds of Erin rife ! roar ye whirlwinds of the heath ! Amidft the tempeft let me die, torn in a cloud by angry ghofts of men ; amidft the tempeft let Calmar die, if ever chace was fport to him fo much as the battle of fhields.

† Cálm-er, *a ftreng man.*

‡ The Galic name of Scandinavia in general ; in a more con- fined fenfe that of the peninfula of Jutland.

|| Innis-tore, *the ifland of wha'es,* the ancient name of the Orkney iflands.

CALMAR !

CALMAR! flow replied the chief, I never fled, O Matha's fon. I was fwift with my friends in battle, but fmall is the fame of Connal. The battle was won in my prefence, and the valiant overcame. But, fon of Semo, hear my voice, regard the ancient throne of Cormac. Give wealth and half the land for peace, till Fingal come with battle. Or, if war be thy choice, I lift the fword and fpear. My joy fhall be in the midft of thoufands, and my foul brighten in the gloom of the fight.

To me, Cuchullin replies, pleafant is the noife of arms : pleafant as the thunder of heaven before the fhower of Spring. But gather all the fhining tribes that I may view the fons of war. Let them move along the heath, bright as the fun-fhine before a ftorm ; when the weft wind collects the clouds, and the oaks of Morven echo along the fhore.

BUT where are my friends in battle? The companions of my arm in danger? Where art thou, white-bofom'd Cathbat? Where is that cloud in war, Duchomar * ? and haft thou left me, O Fergus †! in the day of the ftorm ? Fergus, firft in our joy at the feaft! fon of

* Dubhchomar, *a black well-fhaped man.*
† Fear-guth,—*the man of the word*; or a commander of an army.

Roffa !

Roffa! arm of death! comeft thou like a roe ‡
from Malmor? Like a hart from the ecchoing
hills?——Hail thou fon of Roffa! what fhades
the foul of war?

Four ftones ||, replied the chief, rife on the
grave of Cathbat.——Thefe hands have laid in
earth Duchomar, that cloud in war. Cathbat,
thou fon of Torman, thou wert a fun-beam on
the hill.——And thou, O valiant Duchomar,
like the mift of marfhy Lano; when it fails
over the plains of autumn and brings death to
the people. Morna, thou faireft of maids! calm
is thy fleep in the cave of the rock. Thou haft·
fallen in darknefs like a ftar, that fhoots athwart
the defart, when the traveller is alone, and
mourns the tranfient beam.

Say, faid Semo's blue-eyed fon, fay how fell
the chiefs of Erin? Fell they by the fons of

‡ Be thou like a roe or young hart on the mountains of
Bether.   SOLOMON's Song.

|| This paffage alludes to the manner of burial among the an-
cient Scots. They opened a grave fix or eight feet deep: the
bottom was lined with fine clay; and on this they laid the body
of the deceafed, and, if a warrior, his fword, and the heads of
twelve arrows by his fide. Above they laid another ftratum of
clay, in which they placed the horn of a deer, the fymbol of
hunting. The whole was covered with a fine mold, and four
ftones placed on end to mark the extent of the grave. Thefe
are the four ftones alluded to here.

Lochlin,

Lochlin, ftriving in the battle of heroes? Or what confines the chiefs of Cromla to the dark and narrow houfe * ?

CATHBAT, replied the hero, fell by the fword of Duchomar at the oak of the noify ftreams. Duchomar came to Tura's cave, and fpoke to the lovely Morna.

MORNA †, faireft among women, lovely daughter of Cormac-cairbar. Why in the circle of ftones ; in the cave of the rock alone? The ftream murmurs hoarfely. The old tree's groan is in the wind. The lake is troubled before thee, and dark are the clouds of the fky. But thou art like fnow on the heath ; and thy hair like the mift of Cromla ; when it curls on the rocks, and fhines to the beam of the weft.—— Thy breafts are like two fmooth rocks feen from Branno of the ftreams. Thy arms like two white pillars in the halls of the mighty Fingal.

FROM whence, the white-armed maid replied, from whence, Duchomar the moft gloomy of men ? Dark are thy brows and terrible. Red are thy rolling eyes. Does Swaran appear on the fea ? What of the foe, Duchomar ?

FROM the hill I return, O Morna, from the hill of the dark-brown hinds. Three have I

---

* The grave.——The houfe appointed for all living.   JOB.
† Muirne or Morna, *a woman beloved by all.*

flain

flain with my bended yew. Three with my
long bounding dogs of the chace.——Lovely
daughter of Cormac, I love thee as my foul.
——I have flain one ftately deer for thee.——
High was his branchy head; and fleet his feet of
wind.

DUCHOMAR ! calm the maid replied, I love
thee not, thou gloomy man.——Hard is thy
heart of rock, and dark thy terrible brow.   But
Cathbat, thou fon of Torman *, thou art the
love of Morna.   Thou art like a fun-beam on
the hill in the day of the gloomy ftorm.   Saw-
eft thou the fon of Torman, lovely on the hill
of his hinds ? Here the daughter of Cormac
waits the coming of Cathbat.

AND long fhall Morna wait, Duchomar faid,
his blood is on my fword.——Long fhall Morna
wait for him.   He fell at Branno's ftream.
High on Cromla I will raife his tomb, daughter
of Cormac-cairbar; but fix thy love on Duchomar, his arm is ftrong as a ftorm.——

AND is the fon of Torman fallen ? faid the
maid of the tearful eye.   Is he fallen on his
ecchoing heath ; the youth with the breaft of
fnow ? he that was firft in the chace of the hill ;
the foe of the ftrangers of the ocean.——Du-

* Torman, *Thunder*. This is the true origin of the Jupiter
Taramis of the ancients.

chomar

chomar thou art dark † indeed, and cruel is thy arm to Morna. But give me that fword, my foe; I love the blood of Caithbat.

HE gave the fword to her tears; but fhe pierced his manly breaft. He fell, like the bank of a mountain-ftream; ftretched out his arm and faid;

DAUGHTER of Cormac-cairbar, thou haft flain Duchomar. The fword is cold in my breaft: Morna, I feel it cold. Give me to Moina * the maid; Duchomar was the dream of her night. She will raife my tomb; and the hunter fhall fee it and praife me. But draw the fword from my breaft; Morna, the fteel is cold.

SHE came, in all her tears, fhe came, and drew it from his breaft. He pierced her white fide with fteel; and fpread her fair locks on the ground. Her burfting blood founds from her fide: and her white arm is ftained with red. Rolling in death fhe lay, and Tura's cave an-fwered to her groans.——

PEACE, faid Cuchullin, to the fouls of the heroes; their deeds were great in danger. Let them ride around † me on clouds; and fhew

---

† She alludes to his name——*the dark man.*

* Moina, *foft in temper and perfon.*

† It was the opinion then, as indeed it is to this day, of fome of the highlanders, that the fouls of the deceafed hovered round their living friends; and fometimes appeared to them when they were about to enter on any great undertaking.

I   their

their features of war: that my foul may be
ftrong in danger; my arm like the thunder of
heaven.———But be thou on a moon-beam, O
Morna, near the window of my reft; when my
thoughts are of peace; and the din of arms is
over.———Gather the ftrength of the tribes, and
move to the wars of Erin.———Attend the car
of my battles; rejoice in the noife of my
courfe.———Place three fpears by my fide; follow the bounding of my fteeds; that my foul
may be ftrong in my friends, when the battle
darkens round the beams of my fteel.

As rufhes a ftream * of foam from the dark
fhady fteep of Cromla; when the thunder is
rolling above, and dark-brown night on half
the hill. So fierce, fo vaft, fo terrible rufhed
on the fons of Erin. The chief like a whale

---

* Ὡς δ' ὅτε χείμαρροι ποταμοὶ, κατ' ὄρεσφι ῥέοντες
Ἐς μισγάγκειαν συμβάλλετον ὕβριμον ὕδωρ,
Κρυνῶν ἐκ μεγάλων κοίλης ἔντοσθε χαράδρης.   Hom.

As torrents roll encreas'd by numerous rills
With rage impetuous down the ecchoing hills ;
Rufh to the vales, and pour'd along the plain,
Roar thro' a thoufand channels to the main.   Pope.

Aut ubi decurfu rapido de montibus altis,
Dant fonitum fpumofi amnes, & in æquora currunt,
Quifque fuum populatus iter.   Virg.

of

of ocean, whom all his billows follow, poured valour forth as a ftream, rolling his might along the ſhore.

THE fons of Lochlin heard the noife as the found of a winter-ftream. Swaran ftruck his boffy fhield, and called the fon of Arno. What murmur rolls along the hill like the gathered flies of evening ? The fons of Innis-fail defcend, or ruftling winds roar in the diftant wood. Such is the noife of Gormal before the white tops of my waves arife. O fon of Arno, af-cend the hill and view the dark face of the heath.

HE went, and trembling, fwift returned. His eyes rolled wildly round. His heart beat high againft his fide. His words were faulter-ing, broken, flow.

RISE, fon of ocean, rife chief of the dark-brown fhields. I fee the dark, the mountain-ftream of the battle : the deep-moving ftrength of the fons of Erin.——The car, the car of battle comes, like the flame of death ; the rapid car of Cuchullin, the noble fon of Semo. It bends behind like a wave near a rock ; like the golden mift of the heath. Its fides are emboffed with ftones, and fparkle like the fea round the

boat

boat of night. Of polifhed yew is its beam,
and its feat of the fmootheft bone. The fides
are replenifhed with fpears ; and the bottom is
the footftool of heroes. Before the right fide
of the car is feen the fnorting horfe. The high-
maned, broad-breafted, proud, high-leaping,
ftrong fteed of the hill. Loud and refounding
is his hoof; the fpreading of his mane above is
like that ftream of fmoke on the heath. Bright
are the fides of the fteed, and his name is Sulin-
Sifadda.

BEFORE the left fide of the car is feen the
fnorting horfe. The dark-maned, high-headed,
ftrong-hooffed, fleet, bounding fon of the hill :
his name is Dufronnal among the ftormy fons
of the fword.——A thoufand thongs bind the
car on high. Hard polifhed bits fhine in a
wreath of foam. Thin thongs bright-ftudded
with gems, bend on the ftately necks of the
fteeds.——The fteeds that like wreaths of mift
fly over the ftreamy vales. The wildnefs of deer
is in their courfe, the ftrength of the eagle defcending on her prey. Their noife is like the
blaft of winter on the fides of the fnow-headed
Gormal *.

* A hill of Lochlin.

C   WITHIN

WITHIN the car is feen the chief; the ftrong ftormy fon of the fword; the hero's name is Cuchullin, fon of Semo king of fhells.   His red cheek is like my polifhed yew.   The look of his blue-rolling eye is wide beneath the dark arch of his brow.   His hair flies from his head like a flame, as bending forward he wields the fpear.   Fly, king of ocean, fly; he comes, like a ftorm, along the ftreamy vale.

WHEN did I fly, replied the king, from the battle of many fpears? When did I fly, fon of Arno, chief of the little foul? I met the ftorm of Gormal when the foam of my waves was high; I met the ftorm of the clouds and fhall I fly from a hero? Were it Fingal himfelf my foul fhould not darken before him.——Rife to the battle, my thoufands; pour round me like the echoing main. Gather round the bright fteel of your king; ftrong as the rocks of my land; that meet the ftorm with joy, and ftretch their dark woods to the wind.

As autumn's * dark ftorms pour from two echoing hills, towards each other approached the

_____

* The reader may compare this paffage with a fimilar one in Homer.   Iliad. 4. v. 446.

　　Now fhield with fhield, with helmet helmet clos'd,
　. To armour armour, lance to lance oppos'd,

　　　　　　　　　　　　　　　　　　　Hoft

the heroes.——As two dark ſtreams from high rocks meet, and mix and roar on the plain; loud, rough and dark in battle meet Lochlin and Innis-fail. Chief mixed his ſtrokes with chief, and man with man; ſteel, clanging, ſounded on ſteel, helmets are cleft on high. Blood burſts and ſmoaks around.——Strings twang on the poliſhed yews. Darts ruſh along the ſky. Spears fall like the circles of light that gild the ſtormy face of night.

As the troubled noiſe of the ocean when roll the waves on high; as the laſt peal of the thunder of heaven, ſuch is the noiſe of battle. Though Cormac's hundred bards were there to give the war to ſong; feeble were the voices of a hundred bards to ſend the deaths to future times. For many were the falls of the heroes; and wide poured the blood of the valiant.

Hoſt againſt hoſt, with ſhadowy ſquadrons drew,
The ſounding darts in iron tempeſts flew ;
With ſtreaming blood the ſlipp'ry fields are dy'd,
And ſlaughter'd heroes ſwell the dreadful tide.   **Pope.**
Statius has very happily imitated Homer.
Jam clypeu clypeis, umbone repellitur umbo,
Erſe minax enſis, pede pes, & cuſpide cuſpis, &c.
          Arms on armour craſhing, bray'd
Horrible diſcord, and the madding wheels
Of brazen chariots rag'd, &c.   Milton.

C 2   Mourn,

Mourn, ye fons of fong, the death of the
noble Sithallin *.——Let the fighs of Fiöna rife
on the dark heaths of her lovely Ardan.——
They fell, like two hinds of the defart, by the
hands of the mighty Swaran; when, in the
midft of thoufands he roared; like the fhrill
fpirit of a ftorm, that fits dim, on the clouds of
Gormal, and enjoys the death of the mariner.

·Nor flept thy hand by thy fide, chief of the
ifle of mift †; many were the deaths of thine
arm, Cuchullin, thou fon of Semo.   His fword
was like the beam of heaven when it pierces the
fons of the vale; when the people are blafted
and fall, and all the hills are burning around.
——Dufronnal ‡ fnorted over the bodies of he-
roes; and Sifadda || bathed his hoof in blood.
The battle lay behind them as groves overturned
on the defart of Cromla; when the blaft has
paffed the heath laden with the fpirits of night.

* Sithallin fignifies *a handfome man*;—Fiöna, *a fair maid*;—
and Ardan, *pride*.

† The Ifle of Sky; not improperly called the *ifle of mift*, as
its high hills, which catch the clouds from the weftern ocean,
occafion almoft continual rains.

‡ One of Cuchullin's horfes.   Dubhftron-gheal.

|| Sith-fadda, *i. e. a long ftride*.

WEEP

WEEP on the rocks of roaring winds, O maid of Iniftore *, bend thy fair head over the waves, thou fairer than the fpirit of the hills; when it moves in a fun-beam at noon over the filence of Morven. He is fallen! thy youth is low; pale beneath the fword of Cuchullin. No more fhall valour raife the youth to match the blood of kings.——Trenar, lovely Trenar died, thou maid of Iniftore. His gray dogs are howling at home, and fee his paffing ghoft. His bow is in the hall unftrung. No found is in the heath of his hinds.

As roll a thoufand waves to the rocks, fo Swaran's hoft came on; as meets a rock a thoufand waves, fo Innis-fail met Swaran. Death raifes all his voices around, and mixes with the found of fhields.——Each hero is a pillar of darknefs, and the fword a beam of fire in his hand. The field echoes from wing to wing, as

---

* The maid of Iniftore was the daughter of Gorlo king of Iniftore or Orkney iflands. Trenar was brother to the king of Inifcon, fuppofed to be one of the iflands of Shetland. The Orkneys and Shetland were at that time fubject to the king of Lochlin. We find that the dogs of Trenar are fenfible at home of the death of their mafter, the very inftant he is killed.—— It was the opinion of the times, that the fouls of heroes went immediately after death to the hills of their country, and the fcenes they frequented the moft happy time of their life. It was thought too that dogs and horfes faw the ghofts of the deceafed.

a huna hundred hammers that rife by turns on the red fon of the furnace.

Who are thefe on Lena's heath that are fo gloomy and dark? Who are thefe like two clouds *, and their fwords like lightning above them? The little hills are troubled around, and the rocks tremble with all their mofs.——Who is it but Ocean's fon and the car-borne chief of Erin? Many are the anxious eyes of their friends, as they fee them dim on the heath. Now night conceals the chiefs in her clouds, and ends the terrible fight.

It was on Cromla's fhaggy fide that Dorglas placed the deer †; the early fortune of the chace, before the heroes left the hill.——A hundred youths collect the heath; ten heroes blow the fire; three hundred chufe the polifh'd ftones. The feaft is fmoaking wide.

* As when two black clouds
With heaven's artillery fraught, come rattling on
Over the Cafpian.   Milton.

† The ancient manner of preparing feafts after hunting, is handed down by tradition.—— A pit lined with fmooth ftones was made; and near it ftood a heap of fmooth flat ftones of the flint kind. The ftones as well as the pit were properly heated with heath. Then they laid fome venifon in the bottom, and a ftratum of the ftones above it; and thus they did alternately till the pit was full. The whole was covered over with heath to confine the fteam. Whether this is probable I cannot fay; but fome pits are fhewn, which the vulgar fay, were ufed in that manner.

                          Cuch-

Cuchullin, chief of Erin's war, refumed his mighty foul. He ftood upon his beamy fpear, and.fpoke to the fon of fongs; to Carril of other times, the gray-haired fon of Kin-fena *. Is this feaft fpread for me alone and the king of Lochlin on Ullin's fhore, far from the deer of his hills, and founding halls of his feafts ? Rife, Carril of other times, and carry my words to Swaran; tell him that came from the roaring of waters, that Cuchullin gives his feaft. Here let him liften to the found of my groves amidft the clouds of night.——For cold and bleak the bluftering winds rufh over the foam of his feas. Here let him praife the trembling harp, and hear the fongs of heroes.

Old Carril went, with fofteft voice, and called the king of dark-brown fhields. Rife from the fkins of thy chace, rife, Swaran king of groves.——Cuchullin gives the joy of fhells; partake the feaft of Erin's blue-eyed chief.

He anfwered like the fullen found of Cromla before a ftorm. Though all thy daughters, Innis-fail! fhould extend their arms of fnow; raife high the heavings of their breafts, and foftly roll their eyes of love; yet, fixed as Loch-lin's thoufand rocks, here Swaran fhall re-

* Cean-feana, *i. e. the head of the people.*

main; till morn, with the young beams of my
eaft, fhall light me to the death of Cuchullin.
Pleafant to my ear is Lochlin's wind. It rufhes
over my feas. It fpeaks aloft in all my throwds,
and brings my green forefts to my mind; the
green forefts of Gormal that often echoed to
my winds, when my fpear was red in the chace
of the boar. Let dark Cuchullin yield to me
the ancient throne of Cormac, or Erin's torrents fhall fhew from their hills the red foam of
the blood of his pride.

SAD is the found of Swaran's voice, faid Carril of other times :———.

SAD to himfelf alone, faid the blue-eyed fon
of Semo. But, Carril, raife thy voice on high,
and tell the deeds of other times. Send thou
the night away in fong; and give the joy of
grief. For many heroes and maids of love
have moved on Innis-fail. And lovely are the
fongs of woe that are heard on Albion's rocks;
when the noife of the chace is over, and the
ftreams of Cona anfwer to the voice of Offian *.

* Offian the fon of Fingal and author of the poem. One
cannot but admire the addrefs of the poet in putting his own
praife fo naturally into the mouth of Cuchullin. The Cona here
mentioned is perhaps that fmall river that runs through Glenco
in Argylefhire. One of the hills which environ that romantic
valley is ftill called Scorna-fena, or the hill of Fingal's people.

In other days *, Carril replies, came the fons of Ocean to Erin. A thoufand veffels bounded over the waves to Ullin's lovely plains. The fons of Innis-fail arofe to meet the race of dark-brown fhields. Cairbar, firft of men, was there, and Grudar, ftately youth. Long had they ftrove for the fpotted bull, that lowed on Golbun's † echoing heath. Each claimed him as his own; and death was often at the point of their fteel.

Side by fide the heroes fought, and the ftrangers of Ocean fled. Whofe name was fairer on the hill than the name of Cairbar and Grudar! ——But ah! why ever lowed the bull on Golbun's echoing heath? They faw him leaping like the fnow. The wrath of the chiefs returned.

On Lubar's ‡ graffy banks they fought, and Grudar like a fun-beam, fell. Fierce Cairbar came to the vale of the echoing Tura, where

* This epifode is introduced with propriety. Calmar and Connal, two of the Irifh heroes, had difputed warmly before the battle about engaging the enemy. Carril endeavours to reconcile them with the ftory of Cairbar and Grudar; who, tho' enemies before, fought *fide by fide* in the war. The poet obtained his aim, for we find Calmar and Connal perfectly reconciled in the third book.

† Golb-bhean, as well as Cromleach, fignifies *a crooked hill.* It is here the name of a mountain in the county of Sligo.

‡ Lubar—a river in Ulfter. *Labhar,* loud, noify.

Braffolis,

Braffolis *, faireft of his fifters, all alone, raifed the fong of grief. She fung of the actions of Grudar, the youth of her fecret foul.——She mourned him in the field of blood; but ftill fhe hoped for his return. Her white bofom is feen from her robe, as the moon from the clouds of night. Her voice was fofter than the harp to raife the fong of grief. Her foul was fixed on Grudar; the fecret look of her eye was his.—— When fhalt thou come in thine arms, thou mighty in the war?——

TAKE, Braffolis, Cairbar came and faid, take, Braffolis, this fhield of blood. Fix it on high within my hall, the armour of my foe. Her foft heart beat againft her fide. Diftracted, pale, fhe flew. She found her youth in all his blood; fhe died on Cromla's heath. Here refts their duft, Cuchullin; and thefe two lonely yews, fprung from their tombs, wifh to meet on high. Fair was Braffolis on the plain, and Grudar on the hill. The bard fhall preferve their names, and repeat them to future times.

PLEASANT is thy voice, O Carril, faid the blue-eyed chief of Erin; and lovely are the words of other times. They are like the calm

* Braffolis fignifies *a woman with a white breaft.*

fhower

ſhower * of ſpring, when the ſun looks on the
field, and the light cloud flies over the hills.
O ſtrike the harp in praiſe of my love, the
lonely ſun-beam of Dunſcaich. Strike the harp
in the praiſe of Bragéla †, of her that I left
in the Iſle of Miſt, the ſpouſe of Semo's ſon.
Doſt thou raiſe thy fair face from the rock to
find the ſails of Cuchullin?——The ſea is rolling far diſtant, and its white foam ſhall deceive
thee for my ſails. Retire, for it is night, my
love, and the dark winds ſigh in thy hair. Retire to the halls of my feaſts, and think of the
times that are paſt : for I will not return till the
ſtorm of war is ceaſed. O Connal, ſpeak of
wars and arms, and ſend her from my mind,
for lovely with her raven-hair is the white-boſomed daughter of Sorglan.

---

* Homer compares ſoft piercing words to the fall of ſnow.
—ιπεα νιφαδεσσιν ἑοικότα χειμερίησιν.
But when he ſpeaks, what elocution flows!
Like the ſoft fleeces of deſcending ſnows.   Pope.
† Bragéla was the daughter of Sorglan, and the wife of
Cuchullin.—Cuchullin, upon the death of Artho, ſupreme king
of Ireland, paſſed over into Ireland, probably by Fingal's order,
to take upon him the adminiſtration of affairs in that kingdom
during the minority of Cormac the ſon of Artho. He left his
wife Bragéla in Dunſcaich, the ſeat of the family, in the iſle of
Sky, where the remains of his palace is ſtill ſhewn; and a ſtone,
to which he bound his dog Luath, goes ſtill by his name.

CONNAL, flow to fpeak, replied, Guard
againſt the race of Ocean. Send thy troop of
night abroad, and watch the ſtrength of Swaran.——Cuchullin! I am for peace till the race
of the defart come ; till Fingal come, the firſt
of men, and beam, like the fun, on our fields.

THE hero ſtruck the ſhield of his alarms——
the warriors of the night moved on. The reſt
lay in the heath of the deer, and ſlept amidſt
the duſky wind.——The ghoſts * of the lately
dead were near, and ſwam on gloomy clouds.
And far diſtant, in the dark ſilence of Lena,
the feeble voices of death were heard.

* It was long the opinion of the ancient Scots, that a ghoſt
was heard ſhrieking near the place where a death was to happen
foon after. The accounts given, to this day, among the vulgar, of this extraordinary matter, are very poetical. The ghoſt
comes mounted on a meteor, and furrounds twice or thrice the
place deſtined for the perfon to die; and then goes along the
road through which the funeral is to pafs, ſhrieking at intervals ;
at laſt, the meteor and ghoſt difappear above the burial place.

FINGAL,

FINGAL,

AN ANCIENT

EPIC POEM.

BOOK II.

ARGUMENT to Book II.

The ghoſt of Crugal, one of the Iriſh heroes who was killed in battle, appearing to Connal, foretels the defeat of Cuchullin in the next battle; and earneſtly adviſes him to make peace with Swaran. Connal communicates the viſion; but Cuchullin is inflexible; from a principle of honour he would not be the firſt to ſue for peace, and he reſolved to continue the war. Morning comes; Swaran propoſes diſhonourable terms to Cuchullin, which are rejected. The battle begins, and is obſtinately fought for ſome time, until, upon the flight of Grumal, the whole Iriſh army gave way. Cuchullin and Connal cover their retreat: Carril leads them to a neighbouring hill, whither they are ſoon followed by Cuchullin himſelf, who deſcries the fleet of Fingal making towards the coaſt; but, night coming on, he loſt ſight of it again. Cuchullin, dejected after his defeat, attributes his ill ſucceſs to the death of Ferda his friend, whom he had killed ſome time before. Carril, to ſhew that ill ſucceſs did not always attend thoſe who innocently killed their friends, introduces the epiſode of Comal and Galvina.

F I N G A L,

AN ANCIENT

E P I C   P O E M.

In S I X   B O O K S.

✼✿✼✿✼✿✼✿✼✿✼✿✼✿✼✿✼✿✼✿✼✿✼✿✼✿✿

B O O K   II.

✼✿✼✿✼✿✼✿✼✿✼✿✼✿✼✿✼✿✼✿✼✿✼✿✼✿✿

CONNAL* lay by the found of the mountain ftream, beneath the aged tree. A ftone, with its mofs, fupported his head. Shrill thro'

---

* The fcene of Connal's repofe is familiar to thofe who have been in the Highlands of Scotland. The poet removes him to a diftance from the army, to add more horror to the defcription of Crugal's ghoft by the lonelinefs of the place. It perhaps will not be difagreeable to the reader, to fee how two other ancient poets handled a fimilar fubject.

Ηλθη δ' ιπι ψυχη Πατροκληος δειλοιο
Παητ' αυτω μεγιθος τι και οματα κατ' ιικτια
Και φωνην, &c.   HOM. Il. 23.

When lo! the fhade, before his clofing eyes,
Of fad Patroclus rofe or feem'd to rife,
In the fame robe he living wore, he came
In ftature, voice, and pleafing look the fame.
The form familiar hover'd o'er his head,
And fleeps Achilles thus? the phantom faid.   POPE.

*In fomnis ecce ante oculos mæftiffimus Hector
Vifus addeffe mihi, largofque effundere fletus,
Raptatus bigis, ut quondam, aterque cruento
Pulvere perque pedes trajectus lora tumentes.*

Hei

thro' the heath of Lena, he heard the voice of
night.   At diftance from the heroes he lay, for
the fon of the fword feared no foe.

My hero faw in his reft a dark-red ftream
of fire coming down from the hill.   Crugal
fat upon the beam, a chief that lately fell.
He fell by the hand of Swaran, ftriving in the
battle of heroes.   His face is like the beam of
the fetting moon ; his robes are of the clouds
of the hill : his eyes are like two decaying
flames.   Dark is the wound of his breaft.

Crugal, faid the mighty Connal, fon of
Dedgal famed on the hill of deer.   Why fo
pale and fad, thou breaker of the fhields ?

Hei mihi qualis erat! quantum mutatus ab illo
Hectore, qui redit exuviis indutus Achilli,
Vel Danaüm Phrygios jaculatus puppibus ignes ;
Squalentem barbam & concretos fanguine crines
Vulneraque illa gerens quæ circum plurima muros
Adcepit patrios.   Æn. lib. 2.

      When Hector's ghoft before my fight appears :
A bloody fhroud he feem'd, and bath'd in tears.
Such as he was, when, by Pelides flain,
Theffalian courfers drag'd him o'er the plain.
Swoln were his feet, as when the thongs were thruft
Through the bor'd holes, his body black with duft.
Unlike that Hector, who return'd from toils
Of war triumphant, in Æacian fpoils :
Or him, who made the fainting Greeks retire,
And launch'd againft their navy Phrygian fire.
His hair and beard ftood ftiffen'd with his gore ;
And all the wounds he for his country bore.   Dryden.

                                                   Thou

Thou haft never been pale for fear.——What difturbs the fon of the hill?

DIM, and in tears, he ftood and ftretched his pale hand over the hero.——Faintly he raifed his feeble voice, like the gale of the reedy Lego.

MY ghoft, O Connal, is on my native hills; but my corfe is on the fands of Ullin. Thou fhalt never talk with Crugal, or find his lone fteps in the heath. I am light as the blaft of Cromla, and I move like the fhadow of mift. Connal, fon of Colgar *, I fee the dark cloud of death: it hovers over the plains of Lena. The fons of green Erin fhall fall. Remove from the field of ghofts.——Like the darkened moon † he retired, in the midft of the whiftling blaft.

STAY, faid the mighty Connal, ftay my dark-red friend. Lay by that beam of heaven, fon of the windy Cromla. What cave of the hill is thy lonely houfe? What green-headed

---

* Connal the fon of Caithbat, the friend of Cuchullin, is fometimes, as here, called the fon of Colgar; from one of that name who was the founder of his family.

† Ψυχη δὲ κατα χθονὸς, ηὖτε καπνὸς
Ωχιτο τετριγυῖα   HOM. Il. 23. v. 100.
Like a thin fmoke he fees the fpirit fly,
And hears a feeble, lamentable cry.   POPE.

hill is the place of thy reft? Shall we not hear thee in the ftorm? In the noife of the moun-tain-ftream? When the feeble fons of the wind come forth, and ride on the blaft of the defart.

THE foft-voiced Connal rofe in the midft of his founding arms. He ftruck his fhield above Cuchullin. The fon of battle waked.

WHY, faid the ruler of the car, comes Con-nal through the night? My fpear might turn againft the found; and Cuchullin mourn the death of his friend. Speak, Connal, fon of Colgar, fpeak, thy counfel is like the fon of heaven.

SON of Semo, replied the chief, the ghoft of Crugal came from the cave of his hill.——The ftars dim-twinkled through his form; and his voice was like the found of a diftant ftream.——He is a meffenger of death.——He fpeaks of the dark and narrow houfe. Sue for peace, O chief of Dunfcaich; or fly over the heath of Lena.

HE fpoke to Connal, replied the hero, though ftars dim-twinkled through his form. Son of Colgar, it was the wind that murmured in the caves of Lena.——Or if it was the form * of

Crugal,

* The poet teaches us the opinions that prevailed in his time concerning the ftate of feparate fouls. From Connal's expreffion,
" That

Crugal, why didft thou not force him to my
fight.   Haft thou enquired where is his cave ?
The houfe of the fon of the wind ? My fword
might find that voice, and force his knowledge
from him.   And fmall is his knowledge, Connal, for he was here to day.   He could not
have gone beyond our hills, and who could tell
him there of our death ?

GHOSTS fly on clouds and ride on winds,
faid Connal's voice of wifdom: They reft together in their caves, and talk of mortal men.

THEN let them talk of mortal men ; of every
man but Erin's chief.   Let me be forgot in their
cave ; for I will not fly from Swaran.——If I
muft fall, my tomb fhall rife amidft the fame of
future times.   The hunter fhall fhed a tear on
my ftone ; and forrow dwell round the high-
bofomed Bragéla.   I fear not death, but I fear
to fly, for Fingal faw me often victorious.
Thou dim phantom of the hill, fhew thyfelf
to me ! come on thy beam of heaven, and fhew
me my death in thine hand ; yet will I not fly,
thou feeble fon of the wind.   Go, fon of Colgar, ftrike the fhield of Caithbat, it hangs be-

---

" That the ftars dim-twinkled through the form of Crugal,"
and Cuchullin's reply, we may gather that they both thought
the foul was material ; fomething like the εἴδωλα of the ancient
Greeks.

tween

tween the fpears. Let my heroes rife to the found in the midft of the battles of Erin. Though Fingal delays his coming with the race of the ftormy hills; we fhall fight, O Colgar's fon, and die in the battle of heroes.

THE found fpreads wide; the heroes rife, like the breaking of a blue-rolling wave. They ftood on the heath, like oaks with all their branches round them *; when they eccho to the ftream of froft, and their withered leaves ruftle to the wind.

HIGH Cromla's head of clouds is gray; the morning trembles on the half-enlightened ocean. The blue, gray mift fwims flowly by, and hides the fons of Innis-fail.

RISE ye, faid the king of the dark-brown fhields, ye that came from Lochlin's waves. The fons of Erin have fled from our arms——purfue them over the plains of Lena.——And, Morla, go to Cormac's hall and bid them yield to Swaran; before the people fhall fall into the tomb; and the hills of Ullin be filent.—— They rofe like a flock of fea-fowl when the waves expel them from the fhore. Their found

---

* ——As when heaven's fire
Hath fcath'd the foreft oaks, or mountain pines
With finged tops, their ftately growth tho' bare
Stand on the blafted heath.   MILTON.

was

was like a thoufand ftreams that meet in Cona's
vale, when after a ftormy night, they turn their
dark eddies beneath the pale light of the morning.

As the dark fhades of autumn fly over the
hills of grafs; fo gloomy, dark, fucceffive came
the chiefs of Lochlin's echoing woods. Tall
as the ftag of Morven moved on the king of
groves. His fhining fhield is on his fide like a
flame on the heath at night, when the world is
filent and dark, and the traveller fees fome ghoft
fporting in the beam.

A BLAST from the troubled ocean removed
the fettled mift. The fons of Innis-fail appear
like a ridge of rocks on the fhore.

Go, Morla, go, faid Lochlin's king, and
offer peace to thefe. Offer the terms we give to
kings when nations bow before us. When the
valiant are dead in war, and the virgins weeping on the field.

GREAT Morla came, the fon of Swart, and
ftately ftrode the king of fhields. He fpoke to
Erin's blue-eyed fon, among the leffer heroes.

TAKE Swaran's peace, the warrior fpoke, the
peace he gives to kings, when the nations bow
before him. Leave Ullin's lovely plains to us,
and give thy fpoufe and day. Thy fpoufe
high-bofom'd heaving fair. Thy dog that

D 3   over

overtakes the wind. Give thefe to prove the weaknefs of thine arm, and live beneath our power.

TELL Swaran, tell that heart of pride, that Cuchullin never yields.——I give him the dark-blue rolling of ocean, or I give his people graves in Erin ! Never fhall a ftranger have the lovely fun-beam of Dunfcaich; nor ever deer fly on Lochlin's hills before the nimble-footed Luäth.

VAIN ruler of the car, faid Morla, wilt thou fight the king ; that king whofe fhips of many groves could carry off thine Ifle ? So little is thy green-hilled Ullin to the king of ftormy waves.

IN words I yield to many, Morla ; but this fword fhall yield to none. Erin fhall own the fway of Cormac, while Connal and Cuchullin live. O Connal, firft of mighty men, thou haft heard the words of Morla ; fhall thy thoughts then be of peace, thou breaker of the fhields? Spirit of fallen Crugal ! why didft thou threaten us with death ? The narrow houfe fhall receive me in the midft of the light of renown.—— Exalt, ye fons of Innis-fail, exalt the fpear and bend the bow; rufh on the foe in darknefs, as the fpirits of ftormy nights.

THEN

THEN difmal, roaring, fierce, and deep the
gloom of battle rolled along; as mift * that is
poured on the valley, when ftorms invade the
filent fun-fhine of heaven. The chief moves
before in arms, like an angry ghoft before a
cloud; when meteors inclofe him with fire;
and the dark winds are in his hand.——Carril,
far on the heath, bids the horn of battle found.
He raifes the voice of the fong, and pours his
foul into the minds of heroes.

WHERE, faid the mouth of the fong, where
is the fallen Crugal? He lies forgot on earth,
and the hall of fhells † is filent.——Sad is the
fpoufe of Crugal, for fhe is a ftranger ‡ in the
hall of her forrow. But who is fhe, that, like
a fun-beam, flies before the ranks of the foe?
It is Degrena ‖, lovely fair, the fpoufe of fallen
Crugal. Her hair is on the wind behind. Her

* ——As evening mift
Ris'n from a river o'er the marifh glides
And gathers ground faft at the lab'rers heel
Homeward returning   MILTON.

† The ancient Scots, as well as the prefent highlanders, drunk
in fhells; hence it is that we fo often meet, in the old poetry,
with the *chief of fhells,* and *the halls of fhells.*

‡ Crugal had married Degrena but a little time before the
battle, confequently fhe may with propriety be called a ftranger
in the hall of her forrow.

‖ Deo-ghréna fignifies a *fun-beam.*

eye

eye is red; her voice is fhrill. Green, empty
is thy Crugal now, his form is in the cave of
the hill. He comes to the ear of reft, and raifes
his feeble voice; like the humming of the moun-
tain-bee, or collected flies of evening. But
Degrena falls like a cloud of the morn; the
fword of Lochlin is in her fide. Cairbar, fhe
is fallen, the rifing thought of thy youth. She
is fallen, O Cairbar, the thought of thy youthful hours.

FIERCE Cairbar heard the mournful found,
and rufhed on like ocean's whale; he faw the
death of his daughter; and roared in the midft
of thoufands *. His fpear met a fon of Lochlin, and battle fpread from wing to wing. As
a hundred winds in Lochlin's groves, as fire in
the firs of a hundred hills; fo loud, fo ruinous
and vaft the ranks of men are hewn down.——
Cuchullin cut off heroes like thiftles, and Swaran wafted Erin. Curach fell by his hand, and
Cairbar of the boffy fhield. Morglan lies in
lafting reft; and Ca-olt quivers as he dies. His
white breaft is ftained with his blood; and his
yellow hair firetched in the duft of his native
land. He often had fpread the feaft where he
fell; and often raifed the voice of the harp:

* Mediifque in millibus ardet. VIRG.

when

when his dogs leapt around for joy; and the youths of the chace prepared the bow.

STILL Swaran advanced, as a stream that burfts from the defart. The little hills are rolled in its courfe; and the rocks half-funk by its fide. But Cuchullin ftood before him like a hill *, that catches the clouds of heaven.——The winds contend on its head of pines; and the hail rattles on its rocks. But, firm in its ftrength, it ftands and fhades the filent vale of Cona.

So Cuchullin fhaded the fons of Erin, and ftood in the midft of thoufands. Blood rifes like the fount of a rock, from panting heroes around him. But Erin falls on either wing like fnow in the day of the fun.

---

* Virgil and Milton have made ufe of a comparifon fimilar to this; I fhall lay both before the reader, and let him judge for himfelf which of thefe two great poets have beft fucceeded.

Quantus Athos, aut quantus Eryx, aut ipfe corufcis,
Cum fremit ilicibus, quantus gaudetque nivali
Vertice fe attollens pater Appeninus ad auras.

Like Eryx or like Athos great he fhews
Or father Appenine when white with fnows;
His head divine obfcure in clouds he hides,
And fhakes the founding foreft on his fides.   DRYDEN.

On th' other fide Satan alarm'd,
Collecting all his might, dilated ftood
Like Teneriff or Atlas unremov'd:
His ftature reach'd the fky.   MILTON.

O SONS

O sons of Innis-fail, faid Grumal, Lochlin conquers on the field. Why ftrive we as reeds againft the wind? Fly to the hill of dark-brown hinds. He fled like the ftag of Morven, and his fpear is a trembling beam of light be-hind him. Few fled with Grumal, the chief of the little foul: they fell in the battle of heroes on Lena's echoing heath.

High on his car, of many gems, the chief of Erin ftood; he flew a mighty fon of Loch-lin, and fpoke, in hafte, to Connal. O Con-nal, firft of mortal men, thou haft taught this arm of death! Though Erin's fons have fled, fhall we not fight the foe? O Carril, fon of other times, carry my living friends to that bufhy hill. —— Here, Connal, let us ftand like rocks, and fave our flying friends.

Connal mounts the car of light. They ftretch their fhields like the darkened moon, the daughter of the ftarry fkies, when fhe moves, a dun circle, through heaven. Sithfadda pant-ed up the hill, and Dufronnel haughty fteed. Like waves behind a whale behind them rufhed the foe.

Now on the rifing fide of Cromla ftood Erin's few fad fons; like a grove through which the flame had rufhed hurried on by the winds of the ftormy night.——Cuchullin ftood befide an

oak.

oak. He rolled his red eye in filence, and
heard the wind in his bufhy hair ; when the
fcout of ocean came, Moran the fon of Fithil.
——The fhips, he cried, the fhips of the lonely
ifle ! There Fingal comes, the firft of men, the
breaker of the fhields. The waves foam before
his black prows. His mafts with fails are like
groves in clouds.

Blow, faid Cuchullin, all ye winds that rufh
over my ifle of lovely mift. Come to the death
of thoufands, O chief of the hills of hinds. Thy
fails, my friend, are to me like the clouds of
the morning; and thy fhips like the light of
heaven; and thou thyfelf like a pillar of fire
that giveth light in the night. O Connal, firft
of men, how pleafant are our friends ! But the
night is gathering around ; where now are the
fhips of Fingal ? Here let us pafs the hours of
darknefs, and wifh for the moon of heaven.

The winds came down on the woods. The
torrents rufhed from the rocks. Rain gathered
round the head of Cromla. And the red ftars
trembled between the flying clouds. Sad, by
the fide of a ftream whofe found was echoed by
a tree, fad by the fide of a ftream the chief of
Erin fat. Connal fon of Colgar was there, and
Carril of other times.

Unhappy

UNHAPPY is the hand of Cuchullin, faid the fon of Semo, unhappy is the hand of Cuchullin fince he flew his friend.——Ferda, thou fon of Damman, I loved thee as myfelf.

How, Cuchullin, fon of Semo, fell the breaker of the fhields? Well I remember, faid Connal, the noble fon of Damman. Tall and fair he was like the rain-bow of the hill.

FERDA from Albion came, the chief of a hundred hills. In Muri's * hall he learned the fword, and won the friendfhip of Cuchullin. We moved to the chace together; and one was our bed in the heath.

DEUGALA was the fpoufe of Cairbar, chief of the plains of Ullin. She was covered with the light of beauty, but her heart was the houfe of pride. She loved that fun-beam of youth, the noble fon of Damman. Cairbar, faid the white-armed woman, give me half of the herd. No more I will remain in your halls. Divide the herd, dark Cairbar.

* Muri, fay the Irifh bards, was an academy in Ulfter for teaching the ufe of arms. The fignification of the word is a *clufter of people*; which renders the opinion probable. Cuchullin is faid to have been the firft who introduced into Ireland complete armour of fteel. He is famous, among the Senachies, for teaching horfemanfhip to the Irifh, and for being the firft who ufed a chariot in that kingdom; which laft circumftance was the occafion of Offian's being fo circumftantial in his defcription of Cuchullin's car, in the firft book.

Let Cuchullin, faid Cairbar, divide my herd on the hill.   His breaft is the feat of juftice. Depart, thou light of beauty.——I went and divided the herd.   One fnow-white bull remained.   I gave that bull to Cairbar.   The wrath of Deugala rofe.

Son of Damman, begun the fair, Cuchullin pains my foul.   I muft hear of his death, or Lubar's ftream fhall roll over me.   My pale ghoft fhall wander near thee, and mourn the wound of my pride.   Pour out the blood of Cuchullin or pierce this heaving breaft.

Deugala, faid the fair-haired youth, how fhall I flay the fon of Semo ?   He is the friend of my fecret thoughts, and fhall I lift the fword ? She wept three days before him, on the fourth he confented to fight.

I will fight my friend, Deugala ! but may I fall by his fword.   Could I wander on the hill and behold the grave of Cuchullin ?   We fought on the hills of Muri.   Our fwords avoid a wound.   They flide on the helmets of fteel; and found on the flippery fhields.   Deugala was near with a fmile, and faid to the fon of Damman, thine arm is feeble, thou fon-beam of youth. Thy years are not ftrong for fteel.——Yield to the fon of Semo.   He is like the rock of Malmor.

THE

THE tear is in the eye of youth. He faulter-
ing faid to me, Cuchullin, raife thy boffy
fhield. Defend thee from the hand of thy
friend. My foul is laden with grief: for I muft
flay the chief of men.

I SIGHED as the wind in the chink of a rock.
I lifted high the edge of my fteel. The fun-
beam of the battle fell; the firft of Cuchullin's
friends.——

UNHAPPY is the hand of Cuchullin fince the
hero fell.

MOURNFUL is thy tale, fon of the car, faid
Carril of other times. It fends my foul back to
the ages of old, and to the days of other years.
——Often have I heard of Comal who flew the
friend he loved; yet victory attended his fteel;
and the battle was confumed in his prefence.

COMAL was a fon of Albion; the chief of an
hundred hills. His deer drunk of a thoufand
ftreams. A thoufand rocks replied to the voice
of his dogs. His face was the mildnefs of youth.
His hand the death of heroes. One was his love,
and fair was fhe! the daughter of mighty Conloch. She appeared like a fun-beam among
women. And her hair was like the wing of the
raven. Her dogs were taught to the chace.
Her bow-ftring founded on the winds of the
foreft. Her foul was fixed on Comal. Often

met

met their eyes of love. Their courfe in the chace was one, and happy were their words in fecret.——But Gormal loved the maid, the dark chief of the gloomy Ardven. He watched her lone fteps in the heath; the foe of unhappy Comal.

One day, tired of the chace, when the mift had concealed their friends, Comal and the daughter of Conloch met in the cave of Ronan *. It was the wonted haunt of Comal. Its fides were hung with his arms. A hundred fhields of thongs were there; a hundred helms of founding fteel.

Rest here, he faid, my love Galvina; thou light of the cave of Ronan. A deer appears on Mora's brow. I go; but I will foon return. I fear, fhe faid, dark Grumal my foe; he haunts the cave of Ronan. I will reft among the arms; but foon return, my love.

---

* The unfortunate death of this Ronan is the fubject of the ninth fragment of ancient poetry publifhed laft year ; it is not the work of Offian, though it is writ in his manner, and bears the genuine marks of antiquity.—The concife expreffions of Offian are imitated, but the thoughts are too jejune and confined to be the production of that poet.—Many poems go under his name that have been evidently compofed fince his time ; they are very numerous in Ireland, and fome have come to the tranfla-tor's hands. They are trivial and dull to the laft degree ; fwell-ing into ridiculous bombaft, or finking into the loweft kind of profaic ftyle.

He

He went to the deer of Mora. The daughter
of Conloch would try his love. She cloathed
her white fides with his armour, and ftrode from
the cave of Ronan. He thought it was his foe.
His heart beat high. His colour changed, and
darknefs dimmed his eyes. He drew the bow.
The arrow flew. Galvina fell in blood. He run
with wildnefs in his fteps and called the daughter
of Conloch. No anfwer in the lonely rock.
Where art thou, O my love ! He faw, at length,
her heaving heart beating around the feathered
dart. O Conloch's daughter, is it thou ? He
funk upon her breaft.

The hunters found the haplefs pair ; he afterwards walked the hill. But many and filent were
his fteps round the dark dwelling of his love.
The fleet of the ocean came. He fought ; the
ftrangers fled. He fearched for his death over
the field. But who could kill the mighty Comal ! He threw away his dark-brown fhield.
An arrow found his manly breaft. He fleeps
with his loved Galvina at the noife of the founding furge. Their green tombs are feen by the
mariner, when he bounds on the waves of the
north.

F I N G A L,

FINGAL,

AN ANCIENT

EPIC POEM.

BOOK III.

Æ

ARGUMENT to BOOK III.

Cuchullin, pleafed with the ftory of Carril, infifts with that bard for more of his fongs. He relates the actions of Fingal in Lochlin, and death of Agandecca the beautiful fifter of Swaran. He had fcarce finifhed when Calmar the fon of Matha, who had advifed the firft battle, came wounded from the field, and told them of Swaran's defign to furprife the remains of the Irifh army. He himfelf propofes to withftand fingly the whole force of the enemy, in a narrow pafs, till the Irifh fhould make good their retreat. Cuchullin, touched with the gallant propofal of Calmar, refolves to accompany him, and orders Carril to carry off the few that remained of the Irifh. Morning comes, Calmar dies of his wounds; and, the fhips of the Caledonians appearing, Swaran gives over the purfuit of the Irifh, and returns to oppofe Fingal's landing. Cuchullin afhamed, after his defeat, to appear before Fingal, retires to the cave of Tura. Fingal engages the enemy, puts them to flight; but the coming on of night makes the victory not decifive. The king, who had obferved the gallant behaviour of his grandfon Ofcar, gives him advices concerning his conduct in peace and war. He recommends to him to place the example of his fathers before his eyes, as the beft model for his conduct; which introduces the epifode concerning Fainafóllis, the daughter of the king of Craca, whom Fingal had taken under his protection, in his youth. Fillan and Ofcar are difpatched to obferve the motions of the enemy by night; Gaul the fon of Morni defires the command of the army, in the next battle; which Fingal promifes to give him. Some general reflections of the poet clofe the third day.

F I N G A L,

AN ANCIENT

E P I C   P O E M.

In S I X   B O O K S.

❋❋❋❋❋❋❋❋❋❋❋❋❋❋❋❋❋❋❋❋❋❋❋❋❋❋❋❋❋

B O O K   III *.

❋❋❋❋❋❋❋❋❋❋❋❋❋❋❋❋❋❋❋❋❋❋❋❋❋❋❋❋❋

PLEASANT are the words of the fong, faid
Cuchullin, and lovely are the tales of other
times. They are like the calm dew of the
morning on the hill of roes, when the fun is
faint on its fide, and the lake is fettled and blue
in the vale. O Carril, raife again thy voice,
and let me hear the fong of Tura : which was
fung in my halls of joy, when Fingal king of
fhields was there, and glowed at the deeds of
his fathers.

---

* The fecond night, fince the opening of the poem, continues ; and Cuchullin, Connal, and Carril ftill fit in the place
defcribed in the preceding book. The ftory of Agandecca is introduced here with propriety, as great ufe is made of it in the
courfe of the poem, and as it, in fome meafure, brings about the
cataftrophe.

Fingal! thou man of battle, faid Carril, early were thy deeds in arms. Lochlin was con-fumed in thy wrath, when thy youth ftrove with the beauty of maids. They fmiled at the fair-blooming face of the hero ; but death was in his hands. He was ftrong as the waters of Lora. His followers were like the roar of a thoufand ftreams. They took the king of Lochlin in bat-tle, but reftored him to his fhips. His big heart fwelled with pride ; and the death of the youth was dark in his foul.——For none ever, but Fingal, overcame the ftrength of the mighty Starno *.

He fat in the halls of his fhells in Lochlin's woody land. He called the grey-haired Snivan, that often fung round the circle † of Loda : when the ftone of power heard his cry, and the battle turned in the field of the valiant.

Go ; gray-haired Snivan, Starno faid, to Ardven's fea-furrounded rocks. Tell to Fingal king of the defart ; he that is the faireft among his thoufands, tell him I give him my daughter, the lovelieft maid that ever heaved a breaft of

* Starno was the father of Swaran as well as Agandecca.——His fierce and cruel character is well marked in other poems con-cerning the times.

† This paffage moft certainly alludes to the religion of Loch-lin, and the ftone of power here mentioned is the image of one of the deities of Scandinavia.

fnow.

fnow. Her arms are white as the foam of my
waves. Her foul is generous and mild. Let
him come with his braveft heroes to the daughter of the fecret hall.

SNIVAN came to Albion's windy hills : and
fair-haired Fingal went. His kindled foul flew
before him as he bounded on the wavès of the
north.

WELCOME, faid the dark-brown Starno, welcome, king of rocky Morven ; and ye his heroes of might ; fons of the lonely ifle ! Three
days within my halls fhall ye feaft ; and three
days purfue my boars, that your fame may
reach the maid that dwells in the fecret hall.

THE king of fnow * defigned their death, and
gave the feaft of fhells. Fingal, who doubted
the foe, kept on his arms of fteel. The fons of
death were afraid, and fled from the eyes of the
hero. The voice of fprightly mirth arofe. The
trembling harps of joy are ftrung. Bards fing
the battle of heroes ; or the heaving breaft of
love.——Ullin, Fingal's bard, was there ; the
fweet voice of the hill of Cona. He praifed the
daughter of fnow ; and Morven's † high-de-

---

* Starno is here poetically called the king of fnow, from the
great quantities of fnow that fall in his dominions.

† All the North-weft coaft of Scotland probably went of old
under the name of Merven, which fignifies a ridge of very high
hills.

fcended

fcended chief.——The daughter of fnow overheard, and left the hall of her fecret figh. She
came in all her beauty, like the moon from the
cloud of the eaft.——Lovelinefs was around her
as light. Her fteps were like the mufic of fongs.
She faw the youth and loved him. He was the
ftolen figh of her foul. Her blue eye rolled on
him in fecret : and fhe bleft the chief of Morven.

THE third day, with all its beams, fhone
bright on the wood of boars. Forth moved the
dark-browed Stárno ; and Fingal, king of
fhields. Half the day they fpent in the chace;
and the fpear of Fingal was red in the blood of
Gormal *.

IT was then the daughter of Starno, with
blue eyes rolling in tears, came with her voice
of love and fpoke to the king of Morven.

FINGAL, high-defcended chief, truft not
Starno's heart of pride. Within that wood he
has placed his chiefs; beware of the wood of
death. But, remember, fon of the hill, remember Agandecca : fave me from the wrath of my
father, king of the windy Morven !

* Gormal is the name of a hill in Lochlin, in the neighbour-
head of Starno's palace.

The youth, with unconcern, went on ; his heroes by his fide. The fons of death fell by his hand ; and Gormal echoed around.

Before the halls of Starno the fons of the chace convened. The king's dark brows were like clouds. His eyes like meteors of night. Bring hither, he cries, Agandecca to her lovely king of Morven. His hand is ftained with the blood of my people ; and her words have not been in vain.——

She came with the red eye of tears. She came with her loofe raven locks. Her white breaft heaved with fighs, like the foam of the ftreamy Lubar. Starno pierced her fide with fteel. She fell like a wreath of fnow that flides from the rocks of Ronan ; when the woods are ftill, and the echo deepens in the vale.

Then Fingal eyed his valiant chiefs, his valiant chiefs took arms. The gloom of the battle roared, and Lochlin fled or died.——Pale, in his bounding fhip he clofed the maid of the raven hair. Her tomb afcends on Ardven, and the fea roars round the dark dwelling of Agandecca.

Blessed be her foul, faid Cuchullin, and bleffed be the mouth of the fong.——Strong was the youth of Fingal, and ftrong is his arm of age. Lochlin fhall fall again before the king of echoing Morven. Shew thy face from a

cloud,

cloud, O moon ; light his white fails on the
wave of the night. And if any ftrong fpirit *
of heaven fits on that low-hung cloud ; turn his
dark ihips from the rock, thou rider of the
ftorm !

Such were the words of Cuchullin at the
found of the mountain-ftream, when Calmar af-
cended the hill, the wounded fon of Matha.
From the field he came in his blood. He leaned
on his bending fpear. Feeble is the arm of battle ! but ftrong the foul of the hero !

Welcome ! O fon of Matha, faid Connal,
welcome art thou to thy friends ! Why burfts
that broken figh from the breaft of him that never feared before ?

And never, Connal, will he fear, chief of
the pointed fteel. My foul brightens in danger,
and exults in the noife of battle. I am of the
race of fteel ; my fathers never feared.

Cormar was the firft of my race. He fported
through the ftorms of the waves. His black fkiff
bounded on ocean, and travelled on the wings of

* This is the only paffage in the poem that has the appearance
of religion.—But Cuchullin's apoftrophe to this fpirit is accompanied with a doubt ; fo that it is not eafy to determine whether
the hero meant a fuperior being, or the ghofts of deceafed warriors, who were fuppofed in thofe times to rule the ftorms, and
to tranfport themfelves in a guft of wind from one country to
another.

the

the blaft. A fpirit once embroiled the night.
Seas fwell and rocks refound. Winds drive
along the clouds. The lightning flies on wings
of fire. He feared and came to land : then
blufhed that he feared at all. He rufhed again
among the waves to find the fon of the wind.
Three youths guide the bounding bark ; he
ftood with the fword unfheathed. When the
low-hung vapour paffed, he took it by the curling head, and fearched its dark womb with his
fteel. The fon of the wind forfook the air.
The moon and ftars returned.

SUCH was the boldnefs of my race ; and Calmar is like his fathers. Danger flies from the
uplifted fword. They beft fucceed who dare.

BUT now, ye fons of green-vallyed Erin, retire from Lena's bloody heath. Collect the fad
remnant of our friends, and join the fword of
Fingal. I heard the found of Lochlin's advancing arms ; but Calmar will remain and fight.
My voice fhall be fuch, my friends, as if thoufands were behind me. But, fon of Semo, remember me. Remember Calmar's lifelefs corfe.
After Fingal has wafted the field, place me by
fome ftone of remembrance, that future times
may hear my fame ; and the mother * of Calmar rejoice over the ftone of my renown.

* Alclétha, her lamentation over her fon is introduced in the
poem concerning the death of Cuchullin, printed in this collection.

No : fon of Matha, faid Cuchullin, I will never leave thee. My joy is in the unequal field : my foul increafes in danger. Connal, and Carril of other times, carry off the fad fons of Erin ; and when the battle is over, fearch for our pale corfes in this narrow way. For near this oak we fhall fland in the ftream of the battle of thoufands.——O Fithil's fon, with feet of wind, fly over the heath of Lena. Tell to Fingal that Erin is inthralled, and bid the king of Morven haften. O let him come like the fun in a ftorm, when he fhines on the hills of grafs.

Morning is gray on Cromla ; the fons of the fea afcend. Calmar ftood forth to meet them in the pride of his kindling foul. But pale was the face of the warrior ; he leaned on his father's fpear. That fpear which he brought from Lara's hall, when the foul of his mother was fad.——But flowly now the hero falls like a tree on the plains of Cona. Dark Cuchullin ftands alone like a rock * in a fandy vale. The

---

*
$$\text{—— } \mathring{\eta}\mathring{\upsilon}\tau\varepsilon \ \pi\acute{\varepsilon}\tau\rho\eta$$
Ηλίβατος, μεγάλη, πολλῆς ἁλὸς ἐγγὺς ἐοῦσα, &c.
                                        Hom. Il. 15.
So fome tall rock o'erhangs the hoary main,
By winds affail'd, by billows beat in vain,
Unmov'd it hears, above, the tempefts blow,
And fees the watry mountains break below.   Pope.

fea comes with its waves, and roars on its hardened fides.   Its head is covered with foam, and the hills are echoing around.——Now from the gray mift of the ocean, the white-failed fhips of Fingal appear.   High is the grove of their mafts as they nod, by turns, on the rolling wave.

Swaran faw them from the hill, and returned from the fons of Erin. As ebbs the refounding fea through the hundred ifles of Inistore ; fo loud, fo vaft, fo immenfe returned the fons of Lochlin againft the king of the defert hill.   But bending, weeping, fad, and flow, and dragging his long fpear behind, Cuchullin funk in Cromla's wood, and mourned his fallen friends.   He feared the face of Fingal, who was wont to greet him from the fields of renown.

How many lie there of my heroes ! the chiefs of Innis-fail ! they that were chearful in the hall when the found of the fhells arofe.   No more fhall I find their fteps in the heath, or hear their voice in the chace of the hinds.   Pale, filent, low on bloody beds are they who were my friends ! O fpirits of the lately-dead, meet Cuchullin on his heath.   Converfe with him on the wind, when the ruftling tree of Tura's cave refounds.   There, far remote, I fhall lie unknown.   No bard fhall hear of me, No gray

stone

ftone fhall rife to my renown. Mourn me with
the dead, O Bragela! departed is my fame.

SUCH were the words of Cuchullin when he
funk in the woods of Cromla.

FINGAL, tall in his fhip, ftretched his bright
lance before him. Terrible was the gleam of
the fteel: it was like the green meteor of death,
fetting in the heath of Malmor, when the traveller is alone, and the broad moon is darkened
in heaven.

THE battle is over, faid the king, and I behold the blood of my friends. Sad is the heath
of Lena; and mournful the oaks of Cromla:
the hunters have fallen there in their ftrength;
and the fon of Semo is no more.——Ryno and
Fillan, my fons, found the horn of Fingal's
war. Afcend that hill on the fhore, and call
the children of the foe. Call them from the
grave of Lamdarg, the chief of other times.——
Be your voice like that of your father, when he
enters the battles of his ftrength. I wait for the
dark mighty man; I wait on Lena's fhore for
Swaran. And let him come with all his race;
for ftrong in battle are the friends of the dead.

FAIR Ryno flew like lightning; dark Fillan
as the fhade of autumn. On Lena's heath their
voice is heard; the fons of ocean heard the
horn of Fingal's war. As the roaring eddy of

ocean

ocean returning from the kingdom of fnows ; fo
ftrong, fo dark, fo fudden came down the fons
of Lochlin.   The king in their front appears in
the difmal pride of his arms.   Wrath burns in
his dark-brown face : and his eyes roll in the
fire of his valour.

FINGAL beheld the fon of Starno ; and he
remembered Agandecca.——For Swaran with
the tears of youth had mourned his white-bofomed fifter.   He fent Ullin of the fongs to bid
him to the feaft of fhells.   For pleafant on Fingal's foul returned the remembrance of the firft
of his loves.

ULLIN came with aged fteps, and fpoke to
Starno's fon.   O thou that dwelleft afar, furrounded, like a rock, with thy waves, come to
the feaft of the king, and pafs the day in reft.
To-morrow let us fight, O Swaran, and break
the echoing fhields.

TO-DAY, faid Starno's wrathful fon, we
break the echoing fhields : to-morrow my feaft
will be fpread ; and Fingal lie on earth.

AND to-morrow let his feaft be fpread, faid
Fingal with a fmile ; for to-day, O my fons, we
fhall break the echoing fhields.——Offian, ftand
thou near my arm.   Gaul, lift thy terrible
fword.   Fergus, bend thy crooked yew.   Throw,
Fillan, thy lance through heaven.——Lift your

fhields like the darkened moon. Be your fpears the meteors of death. Follow me in the path of my fame; and equal my deeds in battle.

As a hundred winds on Morven; as the ftreams of a hundred hills; as clouds fly fuccef-five over heaven; or, as the dark ocean affaults the fhore of the defert: fo roaring, fo vaft, fo terrible the armies mixed on Lena's echoing heath.——The groan of the people fpread over the hills; it was like the thunder of night, when the cloud burfts on Cona; and a thoufand ghofts fhriek at once on the hollow wind.

FINGAL rufhed on in his ftrength, terrible as the fpirit of Trenmor; when, in a whirlwind, he comes to Morven to fee the children of his pride. The oaks refound on their hills, and the rocks fall down before him.——Bloody was the hand of my father when he whirled the lightning of his fword. He remembers the battles of his youth, and the field is wafted in his courfe.

RYNO went on like a pillar of fire.——Dark is the brow of Gaul. Fergus rufhed forward with feet of wind; and Fillan like the mift of the hill.——Myfelf *, like a rock, came down, I

* Here the poet celebrates his own actions, but he does it in fuch a manner that we are not difpleafed. The mention of the great actions of his youth immediately fuggefts to him the help-lefs fituation of his age. We do not defpife him for felfifh praife, but feel his misfortunes.

exulted

exulted in the ftrength of the king.   Many were
the deaths of my arm; and difmal was the
gleam of my fword.   My locks were not then
fo gray; nor trembled my hands of age.   My
eyes were not clofed in darknefs; nor failed my
feet in the race.

Who can relate the deaths of the people; or
the deeds of mighty heroes; when Fingal, burning
in his wrath, confumed the fons of Lochlin?
Groans fwelled on groans from hill to hill, till
night had covered all.   Pale, ftaring like a herd
of deer, the fons of Lochlin convene on Lena.

We fat and heard the fprightly harp at Lubar's
gentle ftream.   Fingal himfelf was next to the
foe; and liftened to the tales of bards.   His
godlike race were in the fong, the chiefs of
other times.   Attentive, leaning on his fhield,
the king of Morven fat.   The wind whiftled
through his aged locks, and his thoughts are of
the days of other years.   Near him on his bending fpear, my young, my lovely Ofcar ftood.
He admired the king of Morven: and his actions were fwelling in his foul.

Son of my fon, begun the king, O Ofcar,
pride of youth, I faw the fhining of thy fword
and gloried in my race.   Purfue the glory of
our fathers, and be what they have been; when
Trenmor lived, the firft of men, and Trathal

the

the father of heroes. They fought the battle in their youth, and are the fong of bards.——— O Ofcar ! bend the ftrong in arms : but fpare the feeble hand. Be thou a ftream of many tides againft the foes of thy people ; but like the gale that moves the grafs to thofe who afk thine aid.———So Trenmor lived ; fuch Trathal was ; and fuch has Fingal been. My arm was the fupport of the injured ; and the weak refted behind the lightning of my fteel.

Osc A R ! I was young like thee, when lovely Fainafóllis came : that fun-beam ! that mild light of love ! the daughter of Craca's * king ! I then returned from Cona's heath, and few were in my train. A white-failed boat appeared far off; we faw it like a mift that rode on ocean's blaft. It foon approached ; we faw the fair. Her white breaft heaved with fighs. The wind was in her loofe dark hair ; her rofy cheek had tears.———Daughter of beauty, calm I faid, what figh is in that breaft ? Can I, young as I am, defend thee, daughter of the fea ? My fword is not unmatched in war, but dauntlefs is my heart.

---

* What the Craca here mentioned was, is not, at this diftance of time, eafy to determine. The moft probable opinion is, that it was one of the Shetland ifles.—There is a ftory concerning a daughter of the king of Craca in the fixth book.

To

To thee I fly, with fighs fhe replied, O chief
of mighty men! To thee I fly, chief of fhells,
fupporter of the feeble hand! The king of
Craca's echoing ifle owned me the fun-beam of
his race.   And often did the hills of Cromala
reply to the fighs of love for the unhappy Fainafóllis.   Sora's chief beheld me fair ; and loved
the daughter of Craca.   His fword is like a beam
of light upon the warrior's fide.   But dark is
his brow ; and tempefts are in his foul.   I fhun
him on the rolling fea ; but Sora's chief purfues.

REST thou, I faid, behind my fhield ; reft in
peace, thou beam of light! The gloomy chief
of Sora will fly, if Fingal's arm is like his foul.
In fome lone cave I might conceal thee, daughter of the fea ! But Fingal never flies ; for where
the danger threatens, I rejoice in the ftorm of
fpears.——I faw the tears upon her cheek.   I
pitied Craca's fair.

Now, like a dreadful wave afar, appeared the
fhip of ftormy Borbar.   His mafts high-bended
over the fea behind their fheets of fnow.   White
roll the waters on either fide.   The ftrength of
ocean founds.   Come thou, I faid, from the
roar of ocean, thou rider of the ftorm.   Partake
the feaft within my hall.   It is the houfe of
ftrangers.——The maid ftood trembling by my

F   fide ;

fide; he drew the bow: fhe fell. Unerring is
thy hand, I faid, but feeble was the foe.——
We fought, nor weak was the ftrife of death:
He funk beneath my fword. We laid them in
two tombs of ftones; the unhappy children of
youth.

Such have I been in my youth, O Ofcar;
be thou like the age of Fingal. Never feek the
battle, nor fhun it when it comes.——Fillan and
Ofcar of the dark-brown hair; ye children of
the race; fly over the heath of roaring winds;
and view the fons of Lochlin. Far off I hear
the noife of their fear, like the ftorms of echoing Cona. Go: that they may not fly my
fword along the waves of the north.——For
many chiefs of Erin's race lie here on the dark
bed of death. The children of the ftorm are
low; the fons of echoing Cromla.

The heroes flew like two dark clouds; two
dark clouds that are the chariots of ghofts;
when air's dark children come to frighten haplefs men.

It was then that Gaul *, the fon of Morni,
ftood like a rock in the night. His fpear is
glittering

---

* Gaul, the fon of Morni, was chief of a tribe that difputed
long, the pre-eminence, with Fingal himfelf. They were reduced at laft to obedience, and Gaul, from an enemy, turned
Fingal's beft friend and greateft hero. His character is fomething

glittering to the ftars; his voice like many ftreams.——Son of battle, cried the chief, O Fingal, king of fhells ! let the bards of many fongs footh Erin's friends to reft.   And, Fingal, fheath thy fword of death; and let thy people fight. We wither away without our fame; for our king is the only breaker of fhields. When morning rifes on our hills, behold at a diftance our deeds. Let Lochlin feel the fword of Morni's fon, that bards may fing of me. Such was the cuftom heretofore of Fingal's noble race. Such was thine own, thou king of fwords, in battles of the fpear.

O son of Morni, Fingal replied, I glory in thy fame.——Fight; but my fpear fhall be near to aid thee in the midft of danger. Raife, raife the voice, fons of the fong, and lull me into reft. Here will Fingal lie amidft the wind of night.——And if thou, Agandecca, art near, among the children of thy land; if thou fitteft on a blaft of wind among the high-fhrowded mafts of Lochlin; come to my dreams *, my fair one, and fhew thy bright face to my foul.

thing like that of Ajax in the Iliad ; a hero of more ftrength than conduct in battle. He was very fond of military fame, and here he demands the next battle to himfelf.—The poet, by an artifice, removes Fingal, that his return may be the more magnificent.

  * The poet prepares us for the dream of Fingal in the next book.

MANY a voice and many a harp in tuneful
founds arofe. Of Fingal's noble deeds they
fung, and of the noble race of the hero. And
fometimes on the lovely found was heard the
name of the now mournful Offian.

OFTEN have I fought, and often won in battles of the fpear. But blind, and tearful, and
forlorn I now walk with little men. O Fingal,
with thy race of battle I now behold thee not.
The wild roes feed upon the green tomb of the
mighty king of Morven.——Bleft be thy foul,
thou king of fwords, thou moft renowned on
the hills of Cona !

FINGAL,

AN ANCIENT

EPIC POEM.

BOOK IV.

F 3

ARGUMENT to BOOK IV.

The action of the poem being suspended by night, Ossian takes that opportunity to relate his own actions at the lake of Lego, and his courtship of Evirallin, who was the mother of Oscar, and had died some time before the expedition of Fingal into Ireland. Her ghost appears to him, and tells him that Oscar, who had been sent, the beginning of the night, to observe the enemy, was engaged with an advanced party, and almost overpowered. Ossian relieves his son; and an alarm is given to Fingal of the approach of Swaran. The king rises, calls his army together, and, as he had promised the preceding night, devolves the command on Gaul the son of Morni, while he himself, after charging his sons to behave gallantly and defend his people, retires to a hill, from whence he could have a view of the battle. The battle joins; the poet relates Oscar's great actions. But when Oscar, in conjunction with his father, conquered in one wing, Gaul, who was attacked by Swaran in person, was on the point of retreating in the other. Fingal sends Ullin his bard to encourage him with a war song, but notwithstanding Swaran prevails; and Gaul and his army are obliged to give way. Fingal, descending from the hill, rallies them again: Swaran desists from the pursuit, possesses himself of a rising ground, restores the ranks, and waits the approach of Fingal. The king, having encouraged his men, gives the necessary orders, and renews the battle. Cuchullin, who, with his friend Connal, and Carril his bard, had retired to the cave of Tura, hearing the noise, came to the brow of the hill, which overlooked the field of battle, where he saw Fingal engaged with the enemy. He, being hindered by Connal from joining Fingal, who was himself upon the point of obtaining a complete victory, sends Carril to congratulate that hero on his success.

F I N G A L,

AN ANCIENT

E·P I C   P O E M.

In S I X   B O O K S.

✿✿✿✿✿✿✿✿✿✿✿✿✿✿✿✿✿✿✿✿✿✿✿✿✿✿✿✿✿✿

B O O K   IV *.

✿✿✿✿✿✿✿✿✿✿✿✿✿✿✿✿✿✿✿✿✿✿✿✿✿✿✿✿✿

WHO comes with her fongs from the mountain, like the bow of the fhowery Lena? It is the maid of the voice of love. The white-armed daughter of Tofcar. Often haft thou heard my fong, and given the tear of beauty. Doft thou come to the battles of thy people, and to hear the actions of Ofcar? When

---

* Fingal being afleep, and the action fufpended by night, the poet introduces the ftory of his courtfhip of Evirallin the daughter of Branno. The epifode is neceffary to clear up feveral paffages that follow in the poem; at the fame time that it naturally brings on the action of the book which, may be fuppofed to begin about the middle of the third night from the opening of the poem. ——This book, as many of Offian's other compofitions, is addreffed to the beautiful Malvina the daughter of Tofcar. She appears to have been in love with Ofcar, and to have affected the company of the father after the death of the fon.

fhall I ceafe to mourn by the ftreams of the echoing Cona ? My years have paffed away in battle, and my age is darkened with forrow.

DAUGHTER of the hand of fnow ! I was not fo mournful and blind ; I was not fo dark and forlorn when Everallin loved me. Everallin with the dark-brown hair, the white-bofomed love of Cormac. A thoufand heroes fought the maid, fhe denied her love to a thoufand; the fons of the fword were defpifed; for graceful in her eyes was Offian.

I WENT in fuit of the maid to Lego's fable furge ; twelve of my people were there, the fons of the ftreamy Morven. We came to Branno friend of ftrangers : Branno of the founding mail.——From whence, he faid, are the arms of fteel ? Not eafy to win is the maid that has denied the blue-eyed fons of Erin. But bleft be thou, O fon of Fingal, happy is the maid that waits thee. Tho' twelve daughters of beauty were mine, thine were the choice, thou fon of fame !——Then he opened the hall of the maid, the dark-haired Everallin. Joy kindled in our breafts of fteel and bleft the maid of Branno.

ABOVE us on the hill appeared the people of ftately Cormac. Eight were the heroes of the chief; and the heath flamed with their arms. There Colla, Durra of the wounds, there mighty

Tofcar,

Tofcar, and Tago, there Freftal the victorious flood; Dairo of the happy deeds, and Dala the battle's bulwark in the narrow way.——The fword flamed in the hand of Cormac, and graceful was the look of the hero.

Eight were the heroes of Offian; Ullin ftormy fon of war; Mullo of the generous deeds; the noble, the graceful Scelacha; Oglan, and Cerdal the wrathful, and Duma-riccan's brows of death. And why fhould Ogar be the laft; fo wide renowned on the hills of Ardven?

Ogar met Dala the ftrong, face to face, on the field of heroes. The battle of the chiefs was like the wind on ocean's foamy waves. The dagger is remembered by Ogar; the weapon which he loved; nine times he drowned it in Dala's fide. The ftormy battle turned. Three times I pierced Cormac's fhield: three times he broke his fpear. But, unhappy youth of love! I cut his head away.——Five times I fhook it by the lock. The friends of Cormac fled.

Whoever would have told me, lovely maid *, when then I ftrove in battle; that blind, forfaken, and forlorn I now fhould pafs the night; firm ought his mail to have been, and unmatched his arm in battle.

---

* The poet addreffes himfelf to Malvina the daughter of Tofcar.

Now

Now * on Lena's gloomy heath the voice of mufic died away. The unconftant blaft blew hard, and the high oak fhook its leaves around me ; of Everallin were my thoughts, when fhe, in all the light of beauty, and her blue eyes rolling in tears, ftood on a cloud before my fight, and fpoke with feeble voice.

O Ossian, rife and fave my fon ; fave Ofcar chief of men, near the red oak of Lubar's ftream, he fights with Lochlin's fons.——She funk into her cloud again. I clothed me with my fteel. My fpear fupported my fteps, and my rattling armour rung. I hummed, as I was wont in danger, the fongs of heroes of old. Like diftant thunder † Lochlin heard; they fled ; my fon purfued.

---

* The poet returns to his fubject. If one could fix the time of the year in which the action of the poem happened, from the fcene defcribed here, I fhould be tempted to place it in autumn. —The trees fhed their leaves, and the winds are variable, both which circumftances agree with that feafon of the year.

† Offian gives the reader a high idea of himfelf. His very fong frightens the enemy. This paffage refembles one in the eighteenth Iliad, where the voice of Achilles frightens the Tro- jans from the body of Patroclus.

> Forth march'd the chief, and diftant from the crowd
> High on the rampart rais'd his voice aloud.
> So high his brazen voice the hero rear'd,
> Hofts drop their arms and trembled as they fear'd.
>   Pope.

I called him like a dftiant ftream. My fon return over Lena. No further purfue the foe, though Offian is behind thee.——He came; and lovely in my ear was Ofcar's founding fteel. Why didft thou ftop my hand, he faid, till death had covered all? For dark and dreadful by the ftream they met thy fon and Fillan. They watched the terrors of the night. Our fwords have conquered fome. But as the winds of night pour the ocean over the white fands of Mora, fo dark advance the fons of Lochlin over Lena's ruftling heath. The ghofts of night fhriek afar; and I have feen the meteors of death. Let me awake the king of Morven, he that fmiles in danger; for he is like the fon of heaven that rifes in a ftorm.

Fingal had ftarted from a dream, and leaned on Trenmor's fhield; the dark-brown fhield of his fathers; which they had lifted of old in the battles of their race.——The hero had feen in his reft the mournful form of Agandecca; fhe came from the way of the ocean, and flowly, lonely, moved over Lena. Her face was pale like the mift of Cromla; and dark were the tears of her cheek. She often raifed her dim hand from her robe; her robe which was of the clouds of the defart: fhe raifed her dim hand over Fingal, and turned away her filent eyes.

Why

WHY weeps the daughter of Starno, said Fingal, with a figh ? Why is thy face fo pale, thou daughter of the clouds ?——She departed on the wind of Lena ; and left him in the midft of the night.——She mourned the fons of her people that were to fall by Fingal's hand.

THE hero ftarted from reft, and ftill beheld her in his foul.——The found of Ofcar's fteps approached. The king faw the grey fhield on his fide. For the faint beam of the morning came over the waters of Ullin.

WHAT do the foes in their fear ? faid the rifing king of Morven. Or fly they through ocean's foam, or wait they the battle of fteel ? But why fhould Fingal afk ? I hear their voice on the early wind.---Fly over Lena's heath, O Ofcar, and awake our friends to battle.

THE king ftood by the ftone of Lubar ; and thrice raifed his terrible voice. The deer ftarted from the fountains of Cromla ; and all the rocks fhook on their hills. Like the noife of a hundred mountain-ftreams, that burft, and roar, and foam : like the clouds that gather to a tempeft on the blue face of the fky ; fo met the fons of the defart, round the terrible voice of Fingal. For pleafant was the voice of the king of Morven to the warriors of his land : often had

he

he led them to battle, and returned with the
fpoils of the foe.

COME to battle, faid the king, ye children of
the ftorm. Come to the death of thoufands.
Comhal's fon will fee the fight.——My fword
fhall wave on that hill, and be the fhield of my
people. But never may you need it, warriors;
while the fon of Morni fights, the chief of
mighty men.——He fhall lead my battle; that
his fame may rife in the fong.——O ye ghofts
of heroes dead! ye riders of the ftorm of
Cromla! receive my falling people with joy,
and bring them to your hills.---And may the
blaft of Lena carry them over my feas, that they
may come to my filent dreams, and delight my
foul in reft.

FILLAN and Ofcar, of the dark-brown hair!
fair Ryno, with the pointed fteel! advance with
valour to the fight; and behold the fon of
Morni. Let your fwords be like his in the
ftrife : and behold the deeds of his hands. Pro-
tect the friends of your father : and remember
the chiefs of old. My children, I fhall fee you
yet, though here ye fhould fall in Erin. Soon
fhall our cold, pale ghofts meet in a cloud, and
fly over the hills of Cona.

Now like a dark and ftormy cloud, edged
round with the red lightning of heaven, and

flying

9

flying weftward from the morning's beam, the king of hills removed. Terrible is the light of his armour, and two fpears are in his hand.——— His gray hair falls on the wind.———He often looks back on the war. Three bards attend the fon of fame, to carry his words to the heroes.--- High on Cromla's fide he fat, waving the light-ning of his fword, and as he waved we moved.

Joy rofe in Ofcar's face. His cheek is red. His eye fheds tears. The fword is a beam of fire in his hand. He came, and fmiling, fpoke to Offian.———O ruler of the fight of fteel! my father, hear thy fon. Retire with Morven's mighty chief; and give me Offian's fame. And if here I fall; my king, remember that breaft of fnow, that lonely fun-beam of my love, the white-handed daughter of Tofcar. For with red cheek from the rock, and bending over the ftream, her foft hair flies about her bofom as fhe pours the figh for Ofcar. Tell her I am on my hills a lightly-bounding fon of the wind ; that hereafter, in a cloud, I may meet the lovely maid of Tofcar.

Raise, Ofcar, rather raife my tomb. I will not yield the fight to thee. For firft and bloodieft in the war my arm fhall teach thee how to fight. But, remember, my fon, to place this fword, this bow, and the horn of my

deer,

deer, within that dark and narrow houſe, whoſe
mark is one gray ſtone.   Oſcar, I have no love
to leave to the care of my ſon; for graceful
Evirallin is no more, the lovely daughter of
Branno.

Such were our words, when Gaul's loud
voice came growing on the wind.   He waved on
high the ſword of his father, and ruſhed to
death and wounds.

As waves white-bubbling over the deep come
ſwelling, roaring on; as rocks of ooze meet
roaring waves: ſo foes attacked and fought.
Man met with man, and ſteel with ſteel.
Shields ſound; men fall.   As a hundred hammers on the ſon of the furnace, ſo roſe, ſo
rung their ſwords.

Gaul ruſhed on like a whirlwind in Ardven.
The deſtruction of heroes is on his ſword.
Swaran was like the fire of the deſart in the
echoing heath of Gormal.   How can I give to
the ſong the death of many ſpears?   My ſword
roſe high, and flamed in the ſtrife of blood.
And, Oſcar, terrible wert thou, my beſt, my
greateſt ſon!   I rejoiced in my ſecret ſoul, when
his ſword flamed over the ſlain.   They fled
amain through Lena's heath: and we purſued
and flew.   As ſtones that bound from rock to
rock; as axes in echoing woods; as thunder

rolls

rolls from hill to hill in difmal broken peals; fo blow fucceeded to blow, and death to death, from the hand of Ofcar * and mine.

But Swaran clofed round Morni's fon, as the ftrength of the tide of Iniftore. The king half-rofe from his hill at the fight, and half-affumed the fpear. Go, Ullin, go, my aged bard, begun the king of Morven. Remind the mighty Gaul of battle; remind him of his fathers. Support the yielding fight with fong; for fong enlivens war. Tall Ullin went, with fteps of age, and fpoke to the king of fwords.

Son † of the chief of generous fteeds! high-bounding king of fpears. Strong arm in every perilous toil. Hard heart that never yields. Chief of the pointed arms of death. Cut down the foe; let no white fail bound round dark

---

* Offian never fails to give a fine character of his beloved fon. His fpeech to his father is that of a hero; it contains the fubmiffion due to a parent, and the warmth that becomes a young warrior. There is a propriety in dwelling here on the actions of Ofcar, as the beautiful Malvina, to whom the book is addreffed, was in love with that hero.

† The war-fong of Ullin varies from the reft of the poem in the verfification. It runs down like a torrent; and confifts almoft intirely of epithets. The cuftom of encouraging men in battle with extempore rhymes, has been carried down almoft to our own times. Several of thefe war-fongs are extant, but the moft of them are only a group of epithets, without beauty or harmony, utterly deftitute of poetical merit.

Iniftore.

Iniſtore. Be thine arm like thunder. Thine
eyes like fire, thy heart of ſolid rock. Whirl
round thy ſword as a meteor at night, and lift
thy ſhield like the flame of death. Son of the
chief of generous ſteeds, cut down the foe ; de-
ſtroy.——The hero's heart beat high. But
Swaran came with battle. He cleft the ſhield of
Gaul in twain ; and the ſons of the deſart fled.

Now Fingal aroſe in his might, and thrice he
reared his voice. Cromla anſwered around, and
the ſons of the deſart ſtood ſtill.——They bent
their red faces to earth, aſhamed at the preſence
of Fingal. He came like a cloud of rain in the
days of the ſun, when ſlow it rolls on the hill,
and fields expect the ſhower. Swaran beheld the
terrible king of Morven, and ſtopped in the
midſt of his courſe. Dark he leaned on his
ſpear, rolling his red eyes around. Silent and
tall he ſeemed as an oak on the banks of Lubar,
which had its branches blaſted of o d by the
lightning of heaven. It bends over the ſtream,
and the gray moſs whiſtles in the wind : ſo ſtood
the king. Then ſlowly he retired to the riſing
heath of Lena. His thouſands pour around the
hero, and the darkneſs of battle gathers on the
hill.

Fingal, like a beam from heaven, ſhone in
the midſt of his people. His heroes gather

around

around him, and he fends forth the voice of his power. Raife my ftandards * on high,---fpread them on Lena's wind, like the flames of an hundred hills. Let them found on the winds of Erin, and remind us of the fight. Ye fons of the roaring ftreams, that pour from a thoufand hills, be near the king of Morven : attend to the words of his power. Gaul ftrongeft arm of death ! O Ofcar, of the future fights ; Connal, fon of the blue fteel of Sora ; Dermid of the dark-brown hair, and Offian king of many fongs, be near your father's arm.

WE reared the fun-beam † of battle ; the ftandard of the king. Each hero's foul exulted with joy, as, waving, it flew on the wind. It was ftudded with gold above, as the blue wide fhell of the nightly fky. Each hero had his ftandard too ; and each his gloomy men.

BEHOLD, faid the king of generous fhells, how Lochlin divides on Lena.——They ftand like broken clouds on the hill, or an half confumed grove of oaks ; when we fee the fky through

* Th' imperial enfign, which full high advanc'd,
Shone like a meteor ftreaming to the wind.
                                        MILTON.

† Fingal's ftandard was diftinguifhed by the name of *fun-beam*; probably on account of its bright colour, and its being ftudded with gold. To begin a battle is expreffed, in old compofition, by *lifting of the fun-beam.*

                                                    its

its branches, and the meteor paffing behind. Let every chief among the friends of Fingal take a dark troop of, thofe that frown fo high; nor let a fon of the echoing groves bound on the waves of Iniftore.

MINE, faid Gaul, be the feven chiefs that came from Lano's lake.——Let Iniftore's dark king, faid Ofcar, come to the fword of Offian's fon.——To mine the king of Inifcon, faid Connal, heart of fteel! Or Mudan's chief or I, faid brown-haired Dermid, fhall fleep on clay-cold earth. My choice, though now fo weak and dark, was Terman's battling king; I promifed with my hand to win the hero's dark-brown fhield.——Bleft and victorious be my chiefs, faid Fingal of the mildeft look; Swaran, king of roaring waves, thou art the choice of Fingal.

Now, like an hundred different winds that pour through many vales; divided, dark, the fons of the hill advanced, and Cromla echoed around.

How can I relate the deaths when we clofed in the ftrife of our fteel? O daughter of Tofcar! bloody were our hands! The gloomy ranks of Lochlin fell like the banks of the roaring Cona.——Our arms were victorious on Lena; each chief fulfilled his promife. Befide the murmur of Branno thou didft often fit, O

G 2   maid;

maid; when thy white bofom rofe frequent, like
the down of the fwan when flow fhe fails the
lake, and fidelong winds are blowing.——Thou
haft feen the fun * retire red and flow behind
his cloud; night gathering round on the mountain, while the unfrequent blaft † roared in narrow vales.   At length the rain beats hard; and
thunder rolls in peals.   Lightning glances on
the rocks.   Spirits ride on beams of fire.   And

    * *Sol quoque & exoriens & cum fe condit in undas*
Signa dabit.   Solem certiſſima figna fequuntur,
Ut quæ mane refert, & quæ furgentibus aſtris.
Ille ubi nafcentem maculis variaverit ortum
Conditus in nubem, medicque refugerit orbe;
Sufpecti tibi funt imbres.   Virg.
Above the reft the fun, who never lies,
Foretels the change of weather in the fkies.
For if he rife, unwilling to his race,
Clouds on his brow and fpots upon his face;
Or if thro' mifts he fhoots his fullen beams,
Frugal of light, in loofe and ftraggling ftreams,
Sufpect a drifling day.   Dryden.

    † *Continuo ventis furgentibus aut freta ponti*
Incipiunt agitata tumefcere; & aridus altis
Montibus audiri fragor, aut refonantia longe
Littora mifceri, & nemorum increbefcere murmur.
          Virg.
For ere the rifing winds begin to roar,
The working feas advance to wafh the fhore;
Soft whifpers run along the leafy wood,
And mountains whiftle to the murm'ring flood.
        Dryden.

the

the ftrength of the mountain-ftreams * comes roaring down the hills. Such was the noife of battle, maid of the arms of fnow. Why, daughter of the hill, that tear? the maids of Lochlin have caufe to weep. The people of their country fell, for bloody was the blue fteel of the race of my heroes. But I am fad, for-lorn, and blind ; and no more the companion of heroes. Give, lovely maid, to me thy tears, for I have feen the tombs of all my friends.

IT was then by Fingal's hand a hero fell, to his grief.——Gray-haired he rolled in the duft, and lifted his faint eyes to the king. And is it by me thou haft fallen, faid the fon of Comhal, thou friend of Agandecca! I faw thy tears for the maid of my love in the halls of the bloody Starno. Thou haft been the foe of the foes of my love, and haft thou fallen by my hand? Raife, Ullin, raife the grave of the fon of Ma-thon ; and give his name to the fong of Agan-decca ; for dear to my foul haft thou been, thou darkly-dwelling maid of Ardven.

---

‡ ——*ruunt de montibus amnes.*   VIRG.
The rapid rains, defcending from the hills,
To rolling torrents fwell the creeping rills.

                                      DRYDEN.

CUCHULLIN, from the cave of Cromla, heard
the noife of the troubled war. He called to
Connal chief of fwords, and Carril of other
times. The gray-haired heroes heard his voice,
and took their afpen fpears. They came, and
faw the tide of battle, like the crowded waves of
the ocean ; when the dark wind blows from the
deep, and rolls the billows through the fandy
vale.

CUCHULLIN kindled at the fight, and darknefs gathered on his brow. His hand is on the
fword of his fathers : his red-rolling eyes on the
foe. He thrice attempted to ruſh to battle, and
thrice did Connal ſtop him. Chief of the iſle
of miſt, he faid, Fingal fubdues the foe. Seek
not a part of the fame of the king ; himfelf is
like a ſtorm.

THEN, Carril, go, replied the chief, and
greet the king of Morven. When Lochlin falls
away like a ſtream after rain, and the noife of
the battle is over, then be thy voice fweet in his
ear to praife the king of fwords. Give him the
fword of Caithbat ; for Cuchullin is worthy no
more to lift the arms of his fathers.

BUT, O ye ghoſts of the lonely Cromla ! ye
fouls of chiefs that are no more ! be ye the companions of Cuchullin, and talk to him in the
cave of his forrow. For never more ſhall I be

renowned

renowned among the mighty in the land.   I am
like a beam that has fhone ; like a mift that fled
away, when the blaft of the morniug came,
and brightened the fhaggy fide of the hill.   Connal, talk of arms no more: departed is my
fame.---My fighs fhall be on Cromla's wind,
till my footfteps ceafe to be feen.——And thou,
. white-bofom'd Bragela, mourn over the fall of
my fame ; for, vanquifhed, I will never return
to thee, thou fun-beam of Dunfcaich.

F I N G A L,

AN ANCIENT

E P I C P O E M.

B O O K V.

.

ARGUMENT to Book V.

Cuchullin and Connal still remain on the hill. Fingal and Swaran meet; the combat is described. Swaran is overcome, bound and delivered over as a prisoner to the care of Offian and Gaul the son of Morni; Fingal, his younger sons, and Ofcar, still pursue the enemy. The episode of Orla a chief of Lochlin, who was mortally wounded in the battle, is introduced. Fingal, touched with the death of Orla, orders the pursuit to be dif- continued; and calling his sons together, he is in- formed that Ryno, the youngest of them, was killed. He laments his death, hears the story of Lamdarg and Gelchossa, and returns towards the place where he had left Swaran. Carril, who had been sent by Cuchullin to congratulate Fingal on his victory, comes in the mean time to Offian. The conversation of the two poets closes the action of the fourth day.

F I N G A L,

AN ANCIENT

E P I C   P O E M.

In S I X B O O K S.

✿✿✿✿✿✿✿✿✿✿✿✿✿✿✿✿✿✿✿✿✿✿✿✿✿✿✿✿✿✿
B O O K   V *.
✿✿✿✿✿✿✿✿✿✿✿✿✿✿✿✿✿✿✿✿✿✿✿✿✿✿✿✿✿✿

N O W Connal, on Cromla's windy fide, fpoke to the chief of the noble car. Why that gloom, fon of Semo ? Our friends are the mighty in battle. And renowned art thou, O warrior ! many were the deaths of thy fteel. Often has Bragela met with blue-rolling eyes of

---

* The fourth day ftill continues. The poet by putting the narration in the mouth of Connal, who ftill remained with Cuchullin on the fide of Cromla, gives propriety to the praifes of Fingal. The beginning of this book, in the original, is one of the moft beautiful parts of the poem. The verfification is regular and full, and agrees very well with the fedate character of Connal.——No poet has adapted the cadence of his verfe more to the temper of the fpeaker, than Offian has done. It is more than probable that the whole poem was originally defigned to be fung to the harp, as the verfification is fo various, and fo much fuited to the different paffions of the human mind.

joy,

joy, often has fhe met her hero, returning in
the midft of the valiant; when his fword was red
with flaughter, and his foes filent in the fields of
the tomb.   Pleafant to her ears were thy bards,
when thine actions rofe in the fong.

But behold the king of Morven ; he moves
below like a pillar of fire.   His ftrength is like
the ftream of Lubar, or the wind of the echoing
Cromla ; when the branchy forefts of night are
overturned.

Happy are thy people, O Fingal, thine arm
fhall fight their battles : thou art the firft in their
dangers ; the wifeft in the days of their peace.
Thou fpeakeft and thy thoufands obey ; and
armies tremble at the found of thy fteel.   Happy
are thy people, Fingal, chief of the lonely
hills.

Who is that fo dark and terrible, coming in
the thunder of his courfe? who is it but Starno's
fon to meet the king of Morven ? Behold the
battle of the chiefs: it is like the ftorm of the
ocean, when two fpirits meet far diftant, and
contend for the rolling of the wave.   The hunter hears the noife on his hill ; and fees the high
billows advancing to Ardven's fhore.

Such were the words of Connal, when the
heroes met in the midft of their falling people.
There was the clang of arms! there every blow,

like

like the hundred hammers of the furnace ! Terrible is the battle of the kings, and horrid the look of their eyes. Their dark-brown fhields are cleft in twain; and their fteel flies, broken, from their helmets. They fling their weapons down. Each rufhes * to the grafp of his foe. Their finewy arms bend round each other : they turn from fide to fide, and ftrain and ftretch their large fpreading limbs below. But when the pride of their ftrength arofe, they fhook the hill with their heels; rocks tumble from their places on high; the green-headed bufhes are overturned. At length the ftrength of Swaran fell; and the king of the groves is bound.

THUS have I feen on Cona; (but Cona I behold no more) thus have I feen two dark hills removed from their place by the ftrength of the burfting ftream. They turn from fide to fide, and their tall oaks meet one another on high. Then they fall together with all their rocks and

---

* This paffage refembles one in the twenty-third Iliad.

Clofe lock'd above their heads and arms are mixt ;
Below their planted feet at diftance fixt ;
Now to the grafp each manly body bends ;
The humid fweat from ev'ry pore defcends ;
Their bones refound with blows : fides, fhoulders, thighs,
Swell to each gripe, and bloody tumours rife.

POPE.

trees,

trees. The ftreams are turned by their fides, and the red ruin is feen afar.

Sons of the king of Morven, faid the noble Fingal, guard the king of Lochlin; for he is ftrong as his thoufand waves. His hand is taught to the battle, and his race of the times of old. Gaul, thou firft of my heroes, and Offian king of fongs, attend the friend of Agandecca, and raife to joy his grief.——But, Ofcar, Fillan, and Ryno, ye children of the race! purfue the reft of Lochlin over the heath of Lena; that no veffel may hereafter bound on the dark-rolling waves of Iniftore.

They flew like lightning over the heath. He flowly moved as a cloud of thunder when the fultry plain of fummer is filent. His fword is before him as a fun-beam, terrible as the ftream-ing meteor of night. He came toward a chief of Lochlin, and fpoke to the fon of the wave.

Who is that like a cloud at the rock of the roaring ftream? He cannot bound over its courfe; yet ftately is the chief! his boffy fhield is on his fide; and his fpear like the tree of the defart. Youth of the dark-brown hair, art thou of Fingal's foes?

I am

I am a fon of Lochlin, he cries, and ftrong is my arm in war. My fpoufe is weeping at home, but Orla * will never return.

Or fights or yields the hero, faid Fingal of the noble deeds? foes do not conquer in my prefence: but my friends are renowned in the hall. Son of the wave, follow me, partake the feaft of my fhells, and purfue the deer of my defart.

No: faid the hero, I affift the feeble: my ftrength fhall remain with the weak in arms. My fword has been always unmatched, O warrior: let the king of Morven yield.

I never yielded, Orla, Fingal never yielded to man. Draw thy fword and chufe thy foe. Many are my heroes.

And does the king refufe the combat, faid Orla of the dark-brown hair? Fingal is a match for Orla: and he alone of all his race.——But, king of Morven, if I fhall fall; (as one time the warrior muft die;) raife my tomb in the midft, and let it be the greateft on Lena. And fend, over the dark-blue wave, the fword of

* The ftory of Orla is fo beautiful and affecting in the original, that many are in poffeffion of it in the north of Scotland, who never heard a fyllable more of the poem. It varies the action, and awakes the attention of the reader when he expected nothing bu languor in the conduct of the poem, as the great action was over in the conqueft of Swaran.

Orla

Orla to the spoufe of his love; that she may shew it to her son, with tears, to kindle his soul to war.

Son of the mournful tale, said Fingal, why doft thou awaken my tears? One day the warriors muft die, and the children fee their ufelefs arms in the hall. But, Orla, thy tomb shall rife, and thy white-bofomed fpoufe weep over thy fword.

They fought on the heath of Lena, but feeble was the arm of Orla. The fword of Fingal defcended, and cleft his shield in twain. It fell and glittered on the ground, as the moon on the ftream of night.

King of Morven, said the hero, lift thy fword, and pierce my breaft. Wounded and faint from battle my friends have left me here. The mournful tale shall come to my love on the banks of the ftreamy Loda; when she is alone in the wood; and the ruftling blaft in the leaves.

No; said the king of Morven, I will never wound thee, Orla. On the banks of Loda let her fee thee efcaped from the hands of war. Let thy gray-haired father, who, perhaps, is blind with age, hear the found of thy voice in his hall.——With joy let the hero rife, and fearch for his fon with his hands.

But

2

But never will he find him, Fingal ; said the youth of the ftreamy Loda.——On Lena's heath I fhall die ; and foreign bards will talk of me. My broad belt covers my wound of death. And now I give it to the wind.

The dark blood poured from his fide, he fell pale on the heath of Lena. Fingal bends over him as he dies, and calls his younger heroes.

Oscar and Fillan, my fons, raife high the memory of Orla. Here let the dark-haired hero reft far from the fpoufe of his love. Here let him reft in his narrow houfe far from the found of Loda. The fons of the feeble will find his bow at home, but will not be able to bend it. His faithful dogs howl on his hills, and his boars, which he ufed to purfue, rejoice. Fallen is the arm of battle ; the mighty among the va-liant is low !

Exalt the voice, and blow the horn, ye fons of the king of Morven : let us go back to Swaran, and fend the night away on fong. Fillan, Ofcar, and Ryno, fly over the heath of Lena. Where, Ryno, art thou, young fon of fame ? Thou art not wont to be the laft to an-fwer thy father.

Ryno, faid Ullin firft of bards, is with the awful forms of his fathers. With Trathal king of fhields, and Trenmor of the mighty deeds.

H   The

The youth is low,---the youth is pale,---he lies on Lena's heath.

And fell the fwifteft in the race, faid the king, the firft to bend the bow? Thou fcarce haft been known to me : why did young Ryno fall? But fleep thou foftly on Lena, Fingal fhall foon behold thee. Soon fhall my voice be heard no more, and my footfteps ceafe to be feen. The bards will tell of Fingal's name; the ftones will talk of me. But, Ryno, thou art low indeed, ——thou haft not received thy fame. Ullin, ftrike the harp for Ryno; tell what the chief would have been. Farewel, thou firft in every field. No more fhall I direct thy dart. Thou that haft been fo fair; I behold thee not--- Farewel.

The tear is on the cheek of the king; for terrible was his fon in war. His fon! that was like a beam of fire by night on the hill; when the forefts fink down in its courfe, and the tra- veller trembles at the found.   .

Whose fame is in that dark-green tomb, be- gan the king of generous fhells? four ftones with their heads of mofs ftand there; and mark the narrow houfe of death. Near it let my Ryno reft, and be the neighbour of the valiant. Perhaps fome chief of fame is here to fly with my fon on clouds. O Ullin, raife the fongs of

other

other times. Bring to memory the dark dwellers of the tomb. If in the field of the valiant they never fled from danger, my fon fhall reft with them, far from his friends, on the heath of Lena.

Here, faid the mouth of the fong, here reft the firft of heroes. Silent is Lamderg * in this tomb, and Ullin king of fwords. And who, foft fmiling from her cloud, fhews me her face of love? Why, daughter, why fo pale art thou, firft of the maids of Cromla? Doft thou fleep with the foes in battle, Gelchoffa, white-bofomed daughter of Tuathal?——Thou haft been the love of thoufands, but Lamderg was thy love. He came to Selma's moffy towers, and, ftriking his dark buckler, fpoke :

Where is Gelchoffa, my love, the daughter of the noble Tuathal? I left her in the hall of Selma, when I fought with the gloomy Ulfadda. Return foon, O Lamderg, fhe faid, for here I am in the midft of forrow. Her white breaft rofe with fighs. Her cheek was wet with tears. But I fee her not coming to meet me ; and to footh my foul after battle. Silent is the hall of my joy ; I hear not the voice of the bard.---

* Lamh-dhearg fignifies *bloody hand.* Gelchoffa, *white legged.* Tuathal, *furly.* Ulfadda, *long-beard.* Ferchios, *the conqueror of men.*

Bran * does not fhake his chains at the gate, glad
at the coming of Lamderg. Where is Gelchoffa,
my love, the mild daughter of the generous
Tuathal?

LAMDERG ! fays Ferchios the fon of Aidon,
Gelchoffa may be on Cromla; fhe and the maids
of the bow purfuing the flying deer.

FERCHIOS ! replied the chief of Cromla, no
noife meets the car of Lamderg. No found is in
the woods of Lena. No deer fly in my fight.
No panting dog purfues. I fee not Gelchoffa
my love, fair as the full moon fetting on the
hills of Cromla. Go, Ferchios, go to Allad †
the gray-haired fon of the rock. His dwelling
is in the circle of ftones. He may know of
Gelchoffa.

THE fon of Aidon went; and fpoke to the car
of age. Allad ! thou that dwelleft in the rock,
thou that trembleft alone, what faw thine eyes
of age?

* Bran is a common name of gray-hounds to this day. It is a
cuftom in the north of Scotland, to give the names of the heroes
mentioned in this poem, to their dogs; a proof that they are familiar to the ear, and their fame generally known.

† Allad is plainly a druid: he is called the fon of the rock,
from his dwelling in a cave; and the circle of ftones here mentioned is the pale of the druidical temple. He is here confulted
as one who had a fupernatural knowledge of things; from the
druids, no doubt, came the ridiculous notion of the fecond
fight, which prevailed in the highlands and ifles.

I saw, anfwered Allad the old, Ullin the fon of Cairbar. He came like a cloud from Cromla; and he hummed a furly fong like a blaft in a leaflefs wood. He entered the hall of Selma. ——Lamderg, he faid, moft dreadful of men, fight or yield to Ullin. Lamderg, replied Gel-choffa, the fon of battle, is not here. He fights Ulfadda mighty chief. He is not here, thou firft of men. But Lamderg never yielded. He will fight the fon of Cairbar.

Lovely art thou, faid terrible Ullin, daugh-ter of the generous Tuathal. I carry thee to Cairbar's halls. The valiant fhall have Gel-choffa. Three days I remain on Cromla, to wait that fon of battle, Lamderg. On the fourth Gelchoffa is mine, if the mighty Lamderg flies.

Allad! faid the chief of Cromla, peace to thy dreams in the cave. Ferchios, found the horn of Lamderg that Ullin may hear on Cromla. Lamderg *, like a roaring ftorm, af-cended the hill from Selma. He hummed a furly fong as he went, like the noife of a falling ftream. He ftood like a cloud on the hill, that varies its form to the wind. He rolled a ftone,

---

* The reader will find this paffage altered from what it was in the fragments of ancient poetry.——It is delivered down very differently by tradition, and the tranflator has chofen that read-ing which favours leaft of bombaft.

the

the fign of war. Ullin heard in Cairbar's hall.
The hero heard, with joy, his foe, and took
his father's fpear. A fmile brightens his dark-
brown cheek, as he places his fword by his fide.
The dagger glittered in his hand. He whiftled
as he went.

GELCHOSSA faw the filent chief, as a wreath
of mift afcending the hill.——She ftruck her
white and heaving breaft; and filent, tearful,
feared for Lamderg.

CAIRBAR, hoary chief of fhells, faid the
maid of the tender hand; I muft bend the bow
on Cromla ; for I fee the dark-brown hinds.

SHE hafted up the hill. In vain ! the gloomy
heroes fought.——Why fhould I tell the king of
Morven how wrathful heroes fight !——Fierce
Ullin fell. Young Lamderg came all pale to
the daughter of generous Tuathal.

WHAT blood, my love, the foft-haired woman faid, what blood runs down my warrior's
fide ?——It is Ullin's blood, the chief replied,
thou fairer than the fnow of Cromla ! Gelchoffa,
let me reft here a little while. The mighty
Lamderg died.

AND fleepeft thou fo foon on earth, O chief of
fhady Cromla ? three days fhe mourned befide
her love. —— The hunters found her dead.
They raifed this tomb above the three. Thy

6   fon,

fon, O king of Morven, may reft here with heroes.

And here my fon fhall reft, faid Fingal, the noife of their fame has reached my ears. Fillan and Fergus ! bring hither Orla ; the pale youth of the ftream of Loda. Not unequalled fhall Ryno lie in earth when Orla is by his fide. Weep, ye daughters of Morven ; and ye maids of the ftreamy Loda. Like a tree they grew on the hills ; and they have fallen like the oak * of the defart ; when it lies acrofs a ftream, and withers in the wind of the mountain.

Oscar ! chief of every youth ! thou feeft how they have fallen. Be thou, like them, on earth renowned. Like them the fong of bards. Terrible were their forms in battle ; but calm was Ryno in the days of peace. He was like the bow of the fhower feen far diftant on the ftream ; when the fun is fetting on Mora, and filence on the hill of deer. Reft, youngeft of my fons, reft, O Ryno, on Lena. We too fhall be no more ; for the warrior one day muft fall.

---

* —ὡ ὅτι τις δρὖς ἤριπεν—   Hom. Il. 16.

　　　——as the mountain oak
　Nods to the ax, till with a groaning found
　It finks, and fpreads its honours on the ground.

　　　　　　　　　　　　　　　　Pope.

H 4   Such

Such was thy grief, thou king of hills, when Ryno lay on earth. What muſt the grief of Oſſian be, for thou thyſelf art gone. I hear not thy diſtant voice on Cona. My eyes perceive thee not. Often forlorn and dark I ſit at thy tomb; and feel it with my hands. When I think I hear thy voice; it is but the blaſt of the deſart.——Fingal has long ſince fallen aſleep, the ruler of the war.

Then Gaul and Oſſian ſat with Swaran on the ſoft green banks of Lubar. I touched the harp to pleaſe the king. But gloomy was his brow. He rolled his red eyes towards Lena. The hero mourned his people.

I lifted my eyes to Cromla, and I ſaw the ſon of generous Semo.——Sad and ſlow he re- tired from his hill towards the lonely cave of Tura. He ſaw Fingal victorious, and mixed his joy with grief. The ſun is bright on his armour, and Connal ſlowly followed. They ſunk behind the hill like two pillars of the fire of night : when winds purſue them over the moun- tain, and the flaming heath reſounds. Beſide a ſtream of roaring foam his cave is in a rock. One tree bends above it ; and the ruſhing winds echo againſt its ſides. Here reſts the chief of Dunſcaich, the ſon of generous Semo. His thoughts are on the battle he loſt ; and the tear

is

is on his cheek.   He mourned the departure of
his fame that fled like the mift of Cona.   O Bragela, thou art too far remote to cheer the foul
of the hero.   But let him fee thy bright form in
his foul; that his thoughts may return to the
lonely fun-beam of Dunfcaich.

WHO comes with the locks of age? It is the
fon of fongs.   Hail, Carril of other times, thy
voice is like the harp in the halls of Tura.   Thy
words are pleafant as the fhower that falls on the
fields of the fun.   Carril of the times of old,
why comeft thou from the fon of the generous
Semo?

OSSIAN king of fwords, replied the bard,
thou beft raifeft the fong.   Long haft thou been
known to Carril, thou ruler of battles.   Often
have I touched the harp to lovely Evirallin.
Thou too haft often accompanied my voice in
Branno's hall of generous fhells.   And often,
amidft our voices, was heard the mildeft Evirallin.   One day fhe fung of Cormac's fall, the
youth that died for her love.   I faw the tears on
her cheek, and on thine, thou chief of men.
Her foul was touched for the unhappy, though
fhe loved him not.   How fair among a thoufand
maids was the daughter of the generous Branno!

BRING not, Carril, I replied, bring not her
memory to my mind.   My foul muft melt at

the

the remembrance. My eyes muſt have their
tears. Pale in the earth is ſhe the ſoftly-bluſhing
fair of my love. But ſit thou on the heath, O
Bard, and let us hear thy voice. It is pleaſant
as the gale of ſpring that ſighs on the hunter's
ear ; when he wakens from dreams of joy, and
has heard the muſic of the ſpirits of the hill.

F I N G A L,

AN ANCIENT

E P I C P O E M.

B O O K VI.

ARGUMENT to Book VI.

Night comes on. Fingal gives a feast to his army, at which Swaran is present. The king commands Ullin his bard to give the song of peace; a custom always observed at the end of a war. Ullin relates the actions of Trenmor, great grandfather to Fingal, in Scandinavia, and his marriage with Inibaca, the daughter of a king of Lochlin who was ancestor to Swaran; which consideration, together with his being brother to Agandecca, with whom Fingal was in love in his youth, induced the king to release him, and permit him to return, with the remains of his army, into Lochlin, upon his promise of never returning to Ireland, in a hostile manner. The night is spent in settling Swaran's departure, in songs of bards, and in a conversation in which the story of Grumal is introduced by Fingal. Morning comes. Swaran departs; Fingal goes on a hunting party, and finding Cuchullin in the cave of Tura, comforts him, and sets sail, the next day, for Scotland; which concludes the poem.

F I N G A L,

AN ANCIENT

E P I C   P O E M.

In S I X B O O K S.

✿✿✿✿✿✿✿✿✿✿✿✿✿✿✿✿✿✿✿✿✿✿✿✿✿✿✿✿✿

B O O K VI *.

✿✿✿✿✿✿✿✿✿✿✿✿✿✿✿✿✿✿✿✿✿✿✿✿✿✿✿✿✿

THE clouds of night come rolling down and reſt on Cromla's dark-brown ſteep. The ſtars of the north ariſe over the rolling of the waves of Ullin ; they ſhew their heads of fire through the flying miſt of heaven. A diſtant wind roars in the wood ; but ſilent and dark is the plain of death.

STILL on the darkening Lena aroſe in my ears the tuneful voice of Carril. He ſung of the companions of our youth, and the days of former years ; when we met on the banks of Lego,

---

* This book opens with the fourth night, and ends on the morning of the ſixth day. The time of five days, five nights, and a part of the ſixth day is taken up in the poem. The ſcene lies in the heath of Lena, and the mountain Cromla on the coaſt of Ulſter.

and

and fent round the joy of the fhell. Cromla, with its cloudy fteeps, anfwered to his voice. The ghofts of thofe he fung came in their ruft-ling blafts. They were feen to bend with joy towards the found of their praife.

Be thy foul bleft, O Carril, in the midft of thy eddying winds. O that thou would come to my hall when I am alone by night!---And thou doft come, my friend, I hear often thy light hand on my harp; when it hangs on the diftant wall, and the feeble found touches my ear. Why doft thou not fpeak to me in my grief, and tell when I fhall behold my friends? But thou paffeft away in thy murmuring blaft; and thy wind whiftles through the gray hair of Offian.

Now on the fide of Mora the heroes gathered to the feaft. A thoufand aged oaks are burning to the wind.——The ftrength * of the fhells

---

* By the ftrength of the fhell is meant the liquor the heroes drunk: of what kind it was, cannot be afcertained at this dif-tance of time. The tranflator has met with feveral ancient poems that mention wax-lights and wine as common in the halls of Fingal. The names of both are borrowed from the Latin, which plainly fhews that our anceftors had them from the Ro-mans, if they had them at all. The Caledonians in their fre-quent incurfions to the province, might become acquainted with thofe conveniencies of life, and introduce them into their own country, among the booty which they carried from South Britain.

goes

goes round.   And the fouls of warriors brighten
with joy.   But the king of Lochlin is filent, and
forrow reddens in the eyes of his pride.   He
often turned toward Lena and remembered that
he fell.

F INGAL leaned on the fhield of his fathers.
His gray locks flowly waved on the wind, and
glittered to the beam of night.   He faw the
grief of Swaran, and fpoke to the firft of Bards.

RAISE, Ullin, raife the fong of peace, and
footh my foul after battle, that my ear may forget the noife of arms.   And let a hundred harps
be near to gladden the king of Lochlin.   He
muft depart from us with joy.——None ever
went fad from Fingal.   Ofcar ! the lightning
of my fword is againft the ftrong in battle ; but
peaceful it lies by my fide when warriors yield
in war.

TRENMOR *, faid the mouth of the fongs,
lived in the days of other years.   He bounded
over the waves of the north : companion of the
ftorm.   The high rocks of the land of Lochlin,
and its groves of murmuring founds appeared to
the hero through the mift ;---he bound his white-
bofomed fails.——Trenmor purfued the boar

---

* Trenmor was great grandfather to Fingal.   The ftory is
introduced to facilitate the difmiffion of Swaran.

that

that roared along the woods of Gormal. Many had fled from its prefence; but the fpear of Trenmor flew it.

THREE chiefs, that beheld the deed, told of the mighty ftranger. They told that he ftood like a pillar of fire in the bright arms of his valour. The king of Lochlin prepared the feaft, and called the blooming Trenmor. Three days he feafted at Gormal's windy towers; and got his choice in the combat.

THE land of Lochlin had no hero that yielded not to Trenmor. The fhell of joy went round with fongs in praife of the king of Morven; he that came over the waves, the firft of mighty men.

Now when the fourth gray morn arofe, the hero launched his fhip; and walking along the filent fhore waited for the rufhing wind. For loud and diftant he heard the blaft murmuring in the grove.

COVERED over with arms of fteel a fon of the woody Gormal appeared. Red was his cheek and fair his hair. His fkin like the fnow of Morven. Mild rolled his blue and fmiling eye when he fpoke to the king of fwords.

STAY, Trenmor, ftay thou firft of men, thou haft not conquered Lonval's fon. My

fword

fword has often met the brave. And the wife
thun the ftrength of my bow.

THOU fair-haired youth, Trenmor replied,
I will not fight with Lonval's fon. Thine arm
is feeble, fun-beam of beauty. Retire to Gormal's dark-brown hinds.

BUT I will retire, replied the youth, with the
fword of Trenmor; and exult in the found of
my fame. The virgins fhall·gather with fmiles
around him who conquered Trenmor. They
fhall figh with the fighs of love, and admire the
length of thy fpear; when I fhall carry it
among thoufands, and lift the glittering point
to the fun.

THOU fhalt never carry my fpear, faid the
angry king of Morven.——Thy mother fhall
find thee pale on the fhore of the echoing Gormal; and, looking over the dark-blue deep, fee
the fails of him that flew her fon.

I WILL not lift the fpear, replied the youth,
my arm is not ftrong with years. But with the
feathered dart I have learned to pierce a diftant
foe. Throw down that heavy mail of fteel; for
Trenmor is covered all over.——I firft will lay
my mail on earth.——Throw now thy dart,
thou king of Morven.

HE faw the heaving of her breaft. It was the
fifter of the king.---She had feen him in the

I   halls

halls of Gormal; and loved his face of youth.
——The fpear dropt from the hand of Trenmor : he bent his red cheek to the ground, for
he had feen her like a beam of light that meets
the fons of the cave, when they revifit the fields
of the fun, and bend their aching eyes.

Chief of the windy Morven, begun the maid
of the arms of fnow; let me reft in thy bounding
fhip, far from the love of Corlo. For he, like
the thunder of the defart, is terrible to Inibaca.
He loves me in the gloom of his pride, and
fhakes ten thoufand fpears.

Rest thou in peace, faid the mighty Trenmor, behind the fhield of my fathers. I will
not fly from the chief, though he fhakes ten
thoufand fpears.

Three days he waited on the fhore ; and fent
his horn abroad. He called Corlo to battle
from all his echoing hills. But Corlo came not
to battle. The king of Lochlin defcended. He
,fcafted on the roaring fhore ; and gave the maid
to Trenmor.

King of Lochlin, faid Fingal, thy blood
flows in the veins of thy foe. Our families met
in battle, becaufe they loved the ftrife of fpears.
But often did they feaft in the hall; and fend
round the joy of the fhell.——Let thy face
brighten with gladnefs, and thine ear delight in
                                                    the

the harp. Dreadful as the ftorm of thine ocean thou haft poured thy valour forth; thy voice has been like the voice of thoufands when they engage in battle. Raife, to-morrow, thy white fails to the wind, thou brother of Agandecca. Bright as the beam of noon fhe comes on my mournful foul. I faw thy tears for the fair one, and fpared thee in the halls of Starno; when my fword was red with flaughter, and my eye full of tears for the maid.——Or doft thou chufe the fight ? The combat which thy fathers gave to Trenmor is thine : that thou mayeft depart renowned like the fun fetting in the weft.

King of the race of Morven, faid the chief of the waves of Lochlin ; never will Swaran fight with thee, firft of a thoufand heroes ! I faw thee in the halls of Starno, and few were thy years beyond my own.——When fhall I, faid I to my foul, lift the fpear like the noble Fingal? We have fought heretofore, O warrior, on the fide of the fhaggy Malmor; after my waves had carried me to thy halls, and the feaft of a thoufand fhells was fpread. Let the bards fend him who overcame to future years, for noble was the ftrife of heathy Malmor.

But many of the fhips of Lochlin have loft their youths on Lena. Take thefe, thou king of Morven, and be the friend of Swaran. And

when

when thy fons fhall come to the mofly towers of
Gormal, the feaft of fhells fhall be fpread, and
the combat offered on the vale.

Nor fhip, replied the king, fhall Fingal take,
nor land of many hills. The defart is enough
to me with all its deer and woods. Rife on thy
waves again, thou noble friend of Agandecca.
Spread thy white fails to the beam of the morning, and return to the echoing hills of Gormal.

Blest be thy foul, thou king of fhells, faid
Swaran of the dark-brown fhield. In peace
thou art the gale of fpring. In war the moun-
tain-ftorm. Take now my hand in friendfhip,
thou noble king of Morven. Let thy bards
mourn chofe who fell. Let Erin give the fons
of Lochlin to earth ; and raife the mofly ftones
of their fame. That the children of the north
hereafter may behold the place where their fathers fought. And fome hunter may fay, when
he leans on a mofly tomb, here Fingal and Swaran fought, the heroes of other years. Thus
hereafter fhall he fay, and our fame fhall laft
for ever.

Swaran, faid the king of the hills, to-day
our fame is greateft. We fhall pafs away like a
dream. No found will be in the fields of our
battles. Our tombs will be loft in the heath.
The hunter fhall not know the place of our reft.

Our

Our names may be heard in fong, but the
ftrength of our arms will ceafe. O Oſſian, Carril, and Ullin, you know of heroes that are no
more. Give us the fong of other years. Let
the night pafs away on the found, and morning
return with joy.

WE gave the fong to the kings, and a hundred harps accompanied our voice. The face of
Swaran brightened like the full moon of heaven,
when the clouds vaniſh away, and leave her
calm and broad in the midſt of the ſky.

IT was then that Fingal fpoke to Carril the
chief of other times. Where is the fon of Semo;
the king of the iſle of miſt? has he retired, like
the meteor of death, to the dreary cave of Tura?

CUCHULLIN, faid Carril of other times, lies
in the dreary cave of Tura. His hand is on the
fword of his ftrength. His thoughts on the battle which he loſt. Mournful is the king of
fpears; for he has often been victorious. He
fends the fword of his war to reſt on the fide of
Fingal. For, like the ftorm of the defart, thou
haſt fcattered all his foes. Take, O Fingal,
the fword of the hero; for his fame is departed
like miſt when it flies before the ruftling wind
of the vale.

No: replied the king, Fingal ſhall never take
his fword. His arm is mighty in war; and tell

him

him his fame fhall never fail. Many have been overcome in battle, that have fhone afterwards like the fun of heaven.

O Swaran, king of the refounding woods, give all thy grief away.——The vanquifhed, if brave, are renowned; they are like the fun in a cloud when he hides his face in the fouth, but looks again on the hills of grafs.

Grumal was a chief of Cona. He fought the battle on every coaft. His foul rejoic d in blood; his ear in the din of arms. He poured his warriors on the founding Craca; and Craca's king met him from his grove; for then within the circle of Brumo * he fpoke to the ftone of power.

Fierce was the battle of the heroes, for the maid of the breaft of fnow. The fame of the daughter of Craca had reached Grumal at the ftreams of Cona; he vowed to have the white-bofomed maid, or die on the echoing Craca. Three days they ftrove together, and Grumal cn the fourth was bound.

Far from his friends they placed him in the horrid circle of Brumo; where often, they faid, the ghofts of the dead howled round the ftone of

* This paffage alludes to the religion of the king of Craca. See a note on a fimilar fubject in the third book.

their

their fear. But afterwards he fhone like a pillar
of the light of heaven. They fell by his mighty
hand, and Grumal had his fame.

RAISE, ye bards of other times, raife high
the praife of heroes ; that my foul may fettle on
their fame ; and the mind of Swaran ceafe to be
fad.

THEY lay in the heath of Mora ; the dark
winds ruftled over the heroes.——A hundred
voices at once arofe, a hundred harps were
ftrung ; they fung of other times, and the
mighty chiefs of former years.

WHEN now fhall I hear the bard ; or rejoice
at the fame of my fathers? The harp is not
ftrung on Morven ; nor the voice of mufic raifed
on Cona. Dead with the mighty is the bard ;
and fame is in the defart no more.

MORNING trembles with the beam of the
eaft, and glimmers on gray-headed Cromla.
Over Lena is heard the horn of Swaran, and the
fons of the ocean gather around.——Silent and
fad they mount the wave, and the blaft of Ullin
is behind their fails. White, as the mift of
Morven, they float along the fea.

CALL, faid Fingal, call my dogs, the long-
bounding fons of the chace. Call white-breafted
Bran ; and the furly ftrength of Luath.——
Fillan, and Ryno---but he is not here ; my fon
I 4 refts

refts on the bed of death. Fillan and Fergus, blow my horn, that the joy of the chace may arife; that the deer of Cromla may hear and ftart at the lake of roes.

The fhrill found fpreads along the wood. The fons of heathy Cromla arife.——A thoufand dogs fly off at once, gray-bounding through the heath. A deer fell by every dog, and three by the white-breafted Bran. He brought them, in their flight, to Fingal, that the joy of the king might be great.

One deer fell at the tomb of Ryno; and the grief of Fingal returned. He faw how peaceful lay the ftone of him who was the firft at the chace.——No more fhalt thou rife, O my fon, to partake of the feaft of Cromla. Soon will thy tomb be hid, and the grafs grow rank on thy grave. The fons of the feeble fhall pafs over it, and fhall not know that the mighty lie there.

Ossian and Fillan, fons of my ftrength, and Gaul king of the blue fwords of war, let us afcend the hill to the cave of Tura, and find the chief of the battles of Erin.——Are thefe the walls of Tura? gray and lonely they rife on the heath. The king of fhells is fad, and the halls are de-folate. Come let us find the king of fwords, and give him all our joy.——But is that Cu-

chullin,

chullin, O Fillan, or a pillar of fmoke on the heath ? The wind of Cromla is on my eyes, and I diftinguifh not my friend.

FINGAL! replied the youth, it is the fon of Semo. Gloomy and fad is the hero ; his hand is on his fword. Hail to the fon of battle, breaker of the fhields !

HAIL to thee, replied Cuchullin, hail to all the fons of Morven. Delightful is thy prefence, O Fingal, it is like the fun on Cromla; when the hunter mourns his abfence for a feafon, and fees him between the clouds. Thy fons are like ftars that attend thy courfe, and give light in the night. It is not thus thou haft feen me, O Fingal, returning from the wars of the defart; when the kings of the world * had fled, and joy returned to the hill of hinds.

MANY are thy words, Cuchullin, faid Connan † of fmall renown. Thy words are many, fon of Semo, but where are thy deeds in arms ? Why did we come over the ocean to aid thy

---

* This is the only paffage in the poem, wherein the wars of Fingal againft the Romans are alluded to : —— The Roman emperor is diftinguifhed in old compofitions by the title of *king of the world*.

† Connan was of the family of Morni. He is mentioned in feveral other poems, and always appears with the fame charaſter. The poet paffed him over in filence till now, and his behaviour here deferves no better ufage.

feeble

feeble fword ? Thou flyeft to thy cave of forrow, and Connan fights thy battles : Refign to
me thefe arms of light ; yield them, thou fon of
Erin.

No hero, replied the chief, ever fought the
arms of Cuchullin ; and had a thoufand heroes
fought them it' were in vain, thou gloomy
youth. I fled not to the cave of forrow, as long
as Erin's warriors lived.

YOUTH of the feeble arm, faid Fingal, Connan, fay no more. Cuchullin is renowned in
battle, and terrible over the defart. Often have
I heard thy fame, thou ftormy chief of Innis-
fail. Spread now thy white fails for the ifle of
mift, and fee Bragela leaning on her rock. Her
tender eye is in tears, and the winds lift her
long hair from her heaving breaft. She liftens
to the winds of night to hear the voice of thy
rowers * ; to hear the fong of the fea, and the
found of thy diftant harp.

AND long fhall fhe liften in vain ; Cuchullin
fhall never return. How can I behold Bragela
to raife the figh of her breaft ? Fingal, I was
always victorious in the battles of other fpears !

---

* The practice of finging when they row is univerfal among
the inhabitants of the north-weft coaft of Scotland and the ifles.
It deceives time, and infpirits the rowers.

AND

And hereafter thou fhalt be victorious, faid Fingal king of fhells. The fame of Cuchullin fhall grow like the branchy tree of Cromla. Many battles await thee, O chief, and many fhall be the wounds of thy hand. Bring hither, Ofcar, the deer, and prepare the feaft of fhells; that our fouls may rejoice after danger, and our friends delight in our prefence.

We fat, we feafted, and we fung. The foul of Cuchullin rofe. The ftrength of his arm returned; and gladnefs brightened on his face.' Ullin gave the fong, and Carril raifed the voice. I, often, joined the bards, and fung of battles of the fpear.——Battles! where I often fought; but now I fight no more. The fame of my former actions is ceafed; and I fit forlorn at the tombs of my friends.

Thus they paffed the night in the fong; and brought back the morning with joy. Fingal arofe on the heath, and fhook his glittering fpear in his hand.——He moved firft toward the plains of Lena, and we followed like a ridge of fire. Spread the fail, faid the king of Morven, and catch the winds that pour from Lena.—— We rofe on the wave with fongs, and rufhed, with joy, through the foam of the ocean*.

* It is allowed by the beft critics that an epic poem ought to end happily. This rule, in its moft material circumftances, is

observed

obferved by the three moft defervedly celebrated poets, Homer, Virgil, and Milton ; yet, I know not how it happens, the con- clufions of their poems throw a melancholy damp on the mind. One leaves his reader at a funeral; another at the untimely death of a hero ; and the third in the folitary fcenes of an unpeopled world.

Ὡς οἵγ᾽ ἀμφίεπον ταφον Ἕκλορος ἱπποδαμοιο.

HOMER.

Such honours Ilion to her hero paid,
And peaceful flept the mighty Hector's fhade.

POPE.

——*Ferrum adverfo fub pectore condit*
Fervidus. Aft illi folvuntur frigore membra,
Vitaque cum gemitu fugit indignata fub umbras.

VIRGIL.

He rais'd his arm aloft; and at the word
Deep in his bofom drove the fhining fword.
The ftreaming blood diftain'd his arms around,
And the difdainful foul came rufhing thro' the wound.

DRYDEN.

They, hand in hand, with wand'ring fteps and flow,
Through Eden took their folitary way.

MILTON.

C O M Á L A:

A

DRAMATIC POEM*.

❀❀❀❀❀❀❀❀❀❀❀❀❀❀❀❀❀❀❀❀❀❀❀

The P E R S O N S.

FINGAL.	MELILCOMA, } daughters
HIDALLAN.	DERSAGRENA, } of Morni.
COMALA.	BARDS.

DERSAGRENA.

THE chace is over.---No noife on Ardven but the torrent's roar!——Daughter of Morni, come from Crona's banks. Lay down the bow and take the harp. Let the night come on with fongs, and our joy be great on Ardven.

MELILCOMA.

---

* This poem is valuable on account of the light it throws on the antiquity of Offian's compofitions. The Caracul mentioned here is the fame with Caracalla the fon of Severus, who in the year 211 commanded an expedition againft the Caledonians.—The variety of the meafure fhews that the poem was originally fet to mufic,

COMALA:

MELILCOMA *.

AND night comes on, thou blue-eyed maid, gray night grows dim along the plain. I faw a deer at Crona's ftream; a moffy bank he feemed through the gloom, but foon he bounded away. A meteor played round his branchy horns; and the awful faces † of other times looked from the clouds of Crona.

mufic, and perhaps prefented before the chiefs upon folemn occafions.——Tradition has handed down the ftory more complete
than it is in the poem.—" Comala, the daughter of Sarno king
of Iniftore or Orkney iflands, fell in love with Fingal the fon of
Comhal at a feaft, to which her father had invited him, [Fingal,
B. III.] upon his return from Lochlin, after the death of Agandecca. Her paffion was fo violent, that fhe followed him, difguifed like a youth, who wanted to be employed in his wars.
She was foon difcovered by Hidallan the fon of Lamor, one of
Fingal's heroes, whofe love fhe had flighted fome time before—
Her romantic paffion and beauty recommended her fo much to
the king, that he had refolved to make her his wife; when news
was brought him of Caracul's expedition. He marched to ftop
the progrefs of the enemy, and Comala attended him.——He
left her on a hi'l, within fight of Caracul's army, when he himfelf went to battle, having previoufly promifed, if he furvived, to
return that night." The fequel of the ftory may be gathered
from the poem itfelf.

* Melilcoma.—*foft-rolling eye.*

† *Apparent diræ facies, inimicaque Trojæ*
Numina magna deûm.   VIRG.
          ——dreadful founds I hear,
  And the dire forms of hoftile gods appear.
                                        DRYDEN.

DERSAGRENA.

DERSAGRENA *.

THESE are the figns of Fingal's death.——
The king of fhields is fallen!---and Caracul
prevails. Rife, Comala †, from thy rocks;
daughter of Sarno, rife in tears. The youth
of thy love is low, and his ghoft is already on
our hills.

MELILCOMA.

THERE Comala fits forlorn! two gray dogs
near fhake their rough ears, and catch the flying breeze. Her red cheek refts on her arm,
and the mountain wind is in her hair. She
turns her blue-rolling eyes towards the fields of
his promife.——Where art thou, O Fingal, for
the night is gathering around?

COMALA.

O CARUN ‡ of the ftreams! why do I behold
thy waters rolling in blood? Has the noife of
the

* Derfagrena, *the brightnefs of a fun-beam.*

† Comala, *the maid of the pleafant brow.*

‡ Carun or Cara'on, *a winding river.*—This river retains ftill
the name of Carron, and falls into the Forth fome miles to the
North of Falkirk.

——*Gentefque alias cum pelleret armis*
Sedibus, aut victas vilem fervaret in ufum

the battle been heard on thy banks; and fleeps
the king of Morven?——Rife, moon, thou
daughter of the fky! look from between thy
clouds, that I may behold the light of his fteel,
on the field of his promife.---Or rather let the
meteor, that lights our departed fathers through
the night, come, with its red light, to fhew me
the way to my fallen hero. Who will defend me
from forrow? Who from the love of Hidallan?
Long fhall Comala look before fhe can behold
Fingal in the midft of his hoft; bright as the
beam of the morning in the cloud of an early
fhower.

HIDALLAN *.

ROLL, thou mift of gloomy Crona, roll on
the path of the hunter. Hide his fteps from
mine eyes, and let me remember my friend no
more. The bands of battle are fcattered, and

*Servitii, hic contenta fuos defendere fines
Roma fecurigeris pratendit mænia Scotis:
Hic jpe progreffus pofita, Caronis ad undam
Terminus Aufonii fignat divortia regni.*

BUCHANAN.

† Hidallan was fent by Fingal to give notice to Comala of his
return; he, to revenge himfelf on her for flighting his love fome
time before, told her that the king was killed in battle. He
even pretended that he carried his body from the field to be buried
in her prefence; and this circumftance makes it probable that the
poem was prefented of old.

no

no crowding fteps are round the noife of his fteel. O Carun, roll thy ftreams of blood, for the chief of the people fell.

COMALA.

WHO fell on Carun's graffy banks, fon of the cloudy night? Was he white as the fnow of Ardven? Blooming as the bow of the fhower? Was his hair like the mift of the hill, foft and curling in the day of the fun? Was he like the thunder of heaven in battle? Fleet as the roe of the defart?

HIDALLAN.

O THAT I might behold his love, fair-leaning from her rock! Her red eye dim in tears, and her blufhing cheek half hid in her locks! Blow, thou gentle breeze, and lift the heavy locks of the maid, that I may behold her white arm, and lovely cheek of her forrow!

COMALA.

AND is the fon of Comhal fallen, chief of the mournful tale? The thunder rolls on the hill! ——The lightening flies on wings of fire! But they frighten not Comala; for her Fingal fell. Say, chief of the mournful tale, fell the breaker of fhields?

HIDALLAN.

THE nations are fcattered on their hills; for they fhall hear the voice of the chief no more.

COMALA.

CONFUSION purfue thee over thy plains; and deftruction overtake thee, thou king of the world. Few be thy fteps to thy grave; and let one virgin mourn thee. Let her be, like Comala, tearful in the days of her youth.——Why haft thou told me, Hidallan, that my hero fell? I might have hoped a little while his return, and have thought I faw him on the diftant rock; a tree might have deceived me with his appearance; and the wind of the hill been the found of his horn in mine ear. O that I were on the banks of Carun! that my tears might be warm on his cheek!

HIDALLAN.

HE lies not on the banks of Carun: on Ardven heroes raife his tomb. Look on them, O moon, from thy clouds; be thy beam bright on his breaft, that Comala may behold him in the light of his armour.

COMALA.

STOP, ye fons of the grave, till I behold my love. He left me at the chace alone. I knew

not

A DRAMATIC POEM. 131

not that he went to war. He faid he would return with the night; and the king of Morven is
returned. Why didft thou not tell me that he
would fall, O trembling fon of the rock*! Thou
haft feen him in the blood of his youth, but
thou didft not tell Comala!

MELILCOMA.

WHAT found is that on Ardven? Who is
that bright in the vale? Who comes like the
ftrength of rivers, when their crowded waters
glitter to the moon?

COMALA.

WHO is it but the foe of Comala, the fon of
the king of the world! Ghoft of Fingal! do
thou, from thy cloud, direct Comala's bow.
Let him fall like the hart of the defart.——It is
Fingal in the crowd of his ghofts.---Why doft
thou come, my love, to frighten and pleafe
my foul?

FINGAL.

RAISE, ye bards of the fong, the wars of the
ftreamy Carun. Caracul has fled from my arms

---

* By *the fon of the rock* fhe means a druid. It is probable that
fome of the order of the druids remained as late as the beginning of the reign of Fingal; and that Comala had confulted one
of them concerning the event of the war with Caracul.

K 2

along

along the fields of his pride. He fets far diftant like a meteor that inclofes a fpirit of night, when the winds drive it over the heath, and the dark woods are gleaming around.

I HEARD a voice like the breeze of my hills. Is it the huntrefs of Galmal, the white-handed daughter of Sarno ? Look from thy rocks *, my love ; and let me hear the voice of Comala.

COMALA.

TAKE me to the cave of thy reft, O lovely fon of death !——

FINGAL.

COME to the cave of my reft.——The ftorm is over †, and the fun is on our fields. Come to the cave of my reft, huntrefs of echoing Cona.

COMALA.

HE is returned with his fame ; I feel the right hand of his battles.——But I muft reft befide the rock till my foul fettle from fear.---Let the harp

---

* O my dove *t'at art* in the clefts of the rock, in the fecret *flaces* of the ftairs, let me fee thy countenance, let me hear thy voice.   SOLOMON's Song.

† The winter is paft, the rain is over and gone.
                              SOLOMON's Song.

be

be near; and raife the fong, ye daughters of Morni.

DERSAGRENA.

COMALA has flain three deer on Ardven, and the fire afcends on the rock; go to the feaft of Comala, king of the woody Morven!

FINGAL.

RAISE, ye fons of fong, the wars of the ftreamy Carun; that my white-handed maid may rejoice: while I behold the feaft of my love.

BARDS.

ROLL, ftreamy Carun, roll in joy, the fons of battle fled. The fteed is not feen on our fields; and the wings * of their pride fpread in other lands. The fun will now rife in peace, and the fhadows defcend in joy. The voice of the chace will be heard; and the fhields hang in the hall. Our delight will be in the war of the ocean, and our hands be red in the blood of Lochlin. Roll, ftreamy Carun, roll in joy, the fons of battle fled.

MELILCOMA.

DESCEND, ye light mifts from high; ye moon-beams, lift her foul.——Pale lies the maid at the rock! Comala is no more!

* Perhaps the poet alludes to the Roman eagle.

K 3   FINGAL.

FINGAL.

Is the daughter of Sarno dead; the white-bofomed maid of my love ? Meet me, Comala, on my heaths, when I fit alone at the ftreams of my hills.

HIDALLAN.

CEASED the voice of the huntrefs of Galmal ? Why did I trouble the foul of the maid ? When fhall I fee thee, with joy, in the chace of the dark-brown hinds ?

FINGAL.

YOUTH of the gloomy brow! no more fhalt thou feaft in my halls. Thou fhalt not purfue my chace, and my foes fhall not fall by thy fword *.——Lead me to the place of her reft that I may behold her beauty.——Pale fhe lies at the rock, and the cold winds lift her hair. Her bow-ftring founds in the blaft, and her arrow was broken in her fall. Raife the praife of the daughter of Sarno, and give her name to the wind of the hills.

BARDS.

SEE! meteors roll around the maid; and moon-beams lift her foul ! Around her, from

* The fequel of the ftory of Hidallan is introduced, as an epi-fode, in the poem which immediately follows in this collection.

their

their clouds, bend the awful faces of her fathers; Sarno * of the gloomy brow; and the red-rolling eyes of Fidallan. When fhall thy white-hand arife, and thy voice be heard on our rocks? The maids fhall feek thee on the heath, but they will not find thee. Thou fhalt come, at times, to their dreams, and fettle peace in their foul. Thy voice fhall remain in their ears †, and they fhall think with joy on the dreams of their reft. Meteors roll around the maid, and moon-beams lift her foul!

---

* Sarno the father of Comala died foon after the flight of his daughter.——Fidallan was the firft king that reigned in Iniftore.

† The angel ended, and in Adam's ear
So charming left his voice, that he a while
Thought him ftill fpeaking, ftill ftood fix'd to hear.

MILTON.

THE

THE

WAR of CAROS*:

A POEM.

BRING, daughter of Tofcar, bring the harp; the light of the fong rifes in Offian's foul. It is like the field, when darknefs covers the hills around, and the fhadow grows flowly on the plain of the fun.

I BEHOLD my fon, O Malvina, near the moffy rock of Crona †; but it is the mift ‡ of the de-

---

*.Caros is probably the noted ufurper Caraufius, by birth a Menapian, who affumed the purple in the year 284; and, feizing on Britain, defeated the emperor Maximian Herculius in feveral naval engagements, which gives propriety to his being called in this poem *the king of fhips.*——He repaired Agricola's wall, in order to obftruct the incurfions of the Caledonians; and when he was employed in that work, it appears he was attacked by a party under the command of Ofcar the fon of Offian. This battle is the foundation of the prefent poem, which is addreffed to Malvina the daughter of Tofcar.

† Crona is the name of a fmall ftream which runs into the Carron. On its banks is the fcene of the preceding dramatic poem.

‡ Who is this that cometh out of the wildernefs like pillars of fmoke. SOLOMON's Song.

fart

fart tinged with the beam of the weft : Lovely
is the mift that affumes the form of Ofcar ! turn
from it, ye winds, when ye roar on the fide of
Ardven.

WHO comes towards my fon, with the murmur of a fong ? His ftaff is in his hand, his gray
hair loofe on the wind.   Surly joy lightens his
face; and he often looks back to Caros.   It is
Ryno * of the fong, he that went to view the
foe.

WHAT does Caros king of fhips, faid the fon
of the now mournful Offian ? fpreads he the
wings † of his pride, bard of the times of old ?

HE fpreads them, Ofcar, replied the bard,
but it is behind his gathered heap ‡.   He looks
over his ftones with fear, and beholds thee terrible, as the ghoft of night that rolls the wave to
his fhips.

Go, thou firft of my bards, fays Ofcar, and
take the fpear of Fingal.   Fix a flame on its
point, and fhake it to the winds of heaven.   Bid
him, in fongs, to advance, and leave the rolling of his wave.   Tell to Caros that I long for

---

* Ryno is often mentioned in the ancient poetry.——He
feems to have been a bard, of the firft rank, in the days of
Fingal.

† The Roman eagle.

‡ Agricola's wall which Caraufius repaired.

battle;

battle; and that my bow is weary of the chace of Cona. Tell him the mighty are not here; and that my arm is young.

HE went with the found of his fong. Ofcar reared his voice on high. It reached his heroes on Ardven, like the noife of a cave *; when the fea of Togorma rolls before it; and its trees meet the roaring winds.——They gather round my fon like the ftreams of the hill; when, after rain, they roll in the pride of their courfe.

RYNO came to the mighty Caros, and ftruck his flaming fpear. Come to the battle of Ofcar, O thou that fitteft on the rolling of waters. Fingal is diftant far; he hears the fongs of his bards in Morven : and the wind of his hall is in his hair. His terrible fpear is at his fide; and his fhield that is like that darkened moon. Come to the battle of Ofcar; the hero is alone.

HE came not over the ftreamy Carun †; the bard returned with his fong. Gray night grows dim on Crona. The feaft of fhells is fpread. A hundred oaks burn to the wind, and faint light gleams over the heath. The ghofts of Ardven pafs through the beam, and fhew their

---

* —— As when the hollow rocks retain
The found of bluftering winds.——   MILTON.
† The river Carron.

dim

dim and diftant forms. Comala * is half-unfeen
on her meteor; and Hidallan is fullen and dim,
like the darkened moon behind the mift of
night.

WHY art thou fad? faid Ryno; for he alone
beheld the chief. Why art thou fad, Hidallan,
haft thou not received thy fame? The fongs of
Offian have been heard, and thy ghoft has
brightened in the wind, when thou didft bend
from thy cloud to hear the fong of Morven's
bard.

AND do thine eyes behold the hero, faid Ofcar, like the dim meteor of night? Say, Ryno,
fay, how fell the chief that was fo renowned in
the days of our fathers?——His name remains
on the rocks of Cona; and I have often feen the
ftreams of his hills.

FINGAL, replied the bard, had driven Hidallan from his wars. The king's foul was fad
for Comala, and his eyes could not behold Hidallan.

LONELY, fad, along the heath, he flowly
moved with filent fteps. His arms hang difordered on his fide. His hair flies loofe from his

* This is the fcene of Comala's death, which is the fubject of
the dramatic poem. — The poet mentions her in this place, in
order to introduce the fequel of Hidallan's ftory, who, on account
of her death, had been expelled from the wars of Fingal.

helmet

helmet. The tear is in his down-caſt eyes; and the ſigh half-ſilent in his breaſt.

Three days he ſtrayed unſeen, alone, before he came to Lamor's halls : the moſſy halls of his fathers, at the ſtream of Balva *.——There Lamor ſat alone beneath a tree; for he had ſent his people with Hidallan to war. The ſtream ran at his feet, and his gray head reſted on his· ſtaff. Sightleſs are his aged eyes. He hums the ſong of other times.——The noiſe of Hidallan's feet came to his ear : he knew the tread of· his ſon.

Is the ſon of Lamor returned; or is it the ſound of his ghoſt? Haſt thou fallen on the banks of Carun, ſon of the aged Lamor? Or, if I hear the ſound of Hidallan's feet; where are the mighty in war? where are my people, Hidallan, that were wont to return with their echoing ſhields?——Have they fallen on the· banks of Carun?

No : replied the ſighing youth, the people of Lamor live. They are renowned in battle, my father; but Hidallan is renowned no more. I muſt ſit alone on the banks of Balva, when the roar of the battle grows.

* This is perhaps that ſmall ſtream, ſtill retaining the name of Balva, which runs through the romantic valley of Glentivar in Stirlingſhire. Balva ſignifies a ſilent ſtream; and Glentivar, the ſequeſtered vale.

BUT

But thy fathers never fat alone, replied the rifing pride of Lamor; they never fat alone on the banks of Balva, when the roar of battle rofe: ——Doft thou not behold that tomb? Mine eyes difcern it not : there refts the noble Garmállon who never fled from war.——Come, thou renowned in battle, he fays, come to thy father's tomb.——How am I renowned, Garmállon, for my fon has fled from war?

King of the ftreamy Balva! faid Hidallan with a figh, why doft thou torment my foul? Lamor, I never feared.---Fingal was fad for Comala, and denied his wars to Hidallan : Go to the gray ftreams of thy land, he faid, and moulder like a leaflefs oak, which the winds have bent over Balva, never more to grow.

And muft I hear, Lamor replied, the lonely tread of Hidallan's feet? When thoufands are renowned in battle, fhall he bend over my gray ftreams? Spirit of the noble Garmállon ! carry Lamor to his place; his eyes are dark; his foul is fad: and his fon has loft his fame.

Where, faid the youth, fhall I fearch for fame to gladden the foul of Lamor? From whence fhall I return with renown, that the found of my arms may be pleafant in his ear? ——If I go to the chace of hinds, my name will not be heard.---Lamor will not feel my dogs,

with

with his hands, glad at my arrival from the hill.   He will not enquire of his mountains, or of the dark-brown deer of his defarts.

I MUST fall, faid Lamor, like a leaflefs oak : it grew on a rock, but the winds have overturned it. —— My ghoft will be feen on my hills, mournful for my young Hidallan.   Will not ye, ye mifts, as ye rife, hide him from my fight ? ——My fon!---go to Lamor's hall : there the arms of our fathers hang.---Bring the fword of Garmállon ;---he took it from a foe.

HE went and brought the fword with all its ftudded thongs.——He gave it to his father. The gray-haired hero felt the point with his hand.——

MY fon!---lead me to Garmállon's tomb : it rifes befide that ruftling tree.   The long grafs is withered ;---I heard the breeze whiftling there. ---A little fountain murmurs near, and fends its water to Balva.   There let me reft ; it is noon : and the fun is on our fields.

HE led him to Garmállon's tomb.   Lamor pierced the fide of his fon.——They fleep toge- ther ; and their ancient halls moulder on Balva's banks.---Ghofts are feen there at noon : the valley is filent, and the people fhun the place of Lamor.

MOURNFUL

Mournful is thy tale, said Ofcar, fon of the times of old !---My foul fighs for Hidallan; he fell in the days of his youth. He flies on the blaft of the defart, and his wandering is in a foreign land.——

Sons of the echoing Morven! draw near to the foes of Fingal. Send the night away in fongs ; and watch the ftrength of Caros. Ofcar goes to the people of other times ; to the fhades of filent Ardven ; where His fathers fit dim in their clouds, and behold the future war.---And art thou there, Hidallan, like a half-extinguifhed meteor ? Come to my fight, in thy forrow, chief of the roaring Balva !

The heroes move with their fongs.---Ofcar flowly afcends the hill.---The meteors of night are fetting on the heath before him. A diftant torrent faintly roars.---Unfrequent blafts rufh through aged oaks. The half-enlightened moon finks dim and red behind her hill.---Feeble voices are heard on the heath.——Ofcar drew his fword.

Come, faid the hero, O ye ghofts of my fathers! ye that fought againft the kings of the world !---Tell me the deeds of future times ; and your difcourfe in your caves ; when you talk together and behold your fons in the fields of the valiant.

TRENMOR

TRENMOR came, from his hill, at the voice of his mighty fon.---A cloud, like the fteed of the ftranger, fupported his airy limbs. His robe is of the mift of Lano, that brings death to the people. His fword is a meteor half-extin-tinguifhed. His face is without form, and dark. He fighed thrice over the hero: and thrice the winds of the night roared around. Many were his words to Ofcar : but they only came by halves to our ears : they were dark as the tales of other times, before the light of the fong arofe. He flowly vanifhed, like a mift that melts on the funny hill.

IT was then, O daughter of Tofcar, my fon begun firft to be fad. He forefaw the fall of his race; and, at times, he was thoughtful and dark; like the fun * when he carries a cloud on his face ; but he looks afterwards on the hills of Cona.

OSCAR paffed the night among his fathers, gray morning met him on the banks of Carun.

A GREEN vale furrounded a tomb which arofe in the times of old. Little hills lift their head at a diftance ; and ftretch their old trees to the wind. The warriors of Caros fat there, for

* ————caput obfcura nitidum ferrugine texit.   VIRG.

they

they had paffed the ftream by night. They appeared, like the trunks of aged pines, to the
pale light of the morning.

OSCAR ftood at the tomb, and raifed thrice
his terrible voice. The rocking hills echoed
around : the ftarting roes bounded away. And
the trembling ghofts of the dead fled, fhrieking
on their clouds. So terrible was the voice of
my fon, when he called his friends.

A THOUSAND fpears rofe around ; the people
of Caros rofe.---Why daughter of Tofcar, why
that tear ? My fon, though alone, is brave.
Ofcar is like a beam of the fky ; he turns
around and the people fall. His hand is like the
arm of a ghoft, when he ftretches it from a
cloud : the reft of his thin form is unfeen : but
the people die in the vale.

MY fon beheld the approach of the foe ; and
he ftood in the filent darknefs of his ftrength.
——" Am I alone, faid Ofcar, in the midft of
a thoufand foes ?---Many a fpear is there !---
many a darkly-rolling eye !---Shall I fly to
Ardven ?---But did my fathers ever fly !——
The mark of their arm is in a thoufand battles.
---Ofcar too will be renowned.——Come, ye
dim ghofts of my fathers, and behold my deeds

L   in

in war!---I may fall; but I will be renowned
like the race of the echoing Morven *."

He stood dilated in his place, like a flood
swelling in a narrow vale. The battle came, but
they fell : bloody was the sword of Oscar.——
The noise reached his people at Crona ; they
came like a hundred streams. The warriors of
Caros fled, and Oscar remained like a rock left
by the ebbing sea.

Now dark and deep, with all his steeds, Caros
rolled his might along : the little streams are
lost in his course; and the earth is rocking
round.——Battle spreads from wing to wing :
ten thousand swords gleam at once in the sky.
——But why should Ossian sing of battles?---For
never more shall my steel shine in war. I remember the days of my youth with sorrow ;

* This passage is very like the soliloquy of Ulysses upon a
similar occasion.

Ὤμοι ἐγὼ, τί πάθω ; μέγα μὲν κακὸν, αἰκι φέβωμαι,
Πληθὺν ταρβήσας· το δὲ ῥίγιον αἴκεν ἅλοω
Μῦνος· &c.   Hom. Il. 11.

What farther subterfuge, what hopes remain ?
What shame, inglorious if I quit the plain ?
What danger, singly if I stand the ground,
My friends all scatter'd, all the foes around ?
Yet wherefore doubtful ? let this truth suffice ;
The brave meets danger, and the coward flies :
To die or conquer proves a hero's heart,
And knowing this, I know a soldier's part.
                                              Pope.

9   when

when I feel the weaknefs of my arm. Happy are they who fell in their youth, in the midſt of their renown !---They have not beheld the tombs of their friends : or failed to bend the bow of their ſtrength.——Happy art thou, O Oſcar, in the midſt of thy ruſhing blaſt. Thou often goeſt to the fields of thy fame, where Caros fled from thy lifted ſword.

DARKNESS comes on my ſoul, O fair daughter of Toſcar, I behold not the form of my ſon at Carun ; nor the figure of Oſcar on Crona. The ruſtling winds have carried him far away ; and the heart of his father is ſad.

BUT lead me, O Malvina, to the found of my woods, and the roar of my mountain ſtreams. Let the chace be heard on Cona ; that I may think on the days of other years.---And bring me the harp, O maid, that I may touch it when the light of my ſoul ſhall ariſe.——Be thou near, to learn the ſong ; and future times ſhall hear of Offian.

THE ſons of the feeble hereafter will lift the voice on Cona ; and, looking up to the rocks, ſay, " Here Offian dwelt." They ſhall admire the chiefs of old, and the race that are no more : while we ride on our clouds, Malvina, on the wings of the roaring winds. Our voices ſhall be heard, at times, in the defart ; and we ſhall ſing on the winds of the rock.

WAR of INIS-THONA *:

A P O E M.

O UR youth is like the dream of the hunter
on the hill of heath. He sleeps in the
mild beams of the sun ; but he awakes amidst a
storm ; the red lightning flies around : and the
trees shake their heads to the wind. He looks
back with joy on the day of the sun, and the
pleasant dreams of his rest !

WHEN shall Ossian's youth return, or his ear
delight in the sound of arms? When shall I, like
Oscar, travel † in the light of my steel ?---

* Inis-thona, *i. e. the island of waves,* was a country of Scandinavia subject to its own king, but depending upon the kingdom
of Lochlin.—This poem is an episode introduced in a great
work composed by Ossian, in which the actions of his friends,
and his beloved son Oscar, were interwoven.——The work it-
self is lost, but some episodes, and the story of the poem, are
handed down by tradition. There are some now living, who,
in their youth, have heard the whole repeated.

† Travelling in the greatness of his strength.

ISAIAH lxiii. 1.

Come,

Come, with your ftreams, ye hills of Cona, and liften to the voice of Offian ! The fong rifes, like the fun, in my foul; and my heart feels the joys of other times.

I BEHOLD thy towers, O Selma! and the oaks of thy fhaded wall :---thy ftreams found in my ear; thy heroes gather round. Fingal fits in the midft; and leans on the fhield of Tren-mor :---his fpear ftands againft the wall; he liftens to the fong of his bards.---The deeds of his arm are heard; and the actions of the king in his youth.

OSCAR had returned from the chace, and heard the hero's praife.- -He took the fhield of Branno * from the wall; his eyes were filled with tears. Red was the cheek of youth. His voice was trembling, low. My fpear fhook its bright head in his hand: he fpoke to Morven's king.

FINGAL ! thou king of heroes! Offian, next to him in war! ye have fought the battle in your youth; your names are renowned in fong. ---Ofcar is like the mift of Cona : I appear and vanifh.---The bard will not know my name.---

---

* This is Branno, the father of Everallin, and grandfather to Ofcar ; he was of Irifh extraction and lord of the country round the lake of Lego.—His great actions are handed down by tradi-tion, and his hofpitality has paffed into a proverb.

The

The hunter will not fearch in the heath for my tomb. Let me fight, O heroes, in the battles of Inis-thona. Diſtant is the land of my war !---ye ſhall not hear of Ofcar's fall.——Some bard may find me there, and give my name to the fong.---The daughter of the ſtranger ſhall fee my tomb, and weep over the youth that came from afar. The bard ſhall fay, at the feaſt, hear the fong of Ofcar from the diſtant land.

Oscar, replied the king of Morven; thou ſhalt fight,, fon of my fame !---Prepare my dark-bofomed ſhip to carry my hero to Inis-thona. Son of my fon, regard our fame ;---for thou art of the race of renown. Let not the children of ſtrangers fay, feeble are the fons of Morven !——Be thou, in battle, like the roaring ſtorm : mild as the evening fun in peace.---Tell, Ofcar, to Inis-thona's king, that Fingal remembers his youth ; when we ſtrove in the combat together in the days of Agandecca..

They lifted up the founding fail ; the wind whiſtled through the thongs * of their maſts. Waves laſhed the oozy rocks : the ſtrength of ocean roared.——My fon beheld, from the wave, the land of groves. He ruſhed into the

---

* Leather thongs were ufed in Oſſian's time, inſtead of ropes.

echoing

echoing bay of Runa; and fent his fword to Annir king of fpears.

THE gray-haired hero rofe, when he fáw the fword of Fingal. His eyes were full of tears, and he remembered the battles of their youth. Twice they lifted the fpear before the lovely Agandecca : heroes ftood far diftant, as if two ghofts contended.

BUT now, begun the king, I am old ; the fword lies ufelefs in my hall. Thou who art of Morven's race ! Annir has been in the ftrife of fpears ; but he is pale and withered now, like the oak of Lano. I have no fon to meet thee with joy, or to carry thee to the halls of his fathers. Argon is pale in the tomb, and Ruro is no more.---My daughter is in the hall of ftrangers, and longs to behold my tomb.——Her fpoufe fhakes ten thoufand fpears; and comes * like a cloud of death from Lano.---Come thou,

---

* Cormalo had refolved on a war againft his father-in-law Annir king of Inis-thona, in order to deprive him of his kingdom : the injuftice of his defigns was fo much refented by Fingal, that he fent his grandfon, Ofcar, to the affiftance of Annir. Both armies came foon to a battle, in which the conduct and valour of Ofcar obtained a complete victory. An end was put to the war by the death of Cormalo, who fell in a fingle combat, by Ofcar's hand.—Thus is the ftory delivered down by tradition ; though the poet, to raife the character of his fon, makes Ofcar himfelf propofe the expedition.

L 4

to fhare the feaft of Annir, fon of echoing Morven.

THREE days they feafted together; on the fourth Annir heard the name of Ofcar *.---They rejoiced in the fhell †; and purfued the boars of Runa.

BESIDE the fount of moffy ftones, the weary heroes reft. The tear fteals in fecret from Annir: and he broke the rifing figh.——Here darkly reft, the hero faid, the children of my youth.---This ftone is the tomb of Ruro : that tree founds over the grave of Argon. Do ye hear my voice, O my fons, within your narrow houfe ? Or do ye fpeak in thefe ruftling leaves, when the winds of the defart rife ?

KING of Inis-thona, faid Ofcar, how fell the children of youth ? The wild boar often rufhes over their tombs, but he does not difturb the hunters. They purfue deer ‡ formed of clouds, and

---

* It was thought, in thofe days of heroifm, an infringement upon the laws of hofpitality, to afk the name of a ftranger, before he had feafted three days in the great hall of the family. *He that afks the name of the ftranger*, is, to this day, an opprobrious term applied, in the north, to the inhofpitable.

† *To rejoice in the fhell* is a phrafe for feafting fumptuoufly and drinking freely. I have obferved in a preceding note, that the ancient Scots drunk in fhells.

‡ The notion of Offian concerning the ftate of the deceafed, was the fame with that of the ancient Greeks and Romans.

They

A P O E M.   153

and bend their airy bow.---They ſtill love the
ſport of their youth ; and mount the wind with
joy.

CORMALO, replied the king, is chief of ten
thouſand ſpears ; he dwells at the dark-rolling

They imagined that the ſouls purſued, in their ſeparate ſtate, the
employments and pleaſures of their former life.

> *Arma procul, curruſque virûm miratur inanes.*
> *Stant terra defixæ baſtæ, paſſimque ſoluti*
> *Per campum paſcuntur equi, quæ gratia curruum*
> *Armorumque fuit vivis ; quæ cura nitentes*
> *Paſcere equos, eadem ſequitur tellure repoſtos.*
>
> VIRG.

> The chief beheld their chariots from afar ;
> Their ſhining arms and courſers train'd to war :
> Their lances fix'd in earth, their ſteeds around,
> Free from the harneſs, graze the flow'ry ground.
> The love of horſes which they had, alive,
> And care of chariots, after death ſurvive.
>
> DRYDEN.

> Τὸν δὲ μετ' εἰσενόησα βίην Ἡρακληείην,
> Εἴδωλον.
> ——— ὁ δ', ἐρεμνῇ νυκτὶ ἐοικὼς
> Γυμνὸν τόξον ἔχων, καὶ ἐπὶ νευρῆφιν ὀϊστὸν
> Δεινὸν παπλαίνων, αἰεὶ βαλέοντι ἐοικώς, &c.
>
> HOM. Odyſſ. 11.

> Now I the ſtrength of Hercules behold,
> A tow'ring ſpectre of gigantic mold ;
> Gloomy as night he ſtands in act to throw
> Th' aerial arrow from the twanging bow.
> Around his breaſt a wond'rous zone is roll'd
> Where woodland monſters grin in fretted gold,
> There ſullen lions ſternly ſeem to roar,
> The bear to growl, to foam the tuſky boar,
> There war and havock and deſtruction ſtood,
> And vengeful murder red with human blood.
>
> POPE.

waters

waters of Lano * ; which fend forth the cloud of death. . He came to. Runa's echoing halls, and fought the honour of the fpear †. The youth was lovely as the firft beam of the fun ; and few were they who could meet him in fight !---My heroes yielded to Cormalo : and my daughter loved the fon of Lano.

ARGON and Ruro returned from the chace ; the tears of their pride defcended :---They rolled their filent eyes on Runa's heroes, becaufe they yielded to a ftranger : three days they feafted with Cormalo : on the fourth my Argon fought. ---But who could fight with Argon !---Lano's chief was overcome. His heart fwelled with the grief of pride, and he refolved, in fecret, to behold the death of my fons.

THEY went to the hills of Runa, and purfued the dark-brown hinds. The arrow of Cormalo flew in fecret ; and my children fell. He came to the maid of his love ; to Inis-thona's dark-haired maid.——They fled over the defart---and Annir remained alone.

---

* Lano was a lake of Scandinavia, remarkable, in the days of Offian, for emitting a peftilentiai vapour in autumn. *And thou, O valiant Duchomar, like the mift of marfhy Lano ; when it fails over the plains of autumn, and brings death to the people.*
FINGAL, B. I.

† By *the honour of the fpear* is meant a kind of tournament practiced among the ancient northern nations.

NIGHT

NIGHT came on and day appeared; nor Argon's voice, nor Ruro's came. At length their much-loved dog is feen; the fleet and bounding Runar. He came into the hall and howled; and feemed to look towards the place of their fall. ——We followed him : we found them here : and laid them by this mofly ftream. This is the haunt of Annir, when the chace of the hinds is over. I bend like the trunk of an aged oak above them : and my tears for ever flow.

O RONNAN ! faid the rifing Ofcar, Ogar king of fpears! call my heroes to my fide, the fons of ftreamy Morven. To-day we go to Lano's water, that fends forth the cloud of death. Cormalo will not long rejoice : death is often at the point of our fwords.

THEY came over the defart like ftormy clouds, when the winds roll them over the heath : their edges are tinged with lightning :- and the echoing groves forefee the ftorm. The horn of Ofcar's battle was heard; and Lano fhook in all its waves. The children of the lake convened around the founding fhield of Cormalo.

OSCAR fought, as he was wont in battle. Cormalo fell beneath his fword : and the fons of the difmal Lano fled to their fecret vales.—— Ofcar brought the daughter of Inis-thona to Annir's

nir's echoing halls.   The face of age was bright
with joy; he bleft the king of fwords.

How great was the joy of Offian, when he beheld the diftant fail of his fon! it was like a
cloud of light that rifes in the eaft, when the traveller is fad in a land unknown; and difmal
night, with her ghofts, is fitting around him.

WE brought him, with fongs, to Selma's
halls.   Fingal ordered the feaft of fhells to be
fpread.   A thoufand bards raifed the name of
Ofcar: and Morven anfwered to the noife.   The
daughter of Tofcar was there, and her voice was
like the harp; when the diftant found comes, in
the evening, on the foft-ruftling breeze of the
vale.

O LAY me, ye that fee the light, near fome
rock of my hills: let the thick hazels be around,
let the ruftling oak be near.   Green be the place
of my reft; and let the found of the diftant torrent be heard.   Daughter of Tofcar, take the
harp, and raife the lovely fong of Selma; that
fleep may overtake my foul in the midft of joy;
that the dreams of my youth may return, and
the days of the mighty Fingal.

SELMA! I behold thy towers, thy trees, and
fhaded wall.   I fee the heroes of Morven; and
hear the fong of bards.   Ofcar lifts the fword of
Cormalo; and a thoufand youths admire its

ftudded

ftudded thongs. They look with wonder on my
fon; and admire the ftrength of his arm. They
mark the joy of his father's eyes; they long for
an equal fame.

And ye fhall have your fame, O fons of
ftreamy Morven.---My foul is often brightened
with the fong; and I remember the companions
of my youth.——But fleep defcends with the
found of the harp; and pleafant dreams begin to
rife. Ye fons of the chace ftand far diftant, nor
difturb my reft. The bard of other times con-
verfes now with his fathers, the chiefs of the
days of old.---Sons of the chace, ftand far diftant; difturb not the dreams of Offian.

S O N of the diftant land, who dwelleft in the
fecret cell! do I hear the founds of thy
grove? or is it the voice of thy fongs? The

* This poem is compleat; nor does it appear from tradition,
that it was introduced, as an epifode, into any of Offian's great
works.—It is called, in the original, *Duan a Chuldich*, or the
Culdee's poem, becaufe it was addreffed to one of the firft Chriftian
miffionaries, who were called, from their retired life, Culdees,
or *fequeftered perfons*. —The ftory bears a near refemblance to that
which was the foundation of the Iliad. Fingal, on his return
from Ireland, after he had expelled Swaran from that kingdom,
made a feaft to all his heroes: he forgot to invite Ma-ronnan
and Aldo, two chiefs, who had not been along with him on his
expedition. They refented his negleft; and went over to Erragon king of Sora, a country of Scandinavia, the declared
enemy of Fingal. The valour of Aldo foon gained him a great
reputation in Sora: and Lorma the beautiful wife of Erragon fell
in love with him.—He found means to efcape with her, and to
come to Fingal, who refided then in Selma on the weftern coaft.
—Erragon invaded Scotland, and was flain in battle by Gaul the
fon of Morni, after he had rejefted terms of peace offered him
by Fingal.—In this war Aldo fell, in a fingle combat, by the
hands of his rival Erragon; and the unfortunate Lorma afterwards died of grief.

torrent

torrent was loud in my ear, but I heard a tuneful voice ; doft thou praife the chiefs of thy
land ; or the fpirits * of the wind ?---But, lonely
dweller of the rock ! look over that heathy
plain : thou feeft green tombs, with their rank,
whiftling grafs ; with their ftones of mofly.
heads : thou feeft them, fon of the rock, but
Offian's eyes have failed.

A MOUNTAIN-STREAM comes roaring down
and fends its waters round a green hill : four
mofly ftones, in the midft of withered grafs,
rear their heads on the top : two trees, which
the ftorms have bent, fpread their whiftling
branches around.——This is thy dwelling, Erragon † ; this thy narrow houfe : the found of
thy fhells has been long forgot in Sora : and thy
fhield is become dark in thy hall.——Erragon,
king of fhips ! chief of diftant Sora ! how haft
thou fallen on our mountains ‡ ! How is the
mighty low !

* The poet alludes to the religious hymns of the Culdees.

† Erragon, or Ferg-thonn, fignifies *the rage of the waves* ;
probably a poetical name given him by Offian himfelf ; for he
goes by the name of Annir in tradition.

‡ The beauty of Ifrael is flain on thy high places : how are the
mighty fallen !   2 SAM. ii. 19.

How are the mighty fallen in the midft of the battle ! O
Jonathan, thou waft flain in thine high places..
                                                    2 SAM. ii. 25.

SON

SON of the fecret cell! doft thou delight in fongs? Hear the battle of Lora; the found of its fteel is long fince paft. So thunder on the darkened hill roars and is no more. The fun returns with his filent beams : the glittering rocks, and green heads of the mountains fmile.

THE bay of Cona received our fhips *, from Ullin's rolling waves : our white fheets hung loofe to the mafts : and the boifterous winds roared behind the groves of Morven.——The horn of the king is founded, and the deer ftart from their rocks. Our arrows flew in the woods; the feaft of the hill was fpread. Our joy was great on our rocks, for the fall of the terrible Swaran.

Two heroes were forgot at our feaft; and the rage of their bofoms burned. They rolled their red eyes in fecret : the figh burft from their breafts. They were feen to talk together, and to throw their fpears on earth. They were two dark clouds, in the mift of our joy; like pillars of mift on the fettled fea : it glitters to the fun, but the mariners fear a ftorm.

RAISE my white fails, faid Ma-ronnan, raife them to the winds of the weft; let us rufh, O Aldo, through the foam of the northern wave.

* This was at Fingal's return from his war againft Swaran.

We

We are forgot at the feaft : but our arms have been red in blood.   Let us leave the hills of Fingal, and ferve the king of Sora.——His countenance is fierce, and the war darkens round his fpear.   Let us be renowned, O Aldo, in the battles of echoing Sora.

THEY took their fwords and fhields of thongs; and rufhed to Lumar's founding bay. They came to Sora's haughty king, the chief of bounding fteeds.——Erragon had returned from the chace : his fpear was red in blood.   He bent his dark face to the ground : and whiftled as he went.——He took the ftrangers to his feafts : they fought and conquered in his wars.

ALDO returned with his fame towards Sora's lofty walls.---From her tower looked the fpoufe of Erragon, the humid, rolling eyes of Lorma. ——Her dark-brown hair flies on the wind of ocean : her white breaft heaves, like fnow on the heath ; when the gentle winds arife, and flowly move it in the light.   She faw young Aldo, like the beam of Sora's fetting fun.   Her foft heart fighed : tears filled her eyes ; and her white arm fupported her head.

THREE days fhe fat within the hall, and covered grief with joy.---On the fourth fhe fled with the hero, along the rolling fea.——They

M   came

came to Cona's moffy towers, to Fingal king of fpears.

ALDO of the heart of pride! faid the rifing king of Morven, fhall I defend thee from the wrath of Sora's injured king? who will now receive my people into their halls, or give the feaft of ftrangers, fince Aldo, of the little foul, has carried away the fair of Sora? Go to thy hills, thou feeble hand, and hide thee in thy caves; mournful is the battle we muft fight, with Sora's gloomy king.——Spirit of the noble Trenmor! when will Fingal ceafe to fight? I was born in the midft of battles *, and my fteps muft move in blood to my tomb. But my hand did not injure the weak, my fteel did not touch the feeble in arms.---I behold thy tempefts, O Morven, which will overturn my halls; when my children are dead in battle, and none remains to dwell in Selma. Then will the feeble come, but they will not know my tomb: my renown is in the fong: and my actions fhall be as a dream to future times.

His people gathered around Erragon, as the ftorms round the ghoft of night; when he calls

---

* Comhal the Father of Fingal was flain in battle, againft the tribe of Morni, the very day that Fingal was born; fo that he may, with propriety, be faid to have been *born in the midft of battles.*

     them

them from the top of Morven, and prepares to pour them on the land of the ſtranger.——He came to the ſhore of Cona, and ſent his bard to the king; to demand the combat of thouſands; or the land of many hills.

FINGAL ſat in his hall with the companions of his youth around him. The young heroes were at the chace, and far diſtant in the deſart. The gray-haired chiefs talked of other times, and of the actions of their youth; when the aged Narthmor * came, the king of ſtreamy Lora.

THIS is no time, begun the chief, to hear the ſongs of other years : Erragon frowns on the coaſt, and lifts ten thouſand ſwords. Gloomy is the king among his chiefs! he is like the darkened moon, amidſt the meteors of night.

COME, ſaid Fingal, from thy hall, thou daughter of my love; come from thy hall, Boſmina †, maid of ſtreamy Morven! Narthmor, take the ſteeds ‡ of the ſtrangers, and attend the daughter of Fingal: let her bid the king of Sora

* Neart-mór, great ſtrength. Lora, noiſy.

† Boſ-mhina, ſoft and tender hand. She was the youngeſt of Fingal's children.

‡ Theſe were probably horſes taken in the incurſions of the Caledonians into the Roman province, which ſeems to be intimated in the phraſe of the ſteeds of ſtrangers.

to our feaft, to Selma's fhaded wall.——Offer
him, O Bofmina, the peace of heroes, and
the wealth of generous Aldo: our youths are
far diftant, and age is on our trembling hands.

SHE came to the hoft of Erragon, like a beam
of light to a cloud.——In her right hand fhone
an arrow of gold; and in her left a fparkling
fhell, the fign of Morven's peace.——Erragon
brightened in her prefence as a rock, before the
fudden beams of the fun; when they iffue from
a broken cloud, divided by the roaring wind.

SON of the diftant Sora, begun the mildly
blufhing maid, come to the feaft of Morven's
king, to Selma's fhaded walls. ˙ Take the peace
of heroes, O warrior, and let the dark fword
reft by thy fide.---And if thou chufeft the wealth
of kings, hear the words of the generous Aldo.
——He gives to Erragon an hundred fteeds, the
children of the rein; an hundred maids from
diftant lands; an hundred hawks with fluttering
wing, that fly acrofs the fky. An hundred
girdles * fhall alfo be thine, to bind high-bo-

---

* Sanctified girdles, till very lately, were kept in many families in the north of Scotland; they were bound about women
in labour, and were fuppofed to alleviate their pains, and to ac-
celerate the birth. They were impreffed with feveral myftical
figures, and the ceremony of binding them about the woman's
waift, was accompanied with words and geftures which fhewed
the cuftom to have come originally from the druids.

fomed women; the friends of the births of heroes, and the cure of the fons of toil.---Ten fhells ftudded with gems fhall fhine in Sora's towers: the blue water trembles on their ftars, and feems to be fparkling wine.——They gladdened once the kings of the world *, in the midft of their echoing halls. Thefe, O hero, fhall be thine; or thy white-bofomed fpoufe.——Lorma fhall roll her bright eyes in thy halls; though Fingal loves the generous Aldo : ---Fingal !---who never injured a hero, though his arm is ftrong.

Soft voice of Cona! replied the king, tell him, that he fpreads his feaft in vain.——Let Fingal pour his fpoils around me; and bend beneath my power. Let him give me the fwords of his fathers, and the fhields of other times; that my children may behold them in my halls, and fay, " Thefe are the arms of Fingal."

Never fhall they behold them in thy halls, faid the rifing pride of the maid; they are in the mighty hands of heroes who never yielded in war.---King of the echoing Sora ! the ftorm is gathering on our hills. Doft thou not forfee the fall of thy people, fon of the diftant land?

---

* The Roman emperors. Thefe fhells were fome of the fpoils of the province.

M 3

SHE came to Selma's filent halls; the king beheld her down-caft eyes. He rofe from his
place, in his ftrength, and fhook his aged locks.
———He took the founding mail of Trenmor,
and the dark-brown fhield of his fathers. Darknefs filled Selma's hall, when he ftretched his
hand to his fpear :---the ghofts of thoufands
were near, and forefaw the death of the people.
Terrible joy rofe in the face of the aged heroes :
they rufhed to meet the foe; their thoughts are
on the actions of other years : and on the fame
of the tomb.

Now the dogs of the chace appeared at Trathal's tomb : Fingal knew that his young heroes followed them, and he ftopt in the midft of
his courfe.———Ofcar appeared the firft;---then
Morni's fon, and Nemi's race :---Fercuth *
fhewed his gloomy form : Dermid fpread his
dark hair on the wind. Offian came the laft.
O fon of the rock †, I hummed the fong of
other times : my fpear fupported my fteps over
the little ftreams, and my thoughts were of
mighty men. Fingal ftruck his boffy fhield;
and gave the difmal fign of war; a thoufand

* Fear-cuth, the fame with Fergus, *the man of the word*, or
a commander of an army.
† The poet addreffes himfelf to the Culdee.

fwords

fwords *, at once unfheathed, gleam on the waving heath. Three gray-haired fons of fong raife the tuneful, mournful voice.——Deep and dark with founding fteps, we rufh, a gloomy ridge, along : like the fhower of a ftorm when it pours on the narrow vale.

THE king of Morven fat on his hill: the fun-beam † of battle flew on the wind : the companions of his youth are near, with all their waving locks of age.——Joy rofe in the heroes eyes when he beheld his fons in war ; when he faw them amidft the lightning of fwords, and mindful of the deeds of their fathers.——Erragon came on, in his ftrength, like the roar of a winter ftream : the battle falls in his courfe, and death is at his fide.

WHO comes, faid Fingal, like the bounding roe, like the hart of echoing Cona ? His fhield glitters on his fide ; and the clang of his armour is mournful.——He meets with Erragon in the ftrife !---Behold the battle of the chiefs !---it is like the contending of ghofts in a gloomy ftorm.

---

* He fpake ; and to confirm his words out-flew,
Millions of flaming fwords, drawn from the thighs
Of mighty Cherubim ; the fudden blaze
Far round illumin'd hell.   MILTON.

† I have obferved in a former note, that the ftandard of Fingal was called the fun-beam from its being ftudded with ftones and gold.

——But falleſt thou, ſon of the hill, and is thy white boſom ſtained with blood? Weep, unhappy Lorma, Aldo is no more.

THE king took the ſpear of his ſtrength; for he was ſad for the fall of Aldo: he bent his deathful eyes on the foe; but Gaul met the king of Sora.——Who can relate the fight of the chiefs?---The mighty ſtranger fell.

SONS of Cona! Fingal cried aloud, ſtop the hand of death.---Mighty was he that is now ſo low! and much is he mourned in Sora! The ſtranger will come towards his hall, and wonder why it is ſilent. The king is fallen, O ſtranger, and the joy of his houſe is ceaſed.——Liſten to the ſound of his woods: perhaps his ghoſt is there; but he is far diſtant, on Morven, beneath the ſword of a foreign foe.

SUCH were the words of Fingal, when the bard raiſed the ſong of peace; we ſtopped our uplifted ſwords, and ſpared the feeble foe. We laid Erragon in that tomb; and I raiſed the voice of grief: the clouds of night came rolling down, and the ghoſt of Erragon appeared to ſome.---His face was cloudy and dark; and an half-formed ſigh is in his breaſt.——Bleſt be thy ſoul, O king of Sora! thine arm was terrible in war!

LORMA

LORMA fat, in Aldo's hall, at the light of a flaming oak : the night came, but he did not return ; and the foul of Lorma is fad.---What detains thee, hunter of Cona ? for thou didft promife to return.------Has the deer been diftant far ; and do the dark winds figh, round thee, on the heath ? I am in the land of ftrangers, where is my friend, but Aldo ? Come from thy echoing hills, O my beft beloved!

HER eyes are turned toward the gate, and fhe liftens to the ruftling blaft. She thinks it is Aldo's tread, and joy rifes in her face :---but forrow returns again, like a thin cloud on the moon.------And thou wilt not return, my love ? Let me behold the face of the hill. The moon is in the eaft. Calm and bright is the breaft of the lake! When fhall I behold his dogs returning from the chace ? When fhall I hear his voice, loud and diftant on the wind ? Come from thy echoing hills, hunter of woody Cona !

HIS thin ghoft appeared, on a rock, like the watry beam of the moon, when it rufhes from between two clouds, and the midnight fhower is on the field.------She followed the empty form over the heath, for fhe knew that her hero fell. ---I heard her approaching cries on the wind, like the mournful voice of the breeze, when it fighs on the grafs of the cave.

SHE

SHE came, she found her hero : her voice was heard no more : silent she rolled her sad eyes ; she was pale as a watry cloud, that rises from the lake, to the beam of the moon.

FEW were her days on Cona : she sunk into the tomb : Fingal commanded his bards; and they sung over the death of Lorma. The daughters * of Morven mourned her for one day in the year, when the dark winds of autumn returned.

: SON of the distant land †, thou dwellest in the field of fame : O let thy song rise, at times, in the praise of those that fell : that their thin ghosts may rejoice around thee ; and the soul of Lorma come on a moon-beam ‡, when thou liest down to rest, and the moon looks into thy cave. Then shalt thou see her lovely ; but the tear is still on her cheek.

---

* The daughters of Israel went yearly to lament the daughter of Jephthah the Gileadite four days in a year.

JUDGES xi. 40.

† The poet addresses himself to the Culdee.

‡ Be thou on a moon-beam, O Morna, near the window of my rest ; when my thoughts are of peace ; and the din of arms is over. FINGAL, B. l.

CONLATH

CONLATH and CUTHÓNA:

A P O E M *.

DID not Offian hear a voice? or is it the found of days that are no more? Often does the memory of former times come, like the evening fun, on my foul. The noife of the

* Conlath was the youngeft of Morni's fons, and brother to the celebrated Gaul, who is fo often mentioned in Offian's poems. He was in love with Cuthóna the daughter of Rumar, when Tofcar the fon of Kinfena, accompanied by Fercuth his friend, arrived, from Ireland, at Mora where Conlath dwelt. He was hofpitably received, and according to the cuftom of the times, feafted, three days, with Conlath. On the fourth he fet fail, and coafting the *ifland of waves*, probably, one of the He-brides, he faw Cuthóna hunting, fell in love with her, and carried her away, by force, in his fhip. He was forced, by ftrefs of weather, into I-thona a defart ifle. In the mean time Conlath, hearing of the rape, failed after him, and found him on the point of failing for the coaft of Ireland. They fought ; and they, and their followers fell by mutual wounds. Cuthóna did not long furvive : for fhe died of grief the third day after. Fin-gal, hearing of their unfortunate death, fent Stormal the fon of Moran to bury them, but forgot to fend a bard to fing the fu-neral fong over their tombs. The ghoft of Conlath came, long after, to Offian, to intreat him to tranfmit, to pofterity, his and Cuthóna's fame. For it was the opinion of the times, that the fouls of the deceafed were not happy, till their elegies were com-pofed by a bard.——Thus is the ftory of the poem handed down by tradition.

chace

chace is renewed; and, in thought, I lift the
fpear.——But Offian did hear a voice : Who art
thou, fon of the night? The fons of little men
are afleep, and the midnight wind is in my hall.
Perhaps it is the fhield of Fingal that echoes to
the blaft, it hangs in Offian's hall, and he feels
it fometimes with his hands.——Yes!---I hear
thee, my friend : long has thy voice been abfent
from mine ear! What brings thee, on thy
cloud, to Offian, fon of the generous Morni ?
Are the friends of the aged near thee ? Where is
Ofcar, fon of fame ?---He was often near thee,
O Conlath, when the din of battle rofe.

GHOST of CONLATH.

SLEEPS the fweet voice of Cona, in the midft
of his ruftling hall? Sleeps Offian in his hall, and
his friends without their fame? The fea rolls
round the dark I-thona *, and our tombs are
not feen by the ftranger. How long fhall our
fame be unheard, fon of the echoing Morven?

OSSIAN,

O THAT mine eyes could behold thee, as thou
fitteft, dim, on thy cloud! Art thou like the
mift of Lano ; or an half-extinguifhed meteor ?

* I-thonn, *ifland of waves*, one of the uninhabited weftern
ifles.

Of

Of what are the fkirts of thy robe? Of what is
thine airy bow?——But he is gone on his blaſt
like the ſhadow of miſt.---Come from thy wall,
my harp, and let me hear thy found. Let the
light of memory rife on I-thona; that I may
behold my friends. And Offian does behold his
friends, on the dark-blue ifle.---The cave of
Thona appears, with its moffy rocks and bending trees. A ſtream roars at its mouth, and
Tofcar bends over its courfe. Fercuth is fad by
his fide : and the maid * of his love fits at a diftance, and weeps. Does the wind of the waves
deceive me? Or do I hear them fpeak?

TOSCAR.

THE night was ſtormy. From their hills the
groaning oaks came down. The fea darkly-
tumbled beneath the blaſt, and the roaring
waves were climbing againſt our rocks.---The
lightning came often and ſhewed the blaſted
fern.---Fercuth! I faw the ghoſt of night †.
Silent he ſtood, on that bank ; his robe of miſt

---

* Cuthóna the daughter of Rumar, whom Tofcar had carried
away by force.

† It was long thought, in the north of Scotland, that ſtorms
were raifed by the ghoſts of the deceafed. This notion is ſtill entertained by the vulgar; fo they think that whirlwinds, and
ſudden ſqualls of wind are occafioned by fpirits, who tranfport
themfelves, in that manner, from one place to another.

flew

flew on the wind.---I could behold his tears : an aged man he feemed, and full of thought.

FERCUTH.

IT was thy father, O Tofcar ; and he forefees fome death among his race. Such was his appearance on Cromla, before the great Ma-ronnan * fell.——Ullin ! † with thy hills of grafs, how pleafant are thy vales! Silence is near thy blue ftreams, and the fun is on thy fields. Soft is the found of the harp in Seláma ‡, and pleafant the cry of the hunter on Crómla. But we are in the dark I-thona, furrounded by the ftorm. The billows lift their white heads above our rocks: and we tremble amidft the night.

TOSCAR.

WHITHER is the foul of battle fled, Fercuth with the locks of age? I have feen thee undaunted in danger, and thine eyes burning with joy in the fight. Whither is the foul of battle fled? Our fathers never feared.---Go : view the

---

* Ma-ronnan was the brother of Tofcar: the tranflator has a poem in his poffeffion concerning the extraordinary death of that hero.

† Ulfter in Ireland.

‡ Selámath—beautiful to behold, the name of Tofcar's palace, on the coaft of Ulfter, near the mountain Cromla the fcene of the epic poem.

fettling

fettling fea : the ftormy wind is laid. The billows ftill tremble * on the deep, and feem to fear
the blaft. But view the fettling fea : morning is
gray on our rocks. The fun will look foon
from his eaft; in all his pride of light.

I LIFTED up my fails, with joy, before the
halls of generous Conlath. My courfe was by
the ifle of waves, where his love purfued the
deer. I faw her, like that beam of the fun that
iffues from the cloud. Her hair was on her
heaving breaft; fhe, bending forward, drew the
bow : her white arm feemed, behind her, like
the fnow of Cromla :——Come to my foul, I
faid, thou huntrefs of the ifle of waves! But fhe
fpends her time in tears, and thinks of the generous Conlath. Where can I find thy peace,
Cuthona, lovely maid!

CU-THONA†.

A DISTANT fteep bends over the fea, with
aged trees and moffy rocks : the billows roll at
its feet : on its fide is the dwelling of roes. The

---

* ————the face of ocean fleeps,
And a ftill horror faddens all the deeps.
POPE's Homer.

† Cu-thona, *the mournful found of the waves*; a poetical name
given her by Offian, on account of her mourning to the found of
the waves; her name in tradition is Gorm-huil, *the blue-eyed
maid*.

people

people call it Ardven. There the towers of
Mora rife. There Conlath looks over the fea
for his only love. The daughters of the chace
returned, and he beheld their downcaft eyes.
Where is the daughter of Rumar? But they anfwered not.---My peace dwells on Ardven, fon
of the diftant land!

TOSCAR.

AND Cuthona fhall return to her peace; to
the halls of generous Conlath. He is the friend
of Tofcar : I have feafted in his halls.---Rife, ye
gentle breezes of Ullin, and ftretch my fails towards Ardven's fhores. Cuthona fhall reft on
Ardven : but the days of Tofcar will be fad.---
I fhall fit in my cave in the field of the fun. The
blaft will ruftle in my trees, and I fhall think it
is Cuthona's voice. But fhe is diftant far, in the
halls of the mighty Conlath.

CUTHONA.

OH! what cloud is that? It carries the ghofts
of my fathers. I fee the fkirts of their robes,
like gray and watry mift. When fhall I fall, O
Rumar?---Sad Cuthona fees her death. Will
not Conlath behold me, before I enter the narrow houfe? *

* The grave.

OSSIAN.

OSSIAN.

AND he will behold thee, O maid : he comes
along the rolling fea. The death of Tofcar is
dark on his fpear; and a wound is in his fide.
He is pale at the cave of Thona, and fhews his
ghaftly wound *. Where art thou with thy
tears, Cuthona? the chief of Mora dies.——
The vifion grows dim on my mind :---I behold
the chiefs no more. But, O ye bards of future
times, remember the fall of Conlath with tears :
he fell before his day †; and fadnefs darkened
in his hall. His mother looked to his fhield on
the wall, and it was bloody ‡. She knew that
her hero died, and her forrow was heard on
Mora.

ART thou pale on thy rock, Cuthona, befide
the fallen chiefs? The night comes, and the

* ——*inhumati venit imago*
Conjugis, ora modis adtollens pallida miris :
Crudelis aras, trajectaque pectora ferro
Nudavit.—— VIRG.
——the ghoft appears
Of her unhappy Lord : the fpectre ftares,
And with erected eyes his bloody bofom bares.
DRYDEN.

† *Nam quia nec fato, merita nec morte peribat,*
Sed mifera ante diem, &c. VIRG.
‡ It was the opinion of the times, that the arms left by the
heroes at home, became bloody the very inftant their owners
were killed, though at ever fo great a diftance.

N   day

day returns, but none appears to raife their tomb. Thou frightneft the fcreaming fowls* away, and thy tears for ever flow. Thou art pale as a watry cloud, that rifes from a lake.

THE fons of the defart came, and they found her dead. They raife a tomb over the heroes; and fhe refts at the fide of Conlath.---Come not to my dreams, O Conlath; for thou haft received thy fame. Be thy voice far diftant from my hall; that fleep may defcend at night. O that I could forget my friends : till my footfteps ceafe to be feen ! till I come among them with joy ! and lay my aged limbs in the narrow houfe !

---

* The fituation of Cuthona is like that of Rizpah, Saul's miftrefs, who fat by her fons after they had been hanged by the Gibeonites.

And Rizpah, the daughter of Aiah, took fackcloth, and fpread it for her upon the rock, from the beginning of the harveft until water dropped on them out of heaven, and fuffered neither the birds of the air to reft on them by day, nor the beafts of prey by night.   2 SAM. xxi. 10.

C A R T H O N *:

A P O E M.

A TALE of the times of old! The deeds
of days of other years!---The murmur
of thy ftreams, O Lora, brings back the memory of the paft. The found of thy woods,
Garmallar,

* This poem is compleat, and the fubject of it, as of moft of
Offian's compofitions, tragical. In the time of Comhal the fon
of Trathal, and father of the celebrated Fingal, Clefsámmor the
fon of Thaddu and brother of Morna, Fingal's mother, was
driven by a ftorm into the river Clyde, on the banks of which
ftood Balclutha, a town belonging to the Britons between the
walls. He was hofpitably received by Reuthám'r, the principal
man in the place, who gave him Moina his only daughter in
marriage. Reuda, the fon of Cormo, a Briton who was in love
with Moina, came to Reuthámir's houfe, and behaved haugh-
tily towards Clefsámmor. A quarrel infued, in which Reuda
was killed; the Britons, who attended him preffed fo hard on
Clefsámmor, that he was obliged to throw himfelf into the
Clyde, and fwim to his fhip. He hoifted fail, and the wind being favourable, bore him out to fea. He often endeavoured to
return, and carry off his beloved Moina by night; but the wind
continuing contrary, he was forced to defift.

Moina, who had been left with child by her hufband, brough:
forth a fon, and died foon after ——Reuthámir named the child
Carthon. i. e. the murmur of waves, from the ftorm which car-

N 2   ried

Garmallar, is lovely in mine ear. Doft thou not behold, Malvina, a rock with its head of heath ? Three aged firs bend from its face; green is the narrow plain at its feet; there the flower of the mountain grows, and fhakes its white head in the breeze. The thiftle is there alone, and fheds its aged beard. Two ftones, half funk in the ground, fhew their heads 'of mofs. The deer of the mountain avoids the place, for he beholds the gray ghoft that guards it * : for the mighty lie, O Malvina, in the narrow plain of the rock. A tale of the times of old ! the deeds of days of other years !

sied off Clefsámmor his father, who was fuppofed to have been caft away. When Carthon was three years old, Comhal the father of Fingal, in one of his expeditions againft the Britons, took and burnt Balclutha. Reuthámir was killed in the attack : and Carthon was carried fafe away by his nurfe, who fled farther into the country of the Britons. Carthon, coming to man's eftate was refolved to revenge the fall of Balclutha on Comhal's pofterity. He fet fail, from the Clyde, and, falling on the coaft of Morven, defeated two of Fingal's heroes, who came to oppofe his progrefs. He was, at laft, unwittingly killed by his father Clefsámmor, in a fingle combat. This ftory is the foundation of the prefent poem, which opens on the night preceding the death of Carthon, fo that what paffed before is introduced by way of epifode. The poem is addreffed to Malvina the daughter of Tofcar.

* It was the opinion of the times, that deer faw the ghofts of the dead. To this day, when beafts fuddenly ftart without any apparent caufe, the vulgar think that they fee the fpirits of the deceafed.

Who

Who comes from the land of ftrangers, with his thoufands around him ? the fun-beam pours its bright ftream before him ; and his hair meets the wind of his hills. His face is fettled from war. He is calm as the evening beam that looks, from the cloud of the weft, on Cona's filent vale. Who is it but Comhal's fon *, the king of mighty deeds ! He beholds his hills with joy, and bids a thoufand voices rife.——Ye have fled over your fields, ye fons of the diftant land ! The king of the world fits in his hall, and hears of his people's flight. He lifts his red eye of pride, and takes his father's fword. Ye have fled over your fields, fons of the diftant land !

Such were the words of the bards, when they came to Selma's halls.---A thoufand lights † from the ftranger's land rofe, in the midft of the people. The feaft is fpread around ; and the night paffed away in joy.---Where is the noble Clefsámmor ‡ faid the fair-haired Fingal ? Where is the companion of my father, in the days of my joy ? Sullen and dark he paffes his days in

* Fingal returns here, from an expedition againft the Romans, which was celebrated by Offian in a particular poem which is in the tranflator's poffeffion.

† Probably wax-lights ; which are often mentioned as carried, among other booty, from the Roman province.

‡ Cleffamh-mór, *mighty deeds.*

the vale of echoing Lora: but, behold, he
comes from the hill, like a fteed * in his ftrength,
who finds his companions in the breeze; and
toffes his bright mane in the wind.——Bleft be
the foul of Clefsámmor, why fo long from
Selma ?

Returns the chief, faid Clefsámmor, in the
midft of his fame ? Such was the renown of
Comhal in the battles of his youth.   Often did
we pafs over Carun to the land of the ftrangers :

* Haft thou given the horfe ftrength? Haft thou clothed his
neck with thunder ? He paweth in the valley, and rejoiceth in
his ftrength.   JOB.

"Ὡς δ' ὅτι τις ϛατὸς ἵππος ακοϛησας ἐπι ϛατνη,
Δεσμὸν απορρηξας, &c.   HOM. II. 6.

The wanton courfer thus with reins unbound,
Breaks from his ftall, and beats the trembling ground ;
His head, now freed, he toffes to the fkies;
His mane dihevei'd o'er his fhoulders flies ;
He fnuffs the females in the diftant plain,
And fprings, exulting.   POPE.

Qualis ubi abruptis fugit prafepia vinclis
Tandem liber equus, campoque potitus aporto,
——Ille in paftus armentaque tendit equarum :
——arrectifque fremit cervicibus altè
Luxurians, luduntque Iubæ per colla, per armos.
                                                VIRG.

Freed from his keepers, thus with broken reins,
The wanton courfer prances o'er the plains :
Or in the pride of youth o'erleaps the mounds,
And fnuffs the females in forbidden grounds.
——O'er his fhoulders flows his waving mane :
He neighs, he fnorts, he bears his head on high.
                                                DRYDEN.

our

our fwords returned, not unftained with blood:
nor did the kings of the world rejoice.——Why
do I remember the battles of my youth? My
hair is mixed with gray. My hand forgets to
bend the bow: and I lift a lighter fpear. O
that my joy would return, as when I firft beheld
the maid; the white bofomed daughter of ftrangers, Moina* with the dark-blue eyes!

TELL, faid the mighty Fingal; the tale of thy
youthful days. Sorrow, like a cloud on the
fun, fhades the foul of Clefsámmor. Mournful
are thy thoughts, alone, on the banks of the
roaring Lora. Let us hear the forrow of thy
youth, and the darknefs of thy days.

IT.was in the days of peace, replied the great
Clefsámmor, I came, in my bounding fhip, to
Balclutha's † walls of towers. The winds had
roared behind my fails, and Clutha's ‡ ftreams
received my dark-bofomed veffel. Three days
I remained in Reuthámir's halls, and faw that

* Moina, *foft in temper and perfon.* We find the Britifh names
in this poem derived from the Galic, which is a proof that the
ancient language of the whole ifland was one and the fame.

† Balclutha, *i. e. the town of Clyde*, probably the *Alcluth* of
Bede.

‡ Clutha, or Cluäth, the Galic name of the river Clyde, the
fignification of the word is *bending*, in allufion to the winding
courfe of that river. From Clutha is derived its Latin name,
Glotta.

beam of light, his daughter. The joy of the
ſhell went round, and the aged hero gave the
fair. Her breaſts were like foam on the wave,
and her eyes like ſtars of light : her hair was
dark as the raven's wing : her ſoul was generous
and mild. My love for Moina was great : and
my heart poured forth in joy.

THE ſon of a ſtranger came ; a chief who
loved the white-boſomed Moina. His words
were mighty in the hall, and he often half-un-
ſheathed his ſword.---Where, he ſaid, is the
mighty Comhal, the reſtleſs wanderer * of the
heath ? Comes he, with his hoſt, to Balclutha,
ſince Cleſsámmor is ſo bold ?

MY ſoul, I replied, O warrior ! burns in a
light of its own. I ſtand without fear in the
midſt of thouſands, though the valiant are diftant far.---Stranger ! thy words are mighty, for
Cleſsámmor is alone. But my ſword trembles
by my ſide, and longs to glitter in my hand.---
Speak no more of Comhal, ſon of the winding
Clutha !

THE ſtrength of his pride aroſe. We fought;
he fell beneath my ſword. The banks of Clutha

---

* The word in the original here rendered by reſtleſs wanderer,
is Scuta, which is the true origin of the Scoti of the Romans ; an
opprobrious name impoſed by the Britons, on the Caledonians,
on account of the continual incurſions into their country.

heard

heard his fall, and a thoufand fpears glittered
around. I fought: the ftrangers prevailed: I
plunged into the ftream of Clutha. My white
fails rofe over the waves, and I bounded on the
dark-blue fea.---Moina came to the fhore, and
rolled the red eye of her tears: her dark hair
flew on the wind; and I heard her cries.---Of-
ten did I turn my fhip! but the winds of the
Eaft prevailed. Nor Clutha ever fince have I
feen: nor Moina of the dark brown hair.---
She fell in Balclutha: for I have feen her ghoft.
I knew her as fhe came through the dufky night,
along the murmur of Lora: fhe was like the
new moon * feen through the gathered mift:
when the fky pours down its flaky fnow, and
the world is filent and dark.

* *Inter quas Phœniffa recens volnere Dido*
Errabat fylva in magna: quam Troius heros
Ut primum juxta ftetit, agnovitque perumbram
Obfcuram, qualem primo qui furgere menfe
Aut videt, aut vidiffe putat per nubila lunam, &c.
                                                    VIRG.

Not far from thefe Phœnician Dido ftood,
Frefh from her wound, her bofom bath'd in blood.
Whom when the Trojan hero hardly knew
Obfcure in fhades, and with a doubtful view,
Doubtful as he who runs thro' dufky night,
Or thinks he fees the moon's uncertain light, &c.
                                                    DRYDEN.

RAISE,

RAISE *, ye bards, faid the mighty Fingal, the praife of unhappy Moina. Call her ghoft, with your fongs, to our hills; that fhe may reft with the fair of Morven, the fun-beams of other days, and the delight of heroes of old.---I have feen the walls † of Balclutha, but they were defolate. The fire had refounded in the halls: and the voice of the people is heard no more. The ftream of Clutha was removed from its place, by the fall of the walls.---The thiftle fhook, there, its lonely head: the mofs whiftled to the wind. The fox looked out, from the windows, the rank grafs of the wall waved round his head.---Defolate is the dwelling of Moina, filence is in the houfe of her fathers.--- Raife the fong of mourning, O bards, over the land of ftrangers. They have but fallen before us: for, one day, we muft fall.---Why doft thou build the hall, fon of the winged days?

* The title of this poem, in the original, is *Duan na nlaoi*, i.e. *The Poem of the Hymns:* probably on account of its many digreffions from the fubject, all which are in a lyric meafure, as this fong of Fingal. Fingal is celebrated by the Irifh hiftorians for his wifdom in making laws, his poetical genius, and his foreknowledge of events.—O'Flaherty goes fo far as to fay, that Fingal's laws were extant in his own time.

† The reader may compare this paffage with the three laft verfes of the 13th chapter of Ifaiah, where the prophet foretels the deftruction of Babylon.

Thou

Thou lookeft from thy towers to-day ; yet a few years, and the blaft of the defart comes ; it howls in thy empty court, and whiftles round thy half-worn fhield.---And let the blaft of the de-fart come ! we fhall be renowned in our day. The mark of my arm fhall be in the battle, and my name in the fong of bards.---Raife the fong ; fend round the fhell : and let joy be heard in my hall.---When thou, fun of heaven, fhalt fail ! if thou fhalt fail, thou mighty light ! if thy brightnefs is for a feafon, like Fingal ; our fame fhall furvive thy beams.

SUCH was the fong of Fingal, in the day of his joy. His thoufand bards leaned forward from their feats, to hear the voice of the king. It was like the mufic of the harp on the gale of the fpring.---Lovely were thy thoughts, O Fin-gal ! why had not Offian the ftrength of thy foul ?---But thou ftandeft alone, my father ; and who can equal the king of Morven?

THE night paffed away in fong, and morning returned in joy;---the mountains fhewed their gray heads ; and the blue face of ocean fmiled. ---The white wave is feen tumbling round the diftant rock ; the gray mift rifes, flowly, from the lake. It came, in the figure of an aged man, along the filent plain. Its large limbs did not move in fteps ; for a ghoft fupported it in mid air.

air. It came towards Selma's hall, and diffolved in a fhower of blood.

THE king alone beheld the terrible fight, and he forefaw the death of the people. He came, in filence, to his hall; and took his father's fpear.---The mail rattled on his breaft. The heroes rofe around. They looked, in filence, on each other, marking the eyes of Fingal.---They faw the battle in his face : the death of armies on his fpear.---A thoufand fhields, at once, are placed on their arms; and they drew a thoufand fwords. The hall of Selma brightened around. The clang of arms afcends.---The gray dogs howl in their place. No word is among the mighty chiefs.---Each marked the eyes of the king; and half affumed his fpear.

Sons of Morven, begun the king, this is no time to fill the fhell. The battle darkens near us; and death hovers over the land. Some ghoft, the friend of Fingal, has forewarned us of the foe.——The fons of the ftranger come from the darkly-rolling fea. For, from the wa-ter, came the fign of Morven's gloomy danger. ---Let each * affume his heavy fpear, and gird

on

* Εν μιν τις ὀξυ Θηξασθω ιυ δ'ασπιδα Θισθο.
HOM. ii. 382.
His fharpen'd fpear let every Grecian wield,
And every Grecian fix his brazen fhield, &c.   POPE.

Let

on his father's fword.---Let the dark helmet rife on every head; and the mail pour its lightening from every fide.---The battle gathers like a tempeft, and foon fhall ye hear the roar of death.

THE hero moved on before his hoft, like a cloud before a ridge of heaven's fire; when it pours on the fky of night, and mariners forefee a ftorm.   On Cona's rifing heath they ftood : the white-bofomed maids beheld them above like a grove; they forefaw the death of their youths, and looked towards the fea with fear.---The white wave deceived them for diftant fails, and the tear is on their cheek.

THE fun rofe on the fea, and we beheld a diftant fleet.---Like the mift of ocean they came: and poured their youth upon the coaft.---The chief was among them, like the ftag in the midft of the herd.---His fhield is ftudded with gold, and ftately ftrode the king of fpears.---He moved towards Selma ; his thoufands moved behind.

> Let each
> His adamantine coat gird well, and each
> Fit well his helm, gripe faft his orbed fhield,
> Borne ev'n or high ; for this day will pour down,
> If I conjecture right, no drizling fhower,
> But rattling ftorm of arrows barb'd with fire.
>   MILTON.

Go,

Go, with thy fong of peace, faid Fingal; go, Ullin, to the king of fwords. Tell him that we are mighty in battle; and that the ghofts of our foes are many.---But renowned are they who have feafted in my halls! they fhew the arms * of my fathers in a foreign land: the fons of the ftrangers wonder, and blefs the friends of Morven's race; for our names have been heard afar; the kings of the world fhook in the midft of their people.

ULLIN went with his fong. Fingal refted on his fpear: he faw the mighty foe in his armour: and he bleft the ftranger's fon.

How ftately art thou, fon of the fea! faid the king of woody Morven. Thy fword is a beam of might by thy fide: thy fpear is a fir that defies the ftorm. The varied face of the moon is not broader than thy fhield.---Ruddy is thy face of youth! foft the ringlets of thy hair! ---But this tree may fall; and his memory be forgot!---The daughter of the ftranger will be fad, and look to the rolling fea:---the children will fay, " We fee a fhip; perhaps it is the king " of Balclutha." The tear ftarts from their mo-

---

* It was a cuftom among the ancient Scots, to exchange arms with their guefts, and thofe arms were preferved long in the different families, as monuments of the friendfhip which fubfifted between their anceftors.

ther's

ther's eye.   Her thoughts are of him that fleeps in Morven.

SUCH were the words of the king, when Ullin came to the mighty Carthon : he threw down the fpear before him ; and raifed the fong of peace.

COME to the feaft of Fingal, Carthon, from the rolling fea! partake the feaft of the king, or lift the fpear of war. The ghofts of our foes are many: but renowned are the friends of Morven!

BEHOLD that field, O Carthon; many a green hill rifes there, with moffy ftones and ruftling grafs : thefe are the tombs of Fingal's foes, the fons of the rolling fea.

DOST thou fpeak to the feeble in arms, faid Carthon, bard of the woody Morven ? Is my face pale for fear, fon of the peaceful fong? Why, then, doft thou think to darken my foul with the tales of thofe who fell?---My arm has fought in the battle; my renown is known afar. Go to the feeble in arms, and bid them yield to Fingal.---Have not I feen the fallen Balclutha? And fhall I feaft with Comhal's fon? Comhal ! who threw his fire in the midft of my father's hall ! I was young, and knew not the caufe why the virgins wept. The columns of fmoke pleafed mine eye, when they rofe above my walls;

walls; I often looked back, with gladnefs, when
my friends fled along the hill.——But when the
years of my youth came on, I beheld the niofs
of my fallen walls : my figh arofe with the
morning, and my tears defcended with night.
---Shall I not fight, I faid to my foul, againft
the children of my foes? And I will fight, O
bard; I feel the ftrength of my foul.

His people gathered around the hero, and
drew, at once, their fhining fwords. He ftands,
in the midft, like a pillar of fire; the tear half-
ftarting from his eye; for he thought of the
fallen Balclutha, and the crowded pride of his
foul arofe. Sidelong he looked up to the hill,
where our heroes fhone in arms; the fpear trembled in his hand: and, bending forward, he
feemed to threaten the king.

Shall I, faid Fingal to his foul, meet, at
once, the king? Shall I ftop him, in the midft
of his courfe, before his fame fhall arife? But
the bard, hereafter, may fay, when he fees the
tomb of Carthon; Fingal took his thoufands,
along with him, to battle, before the noble
Carthon fell.——No :---bard of the times to
come! thou fhalt not leffen Fingal's fame. My
heroes will fight the youth, and Fingal behold
the battle. If he overcomes, I rufh, in my
ftrength, like the roaring ftream of Cona.

Who,

WHO, of my heroes, will meet the fon of the rolling fea? Many arc his warriors on the coaft: and ftrong is his afhen fpear !

CATHUL * rofe, in his ftrength, the fon of the mighty Lormar : three hundred youths attend the chief, the race † of his native ftreams. Feeble was his arm againft Carthon, he fell; and his heroes fled.

CONNAL ‡ refumed the battle, but he broke his heavy fpear : he lay bound on the field : and Carthon purfued his people.

CLESSAMMOR ! faid the king || of Morven, where is the fpear of thy ftrength? Wilt thou behold Connal bound; thy friend, at the ftream of Lora? Rife, in the light of thy fteel, thou friend of Comhal. Let the youth of Balclutha feel the ftrength of Morven's race.

HE rofe in the ftrength of his fteel, fhaking his grizly locks. He fitted the fhield to his fide; and rufhed, in the pride of valour.

* Cath-'huil, *the eye of battle.*

† It appears, from this paffage, that clanfhip was eftablifhed, in the days of Fingal, though not on the fame footing with the prefent tribes in the north of Scotland.

‡ This Connal is very much celebrated, in ancient poetry, for his wifdom and valour : there is a fmall tribe ftill fubfifting, in the North, who pretend they are defcended from him.

|| Fingal did not then know that Carthon was the fon of Clefsámmor.

O CARTHON

ARTHON stood, on that heathy rock, and
saw the heroes approach. He loved the terrible
joy of his face : and his strength, in the locks of
age.——Shall I lift that spear, he said, that never strikes, but once, a foe? Or shall I, with
the words of peace, preserve the warrior's life?
Stately are his steps of age!---lovely the remnant
of his years. Perhaps it is the love of Moina;
the father of car-borne Carthon. Often have I
heard, that he dwelt at the echoing stream of
Lora.

S<small>UCH</small> were his words, when Clessámmor
came, and lifted high his spear. The youth received it on his shield, and spoke the words of
peace.——Warrior of the aged locks! Is there
no youth to lift the spear? Hast thou no son, to
raise the shield before his father, and to meet
the arm of youth? Is the spouse of thy love no
more? or weeps she over the tombs of thy sons?
Art thou of the kings of men? What will be the
fame of my sword if thou shalt fall?

I<small>T</small> will be great, thou son of pride! begun
the tall Clessámmor, I have been renowned in
battle; but I never told my name * to a foe.

Yield

---

* To tell one's name to an enemy was reckoned, in those
days of heroism, a manifest evasion of fighting him; for, if it
was once known, that friendship subsisted, of old, between the
ancestors

Yield to me, fon of the wave, and then thou fhalt know, that the mark of my fword is in many a field.

I NEVER yielded, king of fpears! replied the noble pride of Carthon: I have alfo fought in battles; and I behold my future fame. Defpife me not, thou chief of men; my arm, my fpear is ftrong. Retire among thy friends, and let young heroes fight.

WHY doft thou wound my foul, replied Clefsámmor with a tear? Age does not tremble on my hand; I ftill can lift the fword. Shall I fly in Fingal's fight; in the fight of him I loved? Son of the fea! I never fled: exalt thy pointed fpear.

THEY fought, like two contending winds, that ftrive to roll the wave. Carthon bade his fpear to err; for he ftill thought that the foe was the fpoufe of Moina.——He broke Clefsámmor's beamy fpear in twain: and feized his fhining fword. But as Carthon was binding the chief; the chief drew the dagger of his fathers. He faw the foe's uncovered fide; and opened, there, a wound.

---

anceftors of the combatants, the battle immediately ceafed; and the ancient amity of théir forefathers was renewed. _A man who tells his name to his enemy_, was of old an ignominious term for a coward.

FINGAL faw Clefsámmor low : he moved in the found of his fteel. The hoft ftood filent, in his prefence ; they turned their eyes towards the hero.---He came, like the fullen noife of a ftorm, before the winds arife : the hunter hears it in the vale, and retires to the cave of the rock.

CARTHON ftood in his place : the blood is rufhing down his fide : he faw the coming down of the king ; and his hopes of fame arofe * ; but pale was his cheek : his hair flew loofe, his hel-met fhook on high : the force of Carthon failed ; but his foul was ftrong.

FINGAL beheld the heroes blood ; he ftopt the uplifted fpear. Yield, king of fwords ! faid Comhal's fon ; I behold thy blood. Thou haft been mighty in battle ; and thy fame fhall never fade.

ART thou the king fo far renowned, replied the car-borne Carthon ? Art thou that light of death, that frightens the kings of the world ?--- But why fhould Carthon afk ? for he is like the ftream of his defart ; ftrong as a river, in his courfe : fwift as the eagle of the fky.---O that I had fought with the king ; that my fame might

---

* This expreffion admits of a double meaning, either that Carthon hoped to acquire glory by killing Fingal ; or to be ren-dered famous by falling by his hand. The laft is the moft pro-bable, as Carthon is already wounded.

5   be-

be great in the fong ! that the hunter, beholding my tomb, might fay, he fought with the mighty Fingal. But Carthon dies unknown; he has poured out his force on the feeble.

BUT thou fhalt not die unknown, replied the king of woody Morven : my bards are many, O Carthon, and their fongs defcend to future times. The children of the years to come fhall hear the fame of Carthon ; when they fit round the burning oak *, and the night is fpent in the fongs of old. The hunter, fitting in the heath, fhall hear the ruftling blaft ; and, raifing his eyes, behold the rock where Carthon fell. He fhall turn to his fon, and fhew the place where the mighty fought; " There the king of Bal-clutha fought, like the ftrength of a thoufand ftreams."

JOY rofe in Carthon's face : he lifted his heavy eyes.——He gave his fword to Fingal, to lie within his hall, that the memory of Balclutha's king might remain on Morven.---The battle ceafed along the field, for the bard had fung the fong of peace. The chiefs gathered round the falling Carthon, and heard his words, with

---

* In the north of Scotland, till very lately, they burnt a large trunk of an oak at their feftivals; it was called *the trunk of the feaft*. Time had fo much confecrated the cuftom, that the vulgar thought it a kind of facrilege to difufe it.

fighs,

fighs. Silent they leaned on their fpears, while Balclutha's hero fpoke. His hair fighed in the wind, and his words were feeble.

KING of Morven, Carthon faid, I fall in the midft of my courfe. A foreign tomb receives, in youth, the laft of Reuthámir's race.. Dark-nefs dwells in Balclutha : and the fhadows of grief in Crathmo.---But raife my remembrance on the banks of Lora : where my fathers dwelt. Perhaps the hufband of Moina will mourn over his fallen Carthon.

HIS words reached the heart of Clefsámmor : he fell, in filence, on his fon. The hoft ftood darkened around : no voice is on the plains of Lora. Night came, and the moon, from the eaft, looked on the mournful field : but ftill they ftood, like a filent grove that lifts its head on Gormal, when the loud winds are laid, and dark autumn is on the plain.

THREE days they mourned over Carthon ; on the fourth his father died. In the narrow plain of the rock they lie; and a dim ghoft defends their tomb. There lovely Moina is often feen ; when the fun-beam darts on the rock, and all around is dark. There fhe is feen, Malvina, but not like the daughters of the hill. Her robes are from the ftrangers land; and fhe is ftill alone.

FINGAL

FINGAL was fad for Carthon; he defired his bards to mark the day, when fhadowy autumn returned. And often did they mark the day and fing the hero's praife. Who comes fo dark from ocean's roar, like autumn's fhadowy cloud? Death is trembling in his hand! his eyes are flames of fire!——Who roars along dark Lora's heath? Who but Carthon king of fwords? The people fall! fee! how he ftrides, like the fullen ghoft of Morven!---But there he lies a goodly oak, which fudden blafts overturned! When fhalt thou rife, Balclutha's joy! lovely car-borne Carthon?——Who comes fo dark from ocean's roar, like autumn's fhadowy cloud?

SUCH were the words of the bards, in the day of their mourning: I have accompanied their voice; and added to their fong. My foul has been mournful for Carthon; he fell in the days of his valour: and thou, O Clefsámmor! where is thy dwelling in the air?---Has the youth forgot his wound? And flies he, on the clouds, with thee?——I feel the fun, O Malvina, leave me to my reft. Perhaps they may come to my dreams; I think I hear a feeble voice.---The beam of heaven delights to fhine on the grave of Carthon: I feel it warm around.

O THOU

O THOU that rolleft above *, round as the
fhield of my fathers! Whence are thy beams, O
fun! thy everlafting light? Thou comeft forth,
in thy awful beauty, and the ftars hide themfelves in the fky; the moon, cold and pale,
finks in the weftern wave. But thou thyfelf
moveft alone : who can be a companion of thy
course! The oaks of the mountains fall: the
mountains themfelves decay with years; the
ocean fhrinks and grows again : the moon herfelf
is loft in heaven; but thou art for ever the
fame ; rejoicing in the brightnefs of thy courfe.
When the world is dark with tempefts ; when
thunder rolls, and lightning flies; thou lookeft
in thy beauty, from the clouds, and laugheft at
the ftorm. But to Offian, thou lookeft in vain;
for he beholds thy beams no more ; whether thy
yellow hair flows on the eaftern clouds, or thou
trembleft at the gates of the weft. But thou art
perhaps, like me, for a feafon, and thy years
will have an end. Thou fhalt fleep in thy

---

* This paffage is fomething fimilar to Satan's addrefs to the
Sun in the fourth book of Paradife Loft.

O thou that with furpaffing glory crown'd,
Looks from thy fole dominion like the god
Of this new world; at whofe fight all the ftars
Hide their diminifh'd heads; to thee I call,
But with no friendly voice, and add thy name
O Sun!

clouds,

clouds, carelefs of the voice of the morning.
——Exult then, O fun, in the ftrength of thy
youth ! Age is dark and unlovely ; it is like the
glimmering light of the moon, when it fhines
through broken clouds, and the mift is on the
hills; the blaft of the north is on the plain, the
traveller fhrinks in the midft of his journey.

T H E

DEATH of CUCHULLIN:

A P O E M*.

IS the wind on Fingal's ſhield? Or is the
voice of paſt times in my hall? Sing on,
ſweet voice, for thou art pleaſant, and carrieſt
away my night with joy. Sing on, O Bragéla,
daughter of car-borne Songlan!

I⊤

* Tradition throws conſiderable light on the hiſtory of Ireland, during the long reign of Fingal, the ſon of Comhal, in
Morven.—Arth, the ſon of Cairbre, ſupreme king of Ireland,
dying, was ſucceeded by his ſon Cormac, a minor.——The
petty kings and chiefs of the tribes met at Temora, the royal
palace, in order to chuſe, out of their own number, a guardian
to the young king. Diſputes, concerning the choice of a proper
perſon, run high, and it was reſolved to end all differences by
giving the tuition of the young king to Cuchullin, the ſon of
Semo, who had rendered himſelf famous by his great actions,
and who reſided, at the time, with Connal, the ſon of Caithbat, in Ulſter.

Cuchullin was but three and twenty years old, when he aſſumed the management of affairs in Ireland : and the invaſion
of Swaran happened two years after. In the twenty-ſeventh
year of Cuchullin's age, and the third of his adminiſtration,
Torlath, the ſon of Cantéla, one of the chiefs of that colony of
Belgæ,

Iᴛ is the white wave of the rock, and not Cuchullin's fails. Often do the mifts deceive me
for the fhip of my love ! when they rife round
fome

Belgæ, who were in poffeffion of the fouth of Ireland, fet up for
himfelf in Connaught, and advanced towards Temora, in order
to dethrone Cormac, who, excepting Feradath, afterwards king
of Ireland, was the only one of the Scotch race of kings exift-
ing in that country. Cuchullin marched againft him, came up
with him at the lake of Lego, and totally defeated his forces.
Torlath fell in the battle by Cuchullin's hand ; but as he himfelf preffed too eagerly on the flying enemy, he was mortally
wounded by an arrow, and died the fecond day after.

The good fortune of Cormac fell with Cuchullin: many fet up
for themfelves, and anarchy and confufion reigned. At laft
Cormac was taken off ; and Cairbar, lord of Atha, one of the
competitors for the throne, having defeated all his rivals, became fole monarch of Ireland.——The family of Fingal, who
were in the intereft of Cormac's family, were refolved to deprive
Cairbar of the throne he had ufurped ; in particular, Ofcar the
fon of Offian had determined to revenge the death of Cathol, his
friend, who had been affaffinated by Cairbar.—The threats of
Ofcar reached Cairbar's ears : he invited him in a friendly manner
to a feaft which he had prepared at the royal palace of Temora,
refolving to pick a quarrel, and have fome pretext for killing
him.

The quarrel happened ; the followers of both fought, and
and Cairbar and Ofcar fell by mutual wounds : in the mean time
Fingal arrived from Scotland with an army, defeated the friends
of Cairbar, and re-eftablifhed the family of Cormac in the poffeffion of the kingdom.——The prefent poem concerns the
death of Cuchullin. It is, in the original, called *Duan loch*
Leigo, i. e. *The Poem of Lego's Lake*, and is an epifode introduced
in a great poem, which celebrated the laft expedition of Fingal
into Ireland. The greateft part of the poem is loft, and nothing
remains but fome epifodes, which a few old people in the north
of Scotland retain on memory.——Cuchullin is the moft famous
champion

fome ghoft, and fpread their gray fkirts on the
wind. Why doft thou delay thy coming, fon of
the generous Semo?---Four times has autumn
returned with its winds, and raifed the feas of
Togorma *, fince thou haft been in the roar of
battles, and Bragéla diftant far.---Hills of the
ifle of mift! when will ye anfwer to his hounds?
------But ye are dark in your clouds, and fad
Bragéla calls in vain. Night comes rolling
down: the face of ocean fails. The heath-
cock's head is beneath his wing: the hind fleeps
with the hart of the defart. They fhall rife with
the morning's light, and feed on the moffy
ftream. But my tears return with the fun, my

champion in the Irifh traditions and poems; in them he is always called the *redoubtable Cuchullin*; and the fables concerning
his ftrength and valour are innumerable. Offian thought his expedition againft the Fir-bolg, or Belgæ of Britain, a fubject fit
for an epic poem; which was extant till of late, and was called
Tora-na-tana, or a *Difpute about Poffeffions*, as the war which
was the foundation of it, was commenced by the Britifh Belgæ,
who inhabited Ireland, in order to extend their territories.---
The fragments that remain of this poem are animated with the
genuine fpirit of Offian; fo that there can be no doubt that it
was of his compofition.

　* Togorma, *i. e. The ifland of blue waves*, one of the He-
brides, was fubject to Connal, the fon of Caithbat, Cuchullin's
friend.—He is fometimes called the fon of Colgar, from one of
that name who was the founder of the family.——Connal, a few
days before the news of Torlath's revolt came to Temora, had
failed to Togorma, his native ifle; where he was detained by
contrary winds during the war in which Cuchullin was killed.

fighs

fighs come on with the night. When wilt thou come in thine arms, O chief of moſſy Tura?

PLEASANT is thy voice in Oſſian's ear, daughter of car-borne Sorglan! But retire to the hall of ſhells; to the beam of the burning oak.——Attend to the murmur of the ſea: it rolls at Dunſcaich's walls: let ſleep deſcend on thy blue eyes, and the hero come to thy dreams.

CUCHULLIN ſits at Lego's lake, at the dark rolling of waters. Night is around the hero; and his thouſands ſpread on the heath: a hundred oaks burn in the midſt, the feaſt of ſhells is ſmoaking wide.---Carril ſtrikes the harp, beneath a tree; his gray locks glitter in the beam; the ruſtling blaſt of night is near, and lifts his aged hair.---His ſong is of the blue Togorma, and of its chief, Cuchullin's friend.

WHY art thou abſent, Connal, in the day of the gloomy ſtorm? The chiefs of the ſouth have convened againſt the car-borne Cormac: the winds detain thy ſails, and thy blue waters roll around thee. But Cormac is not alone: the ſon of Semo fights his battles. Semo's ſon his battles fights! the terror of the ſtranger! he that

is

is like the vapour of death *, flowly borne by fultry winds. The fun reddens in its prefence, the people fall around.

SUCH was the fong of Carril, when a fon of the foe appeared; he threw down his pointlefs fpear, and fpoke the words of Torlath, Torlath the chief of heroes, from Lego's fable furge: he that led his thoufands to battle, againft car-borne Cormac, Cormac, who was diftant far, in Temora's † echoing halls: he learned to bend the bow of his fathers; and to lift the fpear. Nor long didft thou lift the fpear, mildly-fhining beam of youth! death ftands dim behind thee, like the darkened half of the moon behind its growing light.

CUCHULLIN rofe before the bard ‡, that came from generous Torlath; he offered him

the

* Οἶη δ᾽ ἐκ νεφέων ἐριβωμὴ φαίνεται ἀὴρ
Καύματος ἐξ ἀνέμοιο δυσαέος ὀρνυμένοιο.

HOM. Il. 5.

As vapours blown by Aufter's fultry breath,
Pregnant with plagues, and fhedding feeds of death,
Beneath the rage of burning Sirius rife,
Choke the parch'd earth, and blacken all the fkies.

POPE.

† The royal palace of the Irifh kings; Teamhrath according to fome of the bards.

‡ The bards were the heralds of ancient times; and their perfons were facred on account of their office. In later times they abufed that privilege; and as their perfons were inviolable, they

fatyrifed

4

the fhell of joy, and honoured the fon of fongs. Sweet voice of Lego! he faid, what are the words of Torlath? Comes he to our feaft or battle, the car-borne fon of Cantéla * ?

HE comes to thy battle, replied the bard, to the founding ftrife of fpears.——When morning is gray on Lego, Torlath will fight on the plain: and wilt thou meet him, in thine arms, king of the ifle of mift? Terrible is the fpear of Torlath! it is a meteor of night. He lifts it, and the people fall : death fits in the lightning of his fword.

Do I fear, replied Cuchullin, the fpear of car-borne Torlath? He is brave as a thoufand heroes; but my foul delights in war. The fword refts not by the fide of Cuchullin, bard of the times of old! Morning fhall meet me on the plain, and gleam on the blue arms of Semo's fon.---But fit thou, on the heath, O bard! and let us hear thy voice: partake of the joyful fhell; and hear the fongs of Temora.

THIS is no time, replied the bard, to hear the fong of joy; when the mighty are to meet

fatyrifed and lampooned fo freely thofe who were not liked by their patrons, that they became a public nuifance. Screened under the character of heralds, they grofly abufed the enemy when he would not accept the terms they offered.

* Cean-teola', *head of a family*.

in

in battle like the ftrength of the waves of Lego.
Why art thou fo dark, Slimora *! with all thy
filent woods? No green ftar trembles on thy
top; no moon-beam on thy fide. But the meteors of death are there, and the gray watry
forms of ghofts. Why art thou dark, Slimora!
with thy filent woods?

HE retired, in the found of his fong; Carril
accompanied his voice. The mufic was like the
memory of joys that are paft, pleafant and
mournful to the foul. The ghofts of departed
bards heard it from Slimora's fide. Soft founds
fpread along the wood, and the filent valleys of
night rejoice.——So, when he fits in the filence
of noon, in the valley of his breeze, the humming of the mountain bee comes to Offian's ear:
the gale drowns it often in its courfe; but the
pleafant found returns again.

RAISE, faid Cuchullin, to his hundred bards,
the fong of the noble Fingal : that fong which
he hears at night, when the dreams of his reft
defcend : when the bards ftrike the diftant harp,
and the faint light gleams on Selma's walls. Or
let the grief of Lara rife, and the fighs of the
mother of Calmar†, when he was fought, in
vain,

* Slia'-mór, _great hill_.

† Calmar the fon of Matha. His death is related at large, in
the third book of Fingal. He was the only fon of Matha; and
the

vain, on his hills; and fhe beheld his bow in
the hall.——Carril, place the fhield of Caithbat
on that branch; and let the fpear of Cuchullin
be near; that the found of my battle may rife
with the gray beam of the eaft.

THE hero leaned on his father's fhield : the
fong of Lara rofe. The hundred bards were
diftant far : Carril alone is near the chief. The
words of the fong were his; and the found of
his harp was mournful.

ALCLETHA * with the aged locks! mother of
car-borne Calmar! why doft thou look towards
the defart, to behold the return of thy fon ?
Thefe are not his heroes, dark on the heath :
nor is that the voice of Calmar : it is but the
diftant grove, Alcletha! but the roar of the
mountain wind!

WHO † bounds over Lara's ftream, fifter of
the noble Calmar? Does not Alcletha behold his

---

the family was extinct in him.—The feat of the family was on
the banks of the river Lara, in the neighbourhood of Lego, and
probably near the place where Cuchullin lay; which circumftance fuggefted to him, the lamentation of Alcletha over her
fon.

* Ald-cla'tha, *decaying beauty :* probably a poetical name
given the mother of Calmar, by the bard himfelf.

† Alcletha fpeaks. Calmar had promifed to return, by a certain day, and his mother and his fifter Alona are reprefented by
the bard as looking, with impatience, towards that quarter where
they expected Calmar would make his firft appearance.

P   fpear?

fpear? But her eyes are dim! Is it not the fon of Matha, daughter of my love?

It is but an aged oak, Alclétha! replied the lovely weeping Alona *; it is but an oak, Alclétha, bent over Lara's ftream. But who comes along the plain? forrow is in his fpeed. He lifts high the fpear of Calmar. Alclétha, it is covered with blood!

But it is covered with the blood of foes †, fifter of car-borne Calmar! his fpear never returned unftained with blood ‡, nor his bow from the ftrife of the mighty. The battle is confumed in his prefence: he is a flame of death, Alona!——Youth ‖ of the mournful fpeed! where is the fon of Alclétha? Does he return with his fame? in the midft of his echoing fhields?——Thou art dark and filent!--- Calmar is then no more. Tell me not, warrior, how he fell, for I cannot hear of his wound.——

Why doft thou look towards the defart, mother of car-borne Calmar?——

* Alúine, *exquifitely beautiful.*

† Aclétha fpeaks.

‡ From the blood of the flain, from the fat of the mighty, the bow of Jonathan returned not back, and the fword of Saul returned not empty. 2 Sam. i. 22.

‖ She addreffes herfelf to Larnir, Calmar's friend, who had returned with the news of his death.

Such was the fong of Carril, when Cuchullin lay on his fhield : the bards refted on their harps, and fleep fell foftly around.——The fon of Semo was awake alone ; his foul was fixed on the war.——The burning oaks began to decay ; faint red light is fpread around.---A feeble voice is heard : the ghoft of Calmar came. He ftalked in the beam. Dark is the wound in his fide. His hair is difordered and loofe. Joy fits darkly on his face : and he feems to invite Cuchullin to his cave.

Son of the cloudy night! faid the rifing chief of Erin ; Why doft thou bend thy dark eyes on me, ghoft of the car-borne Calmar ? Wouldeft thou frighten me, O Matha's fon! from the battles of Cormac ? Thy hand was not feeble in war ; neither was thy voice * for peace. How art thou changed, chief of Lara! if thou now doft advife to fly!——But, Calmar, I never fled. I never feared † the ghofts of the de-fart. Small is their knowledge, and weak their hands; their dwelling is in the wind.——But my foul grows in danger, and rejoices in the noife of fteel. Retire thou to thy cave ; thou art not

* See Calmar's fpeech, in the firft book of Fingal.
† See Cuchullin's reply to Connal, concerning Crugal's ghoft. Fing. b. 2.

Calmar's

Calmar's ghoſt ; he delighted in battle, and his arm was like the thunder of heaven.

HE retired in his blaſt with joy, for he had heard the voice of his praiſe. The faint beam of the morning roſe, and the found of Caithbat's buckler ſpréad. Green Ullin's warriors convened, like the roar of many ſtreams.---The horn of war is heard over Lego ; the mighty Torlath came.

WHY doſt thou come with thy thouſands, Cuchullin, faid the chief of Lego. I know the ſtrength of thy arm, and thy foul is an unextinguiſhed fire.---Why fight we not on the plain, and let our hoſts behold our deeds? Let them behold us like roaring waves, that tumble round a rock : the mariners haſten away, and look on their ſtrife with fear.

THOU riſeſt, like the fun, on my foul, replied the fon of Semo. Thine arm is mighty, O Torlath ! and worthy of my wrath. ˙ Retire, ye men of Ullin, to Slimora's ſhady fide ; behold the chief of Erin, in the day of his fame.—— Carril ! tell to mighty Connal, if Cuchullin muſt fall, tell him I accuſed the winds which roar on Togorma's waves.---Never was he abfent in battle, when the ſtrife of my fame aroſe.---Let this ſword be before Cormac, like the beam of
heaven:

heaven : let his counſel found in Temora in the day of danger.

HE ruſhed, in the ſound of his arms, like the terrible ſpirit of Loda *, when he comes in the roar of a thouſand ſtorms, and ſcatters battles from his eyes.---He ſits on a cloud over Lochlin's ſeas: his mighty hand is on his ſword, and the winds lift his flaming locks.---So terrible was Cuchullin in the day of his fame.---Torlath fell by his hand, and Lego's heroes mourned.--- They gather around the chief like the clouds of the deſart.---A thouſand ſwords roſe at once ; a thouſand arrows flew ; but he ſtood like a rock in the midſt of a roaring ſea.——They fell around; he ſtrode in blood : dark Slimora echoed wide.---The ſons of Ullin came, and the battle ſpread over Lego.---The chief of Erin overcame ; he returned over the field with his fame.——

* Loda, in the third book of Fingal, is mentioned as a place of worſhip in Scandinavia: by the *ſpirit of Loda*, the poet probably means Odin, the great deity of the northern nations. He is deſcribed here with all his terrors about him, not unlike Mars, as he is introduced in a ſimile, in the ſeventh Iliad.

———— ———— οἷς τε πελώριος ἔρχεται Ἄρης
Ὅς τ' εἶσιν πόλεμόνδε μετ' ἀνέρας, οὕστε κρονίων
Θυμοϐόρε ἔριδ̅· μανεῖ ξυνέηκε μάχεσθαι.
So ſtalks in arms the griſly god of Thrace,
When Jove to puniſh faithleſs men prepares,
And gives whole nations to the waſte of wars.

POPE.

BUT pale he returned! The joy of his face was dark. He rolled his eyes in filence.---The fword hung, unfheathed, in his hand, and his fpear bent at every ftep.

CARRIL, faid the king in fecret, the ftrength of Cuchullin fails. My days are with the years that are paft: and no morning of mine fhall arife.---They fhall feek me at Temora, but I fhall not be found. Cormac will weep in his hall, and fay, " Where is Tura's chief?"--- But my name is renowned! my fame in the fong of bards.——The youth will fay in fecret, O let me die as Cuchullin died; renown cloathed him like a robe; and the light of his fame is great. Draw the arrow from my fide; and lay Cuchullin beneath that oak. Place the fhield of Caithbat near, that they may behold me amidft the arms of my fathers.---

AND is the fon of Semo fallen *, faid Carril with a figh?——Mournful are Tura's walls; and forrow dwells at Dunfcaich.---Thy fpoufe

---

* The Irifh hiftorians have placed Cuchullin in the firft century.—The tranflator has given his reafons for fixing him in the third, in the differtation which is prefixed to this collection. In other particulars the accounts of Keating and O'Flaherty coincide pretty nearly with Offian's poems, and the traditions of the Highlands and Ifles. They fay that he was killed in the twenty-feventh year of his age, and they give him a great character for his wifdom and valour.

is

is left alone in her youth, the fon * of thy love
is alone.---He fhall come to Bragela, and afk her
why fhe weeps.---He fhall lift his eyes to the
wall, and fee his father's fword.---Whofe fword
is that? he will fay : and the foul of his mother
is fad. Who is that, like the hart of the defart,
in the murmur of his courfe ?---His eyes look
wildly round in fearch of his friend.——Connal,
fon of Colgar, where haft thou been, when the
mighty fell ? Did the feas of Togorma roll
round thee? Was the wind of the fouth in thy
fails? The mighty have fallen in battle, and thou
waft not there.---Let none tell it in Selma, nor
in Morven's woody land; Fingal will be fad,
and the fons of the defart mourn.

By the dark rolling waves of Lego they raifed
the hero's tomb.——Luäth †, at a diftance,
lies, the companion of Cuchullin, at the chace.

* Conloch, who was afterwards very famous for his great exploits in Ireland. He was fo remarkable for his dexterity in
handling the javelin, that when a good markfman is defcribed,
it has paffed into a proverb, in the north of Scotland, *He is unerring as the arm of Conloch.*

† It was of old, the cuftom to bury the favourite dog near
the mafter. This was not peculiar to the ancient Scots, for we
find it practifed by many other nations in their ages of heroifm.
——There is a ftone fhewn ftill at Dunfcaich in the ifle of Sky,
to which Cuchullin commonly bound his dog Luäth.—The ftone
goes by his name to this day.

——Bleft

——Bleft * be thy foul, fon of Semo; thou wert mighty in battle.---Thy ftrength was like the ftrength of a ftream : thy fpeed like the eagle's † wing.——Thy path in the battle was terrible : the fteps of death were behind thy fword.——Bleft be thy foul, fon of Semo; car-borne chief of Dunfcaich !

Thou haft not fallen by the fword of the mighty, neither was thy blood on the fpear of the valiant.---The arrow came, like the fting of death in a blaft : nor did the feeble hand, which drew the bow, perceive it. Peace to thy foul, in thy cave, chief of the ifle of Mift !

The mighty are difperfed at Temora: there is none in Cormac's hall. The king mourns in his youth, for he does not behold thy coming. The found of thy fhield is ceafed : his foes are gathering round. Soft be thy reft in thy cave, chief of Erin's wars !

Bragela will not hope thy return, or fee thy fails in ocean's foam.——Her fteps are not on the fhore : nor her ear open to the voice of thy

---

* This is the fong of the bards over Cuchullin's tomb. Every ftanza clofes with fome remarkable title of the hero, which was always the cuftom in funeral elegies.—The verfe of the fong is a lyric meafure, and it was of old fung to the harp.

† They were fwifter than eagles, they were ftronger than lions. 2 Sam. i. 23.

rowers.---She fits in the hall of fhells, and fees the arms of him that is no more.---Thine eyes are full of tears, daughter of car-borne Sorglan! ——Bleft be thy foul in death, O chief of fhady Cromla!

D AUGHTER of heaven †, fair art thou!
the filence of thy face is pleafant. Thou
comeſt forth in lovelinefs : the ſtars attend thy
blue ſteps in the eaſt. The clouds rejoice in thy
prefence,

* It may not be improper here, to give the ſtory which is the
foundation of this poem, as it is handed down by tradition.—
Uſnoth, lord of Etha, which is probably that part of Argylefhire which is near Loch Eta, an arm of the fea in Lorn, had
three fons, Nathos, Althos, and Ardan by Sliſſama, the daughter of Semo and fiſter to the celebrated Cuchullin. The three
brothers, when very young, were fent over to Ireland, by their
father, to learn the ufe of arms, under their uncle Cuchullin,
who made a great figure in that kingdom. They were juſt
landed in Ulſter when the news of Cuchullin's death arrived.
Nathos, though very young, took the command of Cuchullin's
army, made head againſt Cairbar the ufurper, and defeated him
in feveral battles. Cairbar at laſt having found means to murder Cormac the lawful king, the army of Nathos ſhifted fides,
and he himſelf was obliged to return into Ulſter, in order to pafs
over into Scotland.

Dar-thula, the daughter of Colla, with whom Cairbar was in
love, refided, at that time, in Seláma a caſtle in Ulſter : ſhe faw,
fell in love, and fled with Nathos ; but a ſtorm rifing at fea, they
were unfortunately driven back on that part of the coaſt of Ulſter,
where Cairbar was encamped with his army, waiting for Fingal,
who

prefence, O moon, and brighten their dark-
brown fides. Who is like thee in heaven,
daughter of the night ? The ftars are afhamed in
thy prefence, and turn afide their green, fparkling eyes.---Whither doft thou retire from thy
courfe, when the darknefs * of thy countenance
grows? Haft thou thy hall like Offian? Dwelleft
thou in the fhadow of grief? Have thy fifters
fallen from heaven ? Are they who rejoiced with
thee, at night, no more ?---Yes !---they have
fallen, fair light! and thou doft often retire to
mourn.——But thou thyfelf fhalt fail, one night;
and leave thy blue path in heaven. The ftars
will then lift their green heads : they who were
afhamed in thy prefence, will rejoice.

who meditated an expedition into Ireland, to re-eftablifh the
Scotch race of kings on the throne of that kingdom. The three
brothers, after having defended themfelves, for fome time, with
great bravery, were overpowered and flain, and the unfortunate
Dar-thula killed herfelf upon the body of her beloved Nathos.

Offian opens the poem, on the night preceding the death of
the fons of Ufnoth, and brings in, by way of epifode, what
paffed before. He relates the death of Dar-thula differently
from the common tradition ; his account is the moft probable,
as fuicide feems to have been unknown in thofe early times : for
no traces of it are found in the old poetry.

† The addrefs to the moon is very beautiful in the original.
It is in a lyric meafure, and appears to have been fung to the
harp.

* The poet means the moon in her wane.

THOU

THOU art now clothed with thy brightnefs: look from thy gates in the fky. Burft the cloud, O wind, that the daughter of night may look forth, that the fhaggy mountains may brighten, and the ocean roll its blue waves in light.

NATHOS * is on the deep, and Althos that beam of youth, Ardan is near his brothers; they move in the gloom of their courfe. The fons of Ufnoth move in darknefs, from the wrath of car-borne Cairbar †.

WHO is that dim, by their fide? the night has covered her beauty. Her hair fighs on ocean's wind; her robe ftreams in dufky wreaths. She is like the fair fpirit of heaven, in the midft of his fhadowy mift. Who is it but Dar-thula ‡, the firft of Erin's maids? She has fled from the love of Cairbar, with the car-borne Nathos. But the winds deceive thee, O Dar-thula; and deny the woody Etha to thy fails. Thefe are not thy

---

* Nathos fignifies *youthful*, Ailthos, *exquifite beauty*, Ardan, *pride*.

† Cairbar, who murdered Cormac king of Ireland, and ufurped the throne. He was afterwards killed by Ofcar the fon of Offian in a fingle combat. The poet, upon other occafions, gives him the epithet of red-haired.

‡ Dar-thúla, or Dart-'huile, *a woman with fine eyes*. She was the moft famous beauty of antiquity. To this day, when a woman is praifed for her beauty, the common phrafe is, that *fhe is as lovely as Dar-thula*.

mountains,

mountains, Nathos, nor is that the roar of thy climbing waves. The halls of Cairbar are near; and the towers of the foe lift their heads. Ullin ftretches its green head into the fea ; and Tura's bay receives the fhip. Where have ye been, ye fouthern winds! when the fons of my love were deceived? But ye have been fporting on plains, and purfuing the thiftle's beard. O that ye had been ruftling in the fails of Nathos, till the hills of Etha rofe! till they rofe in their clouds, and faw their coming chief! Long haft thou been abfent, Nathos! and the day of thy return is paft *.

But the land of ftrangers faw thee, lovely : thou waft lovely in the eyes of Dar-thula. Thy face was like the light of the morning, thy hair like the raven's wing. Thy foul was generous and mild, like the hour of the fetting fun. Thy words were the gale of the reeds, or the gliding ftream of Lora.

But when the rage of battle rofe, thou waft like a fea in a ftorm; the clang of arms was terrible : the hoft vanifhed at the found of thy courfe.——It was then Dar-thula beheld thee,

---

* That is, the day appointed by deftiny. We find no deity in Offian's poetry, if fate is not one ; of that he is very full in fome of his poems in the tranflator's hands.

from

4

from the top of her mofly tower: from the tower
of Selâma *, where her fathers dwelt.

LOVELY art thou, O ftranger! fhe faid, for
her trembling foul arofe. Fair art thou in thy
battles, friend of the fallen Cormac! † Why
doft thou rufh on, in thy valour, youth of the
ruddy look? Few are thy hands, in battle,
againft the car-borne Cairbar!---O that I might
be freed of his love! ‡ that I might rejoice in
the prefence of Nathos!——Bleft are the rocks
of Etha; they will behold his fteps at the chace!
they will fee his white bofom, when the winds
lift his raven hair!

SUCH were thy words, Dar-thula, in Selâma's
mofly towers. But, now, the night is round
thee: and the winds have deceived thy fails.
The winds have deceived thy fails, Dar-thula:
their bluftering found is high. Ceafe a little
while, O north wind, and let me hear the voice

---

* The poet does not mean that Selâma which is mentioned as
the feat of Tofcar in Ulfter, in the poem of Conlath and Cuthona. The word in the original fignifies either *beautiful to behold*, or a place *with a pleafant or wide profpect*. In thofe times,
they built their houfes upon eminences, to command a view of
the country, and to prevent their being furprized: many of
them, on that account, were called Selâma. The famous Selma
of Fingal is derived from the fame root.

† Cormac the young king of Ireland, who was murdered by
Cairbar.

‡ That is, of the love of Cairbar.

7　　　　　　　　　　　　　　　　of

of the lovely. Thy voice is lovely, Dar-thula, between the ruftling blafts.

Are thefe the rocks of Nathos, and the roar of his mountain-ftreams? Comes that beam of light from Ufnoth's nightly hall? The mift rolls around, and the beam is feeble : but the light of Dar-thula's foul is the car-borne chief of Etha! Son of the generous Ufnoth, why that broken figh? Are we not in the land of ftrangers, chief of echoing Etha?

These are not the rocks of Nathos, he replied, nor the roar of his ftreams. No light comes from Etha's halls, for they are diftant far. We are in the land of ftrangers, in the land of car-borne Cairbar. The winds have deceived us, Dar-thula. Ullin lifts here her green hills.---Go towards the north, Althos; be thy fteps, Ardan, along the coaft ; that the foe may not come in darknefs, and our hopes of Etha fail.———

I will go towards that moffy tower, and fee who dwells about the beam.---Reft, Dar-thula, on the fhore! reft in peace, thou beam of light! the fword of Nathos is around thee, like the lightning of heaven.

He went. She fat alone, and heard the rolling of the wave. The big tear is in her eye; and fhe looks for the car-borne Nathos.---Her

foul

foul trembles at the blaft. And fhe turns her ear towards the tread of his feet.——The tread of his feet is not heard. Where art thou, fon of my love! The roar of the blaft is around me. Dark is the cloudy night.——But Nathos does not return. What detains thee, chief of Etha? ---Have the foes met the hero in the ftrife of the night?---

HE returned, but his face was dark : he had feen his departed friend.---It was the wall of Tura, and the ghoft of Cuchullin ftalked there. The fighing of his breaft was frequent; and the decayed flame of his eyes terrible. His fpear was a column of mift : the ftars looked dim through his form. His voice was like hollow wind in a cave : and he told the tale of grief. The foul of Nathos was fad, like the fun * in the day of mift, when his face is watry and dim.

WHY art thou fad, O Nathos, faid the lovely daughter of Colla? Thou art a pillar of light to Dar-thula : the joy of her eyes is in Etha's

---

* *Conditus in nubem, medioque refugerit orbe* ;

VIRG.

—Thro' mifts he fhoots his fullen beams,
Frugal of light, in loofe and ftraggling ftreams.

DRYDEN.

chief.

chief.   Where is my friend *, but Nathos ? My
father rests in the tomb.   Silence dwells on Seláma : sadnefs fpreads on the blue ftreams of my
land.   My friends have fallen, with Cormac.
The mighty were flain in the battle of Ullin.

EVENING darkened on the plain.   The blue
ftreams failed before mine eyes.   The unfrequent
blaft came ruftling in the tops of Seláma's
groves.   My feat was beneath a tree on the
walls of my fathers.   Truthil paft before my
foul; the brother of my love; he that was abfent † in battle againft the car-borne Cairbar.

BENDING on his fpear, the gray-haired Colla
came : his downcaft face is dark, and forrow
dwells in his foul.   His fword is on the fide of
the hero : the helmet of his fathers on his head.
---The battle grows in his breaft.   He ftrives to
hide the tear.

DAR-THULA, he fighing faid, thou art the
laft of Colla's race.   Truthil is fallen in battle.
The king ‡ of Seláma is no more.------Cairbar

---

* ————————ἐυ γὰρ ετ᾿ αλλη
Ἐϛαι θαλπωρή,————
————ὐδὲ μει᾿ εϛί ϖατὴρ καὶ ϖὁτνια μὴτηϱ.

HOM. vi. 411.

† The family of Colla preferved their loyalty to Cormac long
after the death of Cuchullin.

‡ It is very common, in Offian's pcetry, to give the title of
King to every chief that was remarkable for his valour.

comes,

comes, with his thoufands, towards Seláma's
walls.---Colla will meet his pride, and revenge
his fon. But where fhall I find thy fafety, Dar-
thula with the dark-brown hair! thou art lovely
as the fun-beam of heaven, and thy friends are
low!

AND is the fon of battle fallen? I faid with a
burfting figh. Ceafed the generous foul of Truthil to lighten through the field?---My fafety,
Colla, is in that bow; I have learned to pierce
the deer. Is not Cairbar like the hart of the defart, father of fallen Truthil?

THE face of age brightened with joy: and the
crouded tears of his eyes poured down. The
lips of Colla trembled. His gray beard whiftled
in the blaft. Thou art the fifter of Truthil, he
faid, and thou burneft in the fire of his foul.
Take, Dar-thula, take that fpear, that brazen
fhield, that burnifhed helmet: they are the
fpoils of a warrior: a fon * of early youth.——
When the light rifes on Seláma, we go to meet
the car-borne Cairbar.——But keep thou near
the arm of Colla; beneath the fhadow of my
fhield. Thy father, Dar-thula, could once de-

---

* The poet, to make the ftory of Dar-thula's arming herfelf
for battle, more probable, makes her armour to be that of a very
young man, otherwife it would fhock all belief, that fhe, who
was very young, fhould be able to carry it.

fend

fend thee; but age is trembling on his hand.——
The ftrength of his arm has failed, and his foul
is darkened with grief.

WE paſſed the night in forrow. The light of
morning rofe. I ſhone in the arms of battle.
The gray-haired hero moved before. The ſons
of Seláma convened around the founding ſhield
of Colla. But few were they in the plain, and
their locks were gray. The youths had fallen
with Truthil, in the battle of car-borne Cormac.

COMPANIONS of my youth! faid Colla, it
was not thus you have feen me in arms. It was
not thus I ſtrode to battle, when the great Con-
fadan fell. But ye are laden with grief. The
darknefs of age comes like the miſt of the defart. My ſhield is worn with years; my fword
is fixed * in its place. I faid to my foul, thy
evening ſhall be calm, and thy departure like a
fading light. But the ſtorm has returned; I
bend like an aged oak. My boughs are fallen
on Seláma, and I tremble in my place.——
Where art thou, with thy fallen heroes, O my
car-borne Truthil! Thou anſwereſt not from thy
ruſhing blaſt; and the foul of thy father is fad.

* It was the cuſtom of thofe times, that every warrior at a certain age, or when he became unfit for the field, fixed his arms,
in the great hall, where the tribe feaſted, upon joyful occaſions.
He was afterwards never to appear in battle; and this ſtage of
life was called the *time of fixing of the arms.*

But

But I will be fad no more, Cairbar or Colla muſt
fall. I feel the returning ſtrength of my arm.
My heart leaps at the ſound of battle.

THE hero drew his ſword. The gleaming
blades of his people roſe. They moved along
the plain. Their gray hair ſtreamed in the
wind.---Cairbar fat, at the feaſt, in the ſilent
plain of Lona *. He faw the coming of the heroes, and he called his chiefs to battle.

WHY † ſhould I tell to Nathos, how the
ſtrife of battle grew! I have feen thee, in the
midſt of thouſands, like the beam of heaven's
fire; it is beautiful, but terrible; the people
fall in its red courſe.——The ſpear of Colla
ſlew, for he remembered the battles of his youth.
An arrow came with its found, and pierced the
hero's ſide. He fell on his echoing ſhield. My
ſoul ſtarted with fear; I ſtretched my buckler
over him; but my heaving breaſt was feen.

* Lona, *a marſhy plain.* It was the cuſtom, in the days of
Oſſian, to feaſt after a victory. Cairbar had juſt provided an en-
tertainment for his army, upon the defeat of Truthil the fon of
Colla, and the reſt of the party of Cormac, when Colla and his
aged warriors arrived to give him battle.

† The poet avoids the deſciiption of the battle of Lona, as it
would be improper in the mouth of a woman, and could have
nothing new, after the numerous deſcriptions, of that kind, in
his other poems. He, at the fame time, gives an opportunity
to Dar-thula to pafs a fine compliment on her lover.

5

Cairbar

Cairbar came, with his fpear, and he beheld Selàma's maid: joy rofe on his dark-brown face; he ftayed the lifted fteel. He raifed the tomb of Colla; and brought me weeping to Selàma. He fpoke the words of love, but my foul was fad. I faw the fhields of my fathers, and the fword of car-borne Truthil. I faw the arms of the dead, and the tear was on my cheek.

THEN thou didft come, O Nathos: and gloomy Cairbar fled. He fled like the ghoft of the defart before the morning's beam. His hofts were not near: and feeble was his arm againft thy fteel.

WHY * art thou fad, O Nathos? faid the lovely maid of Colla.

I HAVE met, replied the hero, the battle in my youth. My arm could not lift the fpear, when firft the danger rofe; but my foul brighten-ed before the war, as the green narrow vale, when the fun pours his ftreamy beams, before he hides his head in a ftorm. My foul bright-ened in danger before I faw Selàma's fair; before I faw thee, like a ftar, that fhines on the hill, at night; the cloud flowly comes, and threatens the lovely light.

---

* It is ufual with Offian, to repeat, at the end of the epifodes, the fentence which introduced them. It brings back the mind of the reader to the main ftory of the poem.

WE

WE are in the land of the foe, and the winds have deceived us, Dar-thula! the ſtrength of our friends is not near, nor the mountains of Etha. Where ſhall I find thy peace, daughter of mighty Colla! The brothers of Nathos are brave : and his own ſword has ſhone in war. But what are the ſons of Uſnoth to the hoſt of car-borne Cairbar! O that the winds had brought thy ſails, Oſcar * king of men! thou didſt promiſe to come to the battles of fallen Cormac. Then would my hand be ſtrong as the flaming arm of death. Cairbar would tremble in his halls, and peace dwell round the lovely Dar-thula. But why doſt thou fall, my ſoul ? The ſons of Uſnoth may prevail.

AND they will prevail, O Nathos, ſaid the riſing ſoul of the maid : never ſhall Dar-thula behold the halls of gloomy Cairbar. Give me thoſe arms of braſs, that glitter to that paſſing meteor ; I ſee them in the dark-boſomed ſhip. Dar-thula will enter the battle of ſteel.---Ghoſt of the noble Colla! do I behold thee on that cloud? Who is that dim beſide thee? It is the car-borne Truthil. Shall I behold the halls of

---

* Oſcar, the ſon of Oſſian, had long reſolved on the expedition, into Ireland, againſt Cairbar, who had aſſaſſinated his friend Cathol, the ſon of Moran, an Iriſhman of noble extraction, and in the intereſt of the family of Cormac.

him

him that flew Seláma's chief! No : I will not
behold them, spirits of my love!

Joy rose in the face of Nathos, when he heard
the white bofomed maid.   Daughter of Seláma!
thou shineft on my foul.   Come, with thy
thoufands, Cairbar! the strength of Nathos is
returned.   And thou, O aged Ufnoth, shalt not
hear that thy son has fled.   I remember thy
words on Etha; when my fails begun to rife :
when I fpread them towards Ullin, towards the
moffy walls of Tura.   Thou goeft, he faid, O
Nathos, to the king of shields; to Cuchullin
chief of men who never fled from danger.   Let
not thine arm be feeble : neither be thy thoughts
of flight; left the fon of Semo fay that Etha's
race are weak.   His words may come to Ufnoth,
and fadden his foul in the hall.——The tear was
on his cheek.   He gave this shining fword.

I came to Tura's bay : but the halls of Tura
were filent.   I looked around, and there was
none to tell of the chief of Dunfcaich.   I went
to the hall of his shells, where the arms of his
fathers hung,   But the arms were gone, and
aged Lamhor * fat in tears.

Whence are the arms of steel, faid the rifing
Lamhor? The light of the fpear has long been

* Lamh-mhor, *mighty hand*,

Q 4   abfent

abfent from Tura's dufky walls.---Come ye from
the rolling fea? Or from the mournful halls of
Temora *.

WE come from the fea, I faid, from Ufnoth's
rifing towers. We are the fons of Slis-sáma †,
the daughter of car-borne Semo. Where is
Tura's chief, fon of the filent hall? But why
fhould Nathos afk? for I behold thy tears.
How did the mighty fall, fon of the lonely
Tura?

HE fell not, Lamhor replied, like the filent
ftar of night, when it fhoots through darknefs
and is no more. But he was like a meteor that
falls in a diftant land; death attends its red
courfe, and itfelf is the fign of wars.——Mournful are the banks of Lego, and the roar of
ftreamy Lara! There the hero fell, fon of the
noble Ufnoth.

AND the hero fell in the midft of flaughter, I
faid with a burfting figh. His hand was ftrong
in battle; and death was behind his fword.---We
came to Lego's mournful banks. We found his

---

* Temora was the royal palace of the fupreme kings of Ireland. It is here called mournful, on account of the death of
Cormac, who was murdered there by Cairbar who ufurped his
throne.

† Slis-feamha, *foft bofom.* She was the wife of Ufnoth and
daughter of Semo the chief of the *ifle of mift.*

rifing

rifing tomb. His companions in battle are there; his bards of many fongs. Three days we mourned over the hero : on the fourth, I ftruck the fhield of Caithbat. The heroes gathered around with joy, and fhook their beamy fpears.

CORLATH was near with his hoft, the friend of car-borne Cairbar. We came like a ftream by night, and his heroes fell. When the people of the valley rofe, they faw their blood with morning's light. But we rolled away, like wreaths of mift, to Cormac's echoing hall. Our fwords rofe to defend the king. But Temora's halls were empty. Cormac had fallen in his youth. The king of Erin was no more.

SADNESS feized the fons of Ullin, they flowly, gloomily retired : like clouds that, long having threatened rain, retire behind the hills. The fons of Ufnoth moved, in their grief, towards Tura's founding bay. We paffed by Seláma, and Cairbar retired like Lano's mift, when it is driven by the winds of the defart.

IT was then I beheld thee, O maid, like the light of Etha's fun. Lovely is that beam, I faid, and the crowded figh of my bofom rofe. Thou cameft in thy beauty, Dar-thula, to Etha's mournful chief.——But the winds have deceived us, daughter of Colla, and the foe is near.

YES!

Yes!---the foe is near, faid the ruftling
ftrength of Althos *. I heard their clanging
arms on the coaft, and faw the dark wreaths of
Erin's ftandard. Diftinét is the voice of Cairbar †, and loud as Cromla's falling ftream. He
had feen the dark fhip on the fea, before the
dufky night came down. His people watch on
Lena's ‡ plain, and lift ten thoufand fwords.

And let them lift ten thoufand fwords, faid
Nathos with a fmile. The fons of car-borne
Ufnoth will never tremble in danger. Why doft
thou roll with all thy foam, thou roaring fea of
Ullin ? Why do ye ruftle, on your dark wings,
ye whiftling tempefts of the fky ?---Do ye think,
ye ftorms, that ye keep Nathos on the coaft ?
No : his foul detains him, children of the
night!——Althos ! bring my father's arms :
thou feeft them beaming to the ftars. Bring the

---

* Althos had juft returned from viewing the coaft of Lena,
whither he had been fent by Nathos, the beginning of the
night.

† Cairbar had gathered an army, to the coaft of Ulfter, in order
to oppofe Fingal, who prepared for an expedition into Ireland to
re-eftablifh the houfe of Cormac on the throne, which Cairbar
had ufurped. Between the wings of Cairbar's army was the bay
of Tura, into which the fhip of the fons of Ufnoth was driven :
fo that there was no poffibility of their efcaping.

‡ The fcene of the prefent poem is nearly the fame with that of
the epic poem in this collection. The heath of Lena and Tura
are often mentioned.

fpear

fpear of Semo*, it ftands in the dark-bofomcd
fhip.

HE brought the arms. Nathos clothed his
limbs in all their fhining fteel. The ftride of
the chief is lovely : the joy of his eyes terrible.
He looks towards the coming of Cairbar. The
wind is ruftling in his hair. Dar-thula is filent
at his fide : her look is fixed on the chief. She
ftrives to hide the rifing figh, and two tears
fwell in her eyes.

ALTHOS! faid the chief of Etha, I fce a cave
in that rock. Place Dar-thula there : and let
thy arm be ftrong. Ardan! we meet the foe,
and call to battle gloomy Cairbar. O that he
came in his founding fteel, to mcet the fon of
Ufnoth !——Dar-thula! if thou fhalt efcape,
look not on the falling Nathos. Lift thy fails,
O Althos, towards the echoing groves of Etha.

TELL to the chief †, that his fon fell with
fame ; that my fword did not fhun the battle.
Tell him I fell in the midft of thoufands, and
let the joy of his grief be great. Daughter of
Colla! call the maids to Etha's echoing hall.

---

* Semo was grandfather to Nathos by the mother's fide. The
fpear mentioned here was given to Ufnoth on his marriage, it
being the cuftom then for the father of the lady to give his arms
to his fon-in-law, The ceremony ufed upon thefe occafions is
mentioned in other poems.

† Ufnoth.

Let

Let their fongs arife from Nathos, when fhadowy
autumn returns.---O that the voice of Cona *
might be heard in my praife ! then would my
fpirit rejoice in the midft of my mountain winds.

AND my voice fhall praife thee, Nathos chief
of the woody Etha ! The voice of Offian fhall
rife in thy praife, fon of the generous Ufnoth !
Why was I not on Lena, when the battle rofe ?
Then would the fword of Offian have defended
thee, or himfelf have fallen low.

WE fat, that night, in Selma round the
ftrength of the fhell. The wind was abroad, in
the oaks ; the fpirit of the mountain † fhrieked.
The blaft came ruftling through the hall, and
gently touched my harp. The found was
mournful and low, like the fong of the tomb.
Fingal heard it firft, and the crowded fighs of
his bofom rofe.——Some of my heroes are low,
faid the gray-haired king of Morven. I hear
the found of death on the harp of my fon.
Offian, touch the founding ftring ; bid the forrow rife ; that their fpirits may fly with joy to
Morven's woody hills.

* Offian, the fon of Fingal, is, often, poetically called the
voice of Cona.

† By the fpirit of the mountain is meant that deep and melancholy found which precedes a ftorm ; well known to thofe
who live in a high country.

I TOUCHED the harp before the king, the found was mournful and low. Bend forward from your clouds, I faid, ghofts of my fathers! bend; lay by the red terror of your courfe, and receive the falling chief; whether he comes from a diftant land, or rifes from the rolling fea. Let his robe of mift be near; his fpear that is formed of a cloud. Place an half-extinguifhed meteor by his fide, in the form of the hero's fword. And, oh! let his countenance be lovely, that his friends may delight in his prefence. Bend from your clouds, I faid, ghofts of my fathers! bend.

SUCH was my fong, in Selma, to the lightly-trembling harp. But Nathos was on Ullin's fhore, furrounded by the night; he heard the voice of the foe amidft the roar of tumbling waves. Silent he heard their voice, and refted on his fpear.

MORNING rofe, with its beams; the fons of Erin appear; like gray rocks, with all their trees, they fpread along the coaft. Cairbar ftood, in the midft, and grimly fmiled when he faw the foe.

NATHOS rufhed forward, in his ftrength; nor could Dar-thula ftay behind. She came with the hero, lifting her fhining fpear. And who are thefe, in their armour, in the pride of youth?

youth ? Who but the fons of Ufnoth, Althos and dark-haired Ardan ?

Come, faid Nathos, come! chief of the high Temora! Let our battle be on the coaft for the white-bofomed maid. His people are not with Nathos; they are behind that rolling fea. Why doft thou bring thy thoufands againft the chief of Etha? Thou didft fly * from him, in battle, when his friends were around him.

Youth of the heart of pride, fhall Erin's king fight with thee? Thy fathers were not among the renowned, nor of the kings of men. Are the arms of foes in their halls? Or the fhields of other times? Cairbar is renowned in Temora, nor does he fight with little men.

The tear ftarts from car-borne Nathos; he turned his eyes to his brothers. Their fpears flew, at once, and three heroes lay on earth. Then the light of their fwords gleamed on high; the ranks of Erin yield; as a ridge of dark clouds before a blaft of wind.

Then Cairbar ordered his people, and they drew a thoufand bows. A thoufand arrows flew; the fons of Ufnoth fell. They fell like three young oaks which ftood alone on the hill; the traveller faw the lovely trees, and wondered how

---

* He alludes to the flight of Cairbar from Selama.

they

they grew fo lonely; the blaft of the defart
came, by night, and laid their green heads low;
next day he returned, but they were withered,
and the heath was bare.

DAR-THULA ftood in filent grief, and beheld
their fall: no tear is in her eye: but her look
is wildly fad. Pale was her cheek; her trembling lips broke fhort an half-formed word. Her
dark hair flew on the wind.——But gloomy
Cairbar came. Where is thy lover now? the
car-borne chief of Etha? Haft thou beheld the
halls of Ufnoth? Or the dark-brown hills of
Fingal? My battle had roared on Morven, did
not the winds meet Dar-thula. Fingal himfelf
would have been low, and forrow dwelling in
Selma.

HER fhield fell from Dar-thula's arm, her
breaft of fnow appeared. It appeared, but it
was ftained with blood for an arrow was fixed in
her fide. She fell on the fallen Nathos, like a
wreath of fnow. Her dark hair fpreads on his
face, and their blood is mixing round.

DAUGHTER of Colla! thou art low! faid
Cairbar's hundred bards; filence is at the blue
ftreams of Seláma, for Truthil's* race have failed.
When wilt thou rife in thy beauty, firft of Erin's

* Truthil was the founder of Dar-thula's family.

maids?

maids? Thy ſleep is long in the tomb, and the morning diſtant far. The ſun ſhall not come to thy bed, and ſay, Awake * Darthula! awake, thou firſt of women! the wind of ſpring is abroad. The flowers ſhake their heads on the green hills, the woods wave their growing leaves. Retire, O ſun, the daughter of Colla is aſleep. She will not come forth in her beauty : ſhe will not move, in the ſteps of her lovelineſs.

Such was the ſong of the bards, when they raiſed the tomb. I ſung, afterwards, over the grave, when the king of Morven came; when he came to green Ullin to fight with car-borne Cairbar.

---

* Riſe up, my love, my fair one, and come away. For lo, the winter is paſt, the rain is over, and gone. The flowers appear on the earth ; the time of ſinging is come, and the voice of the turtle is heard in our land. The fig-tree putteth forth her green figs, and the vines, with the tender grape, give a good ſmell. Ariſe, my love, my fair one, and come away.

Solomon's Song.

T E M O R A:

A N

E P I C P O E M*.

T H E blue waves of Ullin roll in light.
The green hills are covered with day.
Trees shake their dusky heads in the breeze; and
gray torrents pour their noisy streams.---Two
green

* Though the history which is the foundation of the present
poem, was given in the notes on the two pieces preceding, it
may not be here improper to recapitulate some part of what has
been said.—Immediately after the death of Cuchullin, Cairbar,
lord of Atha, openly set up for himself in Connaught, and having
privately murdered young king Cormac, became, without oppo-
sition, sole monarch of Ireland.   The murder of Cormac was so
much resented by Fingal, that he resolved on an expedition into
Ireland against Cairbar.   Early intelligence of his designs came
to Cairbar, and he had gathered the tribes together into Ulster, to
oppose Fingal's landing; at the same time his brother Cathmor
kept himself with an army near Temora.—This Cathmor is one
of the finest characters in the old poetry.   His humanity, gene-
rosity, and hospitality, were unparalleled: in short, he had no
fault, but too much attachment to so bad a brother as Cairbar.—
The present poem has its name from Temora, the royal palace
of the Irish kings, near which the last and decisive battle was
fought between Fingal and Cathmor.   What has come to the

R   translator's

green hills, with their aged oaks, furround a
narrow plain. The blue courfe of the mountain-ftream is there; Cairbar ftands on its banks.
——His fpear fupports the king : the red eyes
of his fear are fad. Cormac rifes in his foul,
with all his ghaftly wounds. The gray form of

tranflator's hands, in a regular connection, is little more, than
the opening of the poem.—This work appears, from the ftory of
it, which is ftill preferv'd, to have been one of the greateft of
Offian's compofitions. The variety of the characters makes it in-
terefting ; and the war, as it is carried on by Fingal and Cathmor, affords inftances of the greateft bravery, mixed with in-
comparably generous actions and fentiments. One is at a lofs
for which fide to declare himfelf: and often wifhes, when both
commanders march to battle, that both may return victorious.
At length the good fortune of Fingal preponderates, and the family of Cormac are re-eftablifhed on the Irifh throne.

The Irifh traditions relate the affair in another light, and ex-
claim againft Fingal for appointing thirty judges, or rather ty-
rants, at Temora, for regulating the affairs of Ireland. They
pretend to enumerate many acts of oppreffion committed by thofe
judges ; and affirm, that both they and a part of Fingal's army,
which was left in Ireland to enforce their laws, were at laft expelled the kingdom.—Thus the Irifh traditions, fay the hiftorians of that nation. It is faid, however, that thofe gentlemen
fometimes create facts, in order afterwards to make remarks
upon them ; at leaft, that they adopt for real facts, the traditions
of their bards, when they throw luftre on the ancient ftate of
their country.

The prefent poem opens in the morning. Cairbar is reprefented as retired from the reft of the Irifh chiefs, and tormented
with remorfe for the murder of Cormac, when news was brought
him of Fingal's landing. What paffed, preceding that day, and
is neceffary to be known for carrying on the poem, is afterwards
introduced by way of epifode.

the

the youth appears in the midſt of darkneſs, and the blood pours from his airy ſides.---Cairbar thrice threw his ſpear on earth; and thrice he ſtroked his beard. His ſteps are ſhort; he often ſtopt: and toſſed his ſinewy arms. He is like a cloud in the deſart; that varies its form to every blaſt: the valleys are ſad around, and fear, by turns, the ſhower.

THE king, at length, reſumed his ſoul, and took his pointed ſpear. He turned his eyes towards Lena *. The ſcouts of the ocean appeared. They appeared with ſteps of fear, and often looked behind. Cairbar knew that the mighty were near, and called his gloomy chiefs. The ſounding ſteps of his heroes came. They drew, at once, their ſwords. There Morlath † ſtood with darkened face. Hidalla's buſhy hair ſighs in the wind. Red-haired Cormar bends on his ſpear, and rolls his ſide-long-looking eyes. Wild is the look of Malthos from beneath two ſhaggy brows.---Foldath ſtands like an oozy rock; that covers its dark ſides with foam; his

---

* The ſcene deſcribed here is nearly that of the epic poem, Fingal. In this neighbourhood alſo the ſons of Uſnoth werd killed.

† Mór-lath, *great in the day of battle.* Hidalla', *wildly looking hero.* Cor-mar, *expert at ſea.* Málth-os, *ſlow to ſpeak.* Foldath, *generous.*

ſpear

fpear is like Slimora's fir, that meets the wind
of heaven. His fhield is marked with the ftrokes
of battle; and his red eye defpifes danger.
Thefe and a thoufand other chiefs furrounded
car-borne Cairbar, when the fcout of ocean
came, Mor-annal *, from ftreamy Lena.---His
eyes hang forward from his face, his lips are
trembling, pale.

Do the chiefs of Erin ftand, he faid, filent as
the grove of evening? Stand they, like a filent
wood, and Fingal on the coaft? Fingal, who is
terrible in battle, the king of ftreamy Morven.

AND haft thou feen the warrior, faid Cairbar
with a figh? Are his heroes many on the coaft?
Lifts he the fpear of battle? Or comes the king
in peace?

HE comes not in peace, O Cairbar: for I
have feen his forward fpear †. It is a meteor of
death: the blood of thoufands is on its fteel.
——He came firft to the fhore, ftrong in the

* Mér-annail, *ftrong breath*; a very proper name for a
fcout.

† Mor-annal here alludes to the particular appearance of Fingal's fpear.——If a man, upon his firft landing in a ftrange
country, kept the point of his fpear forward, it denoted in thofe
days that he came in a hoftile manner, and accordingly he was
treated as an enemy; if he kept the point behind him, it was a
token of friendfhip, and he was immediately invited to the feaft
according to the hofpitality of the times.

3   gray

gray hair of age. Full rofe his finewy limbs, as he ftrode in his might. That fword is by his fide which gives no fecond * wound. His fhield is terrible, like the bloody moon, when it rifes in a ftorm.——Then came Offian king of fongs; and Morni's fon, the firft of men. Connal leaps forward on his fpear : Dermid fpreads his dark-brown locks.---Fillan bends his bow : Fergus ftrides in the pride of youth. Who is that with aged locks ? A dark fhield is on his fide. His fpear trembles at every ftep ; and age is on his limbs. He bends his dark face to the ground ; the king of fpears is fad!——It is Ufnoth, O Cairbar, coming to revenge his fons. He fees green Ullin with tears, and he remembers the tombs of his children. But far before the reft, the fon of Offian comes, bright in the fmiles of youth, fair as the firft beams of the fun. His long hair falls on his back.---His dark brows are half hid beneath his helmet of fteel. His fword hangs loofe on the hero's fide. His fpear glitters as he moves. I fled from his terrible eyes, king of high Temora !

---

* This was the famous fword of Fingal, made by Luno, a fmith of Lochlin, and after him poetically called the *fon of Luno:* it is faid of this fword, that it killed a man at every ftroke ; and that Fingal never ufed it, but in times of the greateft danger.

THEN fly, thou feeble man, faid the gloomy wrath of Foldath : fly to the grey ftreams of thy land, fon of the little foul! Have not I feen that Ofcar ? I beheld the chief in battle. He is of the mighty in danger : but there are others who lift the fpear.---Erin has many fons as brave : yes---more brave, O car-borne Cairbar ?---Let Foldath meet him in the ftrength of his courfe, and ftop this mighty ftream.---My fpear is co-vered with the blood of the valiant ; my fhield is like Tura's wall.

SHALL Foldath alone meet the foe, replied the dark-browed Malthos? Are not they nu-merous on our coaft, like the waters of a thou-fand ftreams ? Are not thefe the chiefs who van-quifhed Swaran, when the fons of Erin fled? And fhall Foldath meet their braveft hero ? Fol-dath of the heart of pride ! take the ftrength of the people by thy fide; and let Malthos come. My fword is red with flaughter, but who has heard my words ? *

SONS of green Erin, begun the mild Hidalla, let not Fingal hear your words : leaft the foe re-joice, and his arm be ftrong in the land.---Ye are brave, O warriors, and like the tempefts of the defart; they meet the rocks without fear, and

---

* That is, who has heard my vaunting ? He intended the ex-preffion as a rebuke to the felf-praife of Foldath.

overturn

overturn the woods in their courfe.---But let us move in our ftrength, and flow as a gathered cloud, when the winds drive it from behind.——— Then fhall the mighty tremble, and the fpear drop from the hand of the valiant.---We fee the cloud of death, they will fay; and their faces will turn pale. Fingal will mourn in his age; and fay that his fame is ceafed.——Morven will behold his chiefs no more: the mofs of years fhall grow in Selma.

CAIRBAR heard their words, in filence, like the cloud of a fhower: it ftands dark on Cromla, till the lightning burfts its fide; the valley gleams with red light; the fpirits of the ftorm rejoice. ——So ftood the filent king of Temora; at length his words are heard.

SPREAD the feaft on Lena: and let my hundred bards attend. And thou, red-hair'd Olla, take the harp of the king. Go to Ofcar king of fwords, and bid him to our feaft. To-day we feaft and hear the fong; to-morrow break the. fpears. Tell him that I have raifed the tomb of Cathol *; and that my bards have fung to his ·ghoft.

---

* Cathol the fon of Maronnan, or Moran, was murdered by Cairbar, for his attachment to the family of Cormac. He had attended Ofcar to the *war of Inis-thona*, where they contracted a great friendfhip for one another. Ofcar, immediately after the death of Cathol, had fent a formal challenge to Cairbar, which

he

ghoft.----Tell him that Cairbar has heard his fame at the ftream of diftant Carun *.

CATHMOR † is not here; the generous bro-ther of Cairbar; he is not here with his thou-fands, and our arms are weak. Cathmor is a foe to ftrife at the feaft : his foul is bright as the fun. But Cairbar fhall fight with Ofcar, chiefs of the high Temora ! His words for Cathol were many; and the wrath of Cairbar burns. He fhall fall on Lena : and my fame fhall rife in blood.

THE faces of the heroes brightened. They fpread over Lena's heath. The feaft of fhells is prepared. The fongs of the bards arofe.

WE heard ‡ the voice of joy on the coaft, and we thought that the mighty Cathmor came.

Cathmor

he prudently declined, but conceived a fecret hatred againft Of-car, and had beforehand contrived to kill him at the feaft, to which he here invites him.

* He alludes to the battle of Ofcar againft Caros, *king of fhips*; who is fuppofed to be the fame with Caraufius the ufurper.

† Cath-mór, *great in battle*. Cairbar takes advantage of his brother's abfence, to perpetrate his ungenerous defigns againft Ofcar; for the noble fpirit of Cathmor, had he been prefent, would not have permitted the laws of that hofpitality, for which he was fo renowned himfelf, to be violated. The brothers form a contraft; we do not deteft the mean foul of Cairbar more, than we admire the difinterefted and generous mind of Cathmor.

‡ Fingal's army heard the joy that was in Cairbar's camp. The character given of Cathmor is agreeable to the times.

Some.

Cathmor the friend of ſtrangers! the brother of red-haired Cairbar. But their ſouls were not the ſame : for the light of heaven was in the boſom of Cathmor. His towers roſe on the banks of Atha : ſeven paths led to his halls. Seven chiefs ſtood on thoſe paths, and called the ſtranger to the feaſt ! But Cathmor dwelt in the wood to avoid the voice of praiſe.

OLLA came with his ſongs. Oſcar went to Cairbar's feaſt. Three hundred heroes attended the chief, and the clang of their arms is terrible. The gray dogs bounded on the heath, and their

Some, through oſtentation, were hoſpitable ; and others fell naturally into a cuſtom handed down from their anceſtors. But what marks ſtrongly the character of Cathmor, is his averſion to praiſe ; for he is repreſented to dwell in a wood to avoid the thanks of his gueſts ; which is ſtill a higher degree of generoſity than that of Axylus in Homer : for the poet does not ſay, but the good man might, at the head of his own table, have heard with pleaſure the praiſe beſtowed on him by the people he entertained.

"Αξυλον δ' αρ' επεφνε βοην αγαθος Διομηδης
Τευθρανιδην, ος εναιεν ευκλιμενη εν Αρισβη,
'Αφνειος βιοτοιο, φιλ☉ δ' ην ανθρωποισι·
Πάντας γαρ φιλεεσκεν, οδω επι οικια ναιων.

HOM. 6. 12.

Next Teuthra's ſon diſtain'd the ſands with blood,
Axylus, hoſpitable, rich and good :
In fair Ariſbe's walls, his native place,
He held his ſeat ; a friend to human race.
Faſt by the road, his ever open door
Oblig'd the wealthy, and reliev'd the poor: POPE.

howling

howling is frequent. Fingal faw the departure of the hero: the foul of the king was fad. He dreads the gloomy Cairbar: but who of the race of Trenmor feared the foe?

My fon lifted high the fpear of Cormac: an hundred bards met him with fongs. Cairbàr concealed with fmiles the death that was dark in his foul. The feaft is fpread, the fhells refound; joy brightens the face of the hoft. But it was like the parting beam of the fun, when he is to hide his red head, in a ftorm.

CAIRBAR rofe in his arms; darknefs gathers on his brow. The hundred harps ceafed at once. The clang * of fhields is heard. Far diftant on the heath Olla raifed his fong of woe. My fon knew the fign of death; and rifing feized his fpear.

OSCAR! faid the dark-red Cairbar, I behold the fpear † of Erin's kings. The fpear of Te-

---

* When a chief was determined to kill a man that was in his power already, it was ufual to fignify, that his death was intended, by the found of a fhield ftruck with the blunt end of a fpear; at the fame time that a bard at a diftance raifed the *death-fong*. A ceremony of another kind was long ufed in Scotland upon fuch occafions. Every body has heard that a bull's head was ferved up to Lord Douglas in the caftle of Edinburgh, as a certain fignal of his approaching death.

† Cormac, the fon of Arth, had given the fpear, which is here the foundation of the quarrel, to Ofcar when he came to congratulate him, upon Swaran's being expelled from Ireland.

mora

mora * glitters in thy hand, fon of the woody
Morven! It was the pride of an hundred kings,
the death of heroes of old. Yield it, fon of
Offian, yield it to car-borne Cairbar.

SHALL I yield, Ofcar replied, the gift of
Erin's injured king: the gift of fair-haired Cormac, when Ofcar fcattered his foes? I came to
his halls of joy, when Swaran fled from Fingal.
Gladnefs rofe in the face of youth : he gave the
fpear of Temora. Nor did he give it to the feeble, O Cairbar, neither to the weak in foul.
The darknefs of thy face is not a florm to me ;
nor are thine eyes the flames of death. Do I
fear thy clanging fhield ? Does my foul tremble
at Olla's fong ? No : Cairbar, frighten thou the
feeble ; Ofcar is like a rock.

AND wilt thou not yield the fpear, replied
the rifing pride of Cairbar ? Are thy words
mighty becaufe Fingal is near, the gray-haired
warrior of Morven. He has fought with little
men. But he muft vanifh before Cairbar, like
a thin pillar of mift before the winds of Atha†.

WERE he who fought with little men near the
chief of Atha : Atha's chief would yield green

---

* Ti'-mór-ri', *the houfe of the great king*, the name of the royal
palace of the fupreme kings of Ireland.

† Atha, *fhallow river:* the name of Cairbar's feat in Connaught.   I

Erin

Erin to avoid his rage. Speak not of the mighty,
O Cairbar! but turn thy fword on me. Our
ftrength is equal : but Fingal is renowned ! the
firft of mortal men !

THEIR people faw the darkening chiefs.
Their crowding fteps are heard around. Their
eyes roll in fire. A thoufand fwords are half unfheathed. Red-haired Olla raifed the fong of
battle : the trembling joy of Ofcar's foul arofe :
the wonted joy of his foul when Fingal's horn
was heard.

DARK as the fwelling wave of ocean before
the rifing winds, when it bends its head near the
coaft, came on the hoft of Cairbar.——Daughter of Tofcar *! why that tear ? He is not fallen
yet. Many were the deaths of his arm before
my hero fell!---Behold they fall before my fon
like the groves in the defart, when an angry
ghoft rufhes through night, and takes their
green heads in his hand! Morlath falls : Maronnan dies: Conachar trembles in his blood. Cairbar fhrinks before Ofcar's fword; and creeps in
darknefs behind his ftone. He lifted the fpear
in fecret, and pierced my Ofcar's fide. He falls
forward on his fhield: his knee fuftains the

* The poet means Malvina, the daughter of Tofcar, to whom
he addreffed that part of the poem, which related to the death
of Ofcar her lover.

chief :

chief: but his fpear is in his hand. See gloomy Cairbar * falls. The fteel pierced his forehead, and divided his red hair behind. He lay, like a fhattered rock, which Cromla fhakes from its fide. But never more fhall Ofcar rife! he leans on his boffy fhield. His fpear is in his terrible hand: Erin's fons ftood diftant and dark. Their fhouts arofe, like the crowded noife of ftreams, and Lena echoed around.

FINGAL heard the found; and took his father's fpear. His fteps are before us on the heath. He fpoke the words of woe. I hear the noife of battle: and Ofcar is alone. Rife, ye fons of Morven, and join the hero's fword.

OSSIAN rufhed along the heath. Fillan bounded over Lena. Fergus flew with feet of wind. Fingal ftrode in his ftrength, and the light of his fhield is terrible. The fons of Erin faw it far diftant; they trembled in their fouls. They knew that the wrath of the king arofe: and they forefaw their death. We firft arrived; we fought; and Erin's chiefs withftood our rage.

---

* The Irifh hiftorians place the death of Cairbar, in the latter end of the third century: they fay, he was killed in battle againft Ofcar the fon of Offian, but deny that he fell by his hand. As they have nothing to go upon but the traditions of their bards, the tranflator thinks that the account of Offian is as probable: at the worft, it is but oppofing one tradition to another.

But

But when the king came, in the found of his courfe, what heart of fteel could ftand ! Erin fled over Lena. Death purfued their flight.

We faw Ofcar leaning on his fhield. We faw his blood around. Silence darkened on every hero's face. Each turned his back and wept. The king ftrove to hide his tears. His gray beard whiftled in the wind. He bends his head over his fon : and his words are mixed with fighs.

And art thou fallen, Ofcar, in the midft of thy courfe? the heart of the aged beats over thee ! He fees thy coming battles. He beholds the battles which ought to come, but they are cut off from thy fame. When fhall joy dwell at Selma ? When fhall the fong of grief ceafe on Morven ? My fons fall by degrees : Fingal fhall be the laft of his race. The fame which I have received fhall pafs away : my age will be without friends. I fhall fit like a grey cloud in my hall : nor fhall I·expect the return of a fon, in the midft of his founding arms. Weep, ye heroes of Morven ! never more fhall Ofcar rife !

And they did weep, O Fingal; dear was the hero to their fouls. He went out to battle, and the foes vanifhed ; he returned, in peace, amidft their joy. No father mourned his' fon flain in youth ; no brother his brother of love. They fell,

fell, without tears, for the chief of the people was low! Bran * is howling at his feet: gloomy Luäth is fad, for he had often led them to the chace; to the bounding roes of the defart.

WHEN Ofcar beheld his friends around, his white breaft rofe with a figh.---The groans, he faid, of my aged heroes, the howling of my dogs, the fudden burfts of the fong of grief, have melted Ofcar's foul. My foul, that never melted before; it was like the fteel of my fword. ---Offian, carry me to my hills! Raife the ftones of my fame. Place the horn of the deer, and my fword within my narrow dwelling.---The torrent hereafter may wafh away the earth of my tomb: the hunter may find the fteel and fay, " This has been Ofcar's fword."

AND falleft thou, fon of my fame! And fhall I never fee thee, Ofcar! When others hear of their fons, I fhall not hear of thee. The mofs is on the ftones of his tomb, and the mournful wind is there. The battle fhall be fought without him: he fhall not purfue the dark-brown hinds. When the warrior returns from battles, and tells of other lands, he will fay, I have feen

* Bran was one of Fingal's dogs.—He was fo remarkable for his fleetnefs, that the poet, in a piece which is not juft now in the tranflator's hands, has given him the fame properties with Virgil's Camilla.

a tomb, by the roaring ftream, where a warrior darkly dwells : he was flain by car-borne Ofcar, the firft of mortal men.---I, perhaps, fhall hear him, and a beam of joy will rife in my foul.

THE night would have defcended in forrow, and morning returned in the fhadow of grief: our chiefs would have ftood like cold dropping rocks on Lena, and have forgot the war, had not the king difperfed his grief, and raifed his mighty voice. The chiefs, as new-wakened from dreams, lift their heads around.

How long fhall we weep on Lena; or pour our tears in Ullin? The mighty will not return. Ofcar fhall not rife in his ftrength. The valiant muft fall one day, and be no more known on his hills.---Where are our fathers, O warriors! the chiefs of the times of old? They have fet like ftars that have fhone, we only hear the found of their praife. But they were renowned in their day, and the terror of other times. Thus fhall we pafs, O warriors, in the day of our fall. Then let us be renowned when we may; and leave our fame behind us, like the laft beams of the fun, when he hides his red head in the weft.

ULLIN, my aged bard! take the fhip of the king. Carry Ofcar to Selma, and let the daughters of Morven weep. We fhall fight in Erin

for

for the race of fallen Cormac. The days of my years begin to fail : I feel the weaknefs of my arm. My fathers bend from their clouds, to receive their gray-haired fon. But, Trenmor! before I go hence, one beam of my fame fhall rife : fo fhall my days end, as my years begun, in fame : my life fhall be one ftream of light to other times.

ULLIN rais'd his white fails : the wind of the fouth came forth. He bounded on the waves towards Selma's walls.---I remained in my grief, but my words were not heard.——The feaſt is fpread on Lena : an hundred heroes reared the tomb of Cairbar : but no fong is raifed over the chief; for his foul had been dark and bloody. We remembered the fall of Cormac! and what could we fay in Cairbar's praife ?

THE night came rolling down. The light of an hundred oaks arofe. Fingal fat beneath a tree. The chief of Etha fat near the king, the gray-hair'd ftrength of Ufnoth.

OLD Althan * ftood in the midft, and told the tale of fallen Cormac. Althan the fon of Co-

---

* Althan, the fon of Conachar, was the chief bard of Arth king of Ireland. After the death of Arth, Althan attended his fon Cormac, and was prefent at his death.—He had made his efcape from Cairbar, by the means of Cathmor, and coming to Fingal, related, as here, the death of his mafter Cormac.

nachar, the friend of car-borne Cuchullin : he
dwelt with Cormac in windy Temora, when
Semo's fon fought with generous Torlath.---
The tale of Althan was mournful, and the tear
was in his eye.

 * THE fetting fun was yellow on Dora †.
Gray evening began to   . Temora's
woods fhook with the blaft of   inconftant
wind. A cloud, at length, gathered in the
weft, and a red ftar looked from behind its
edge.---I ftood in the wood alone, and faw a
ghoft on the darkening air. His ftride extended
from hill to hill : his fhield was dim on his fide.
It was the fon of Semo : I knew the fadnefs of
his face. But he paffed away in his blaft ; and
all was dark around.——My foul was fad. I
went to the hall of fhells. A thoufand lights
arofe : the hundred bards had ftrung the harp.
Cormac ftood in the midft, like the morning
ftar ‡, when it rejoices on the eaftern hill, and
                                                   its

 * Althan fpeaks.

 † Doira, *the woody fide of a mountain* ; it is here a hill in the
neighbourhood of Temora.

 ‡ *Qualis, ubi oceani perfufus Lucifer unda,*
Quem Venus ante alios aftrorum diligit ignes,
Extulit os facrum cælo, tenebrafque refolvit.
                                             VIRG.

                                                   So

its young beams are bathed in fhowers.---The fword of Artho * was in the hand of the king; and he looked with joy on its polifhed ftuds: thrice he attempted to draw it, and thrice he failed: his yellow locks are fpread on his fhoulders: his cheeks of youth are red.---I mourned over the beam of youth, for he was foon to fet.

ALTHAN ! he faid, with a fmile, haft thou beheld my father ? Heavy is the fword of the king, furely his arm was ftrong. O that I were like him in battle, when the rage of his wrath arofe ! then would I have met, like Cuchullin, the car-borne fon of Cantéla ! But years may come on, O Althan ! and my arm be ftrong.--- Haft thou heard of Semo's fon, the chief of high Temora ? He might have returned with his fame; for he promifed to return to-night. My bards wait him with their fongs, and my feaft is fpread.---

I HEARD the king in filence. My tears began to flow. I hid them with my gray locks; but he perceived my grief.

So from the feas exerts his radiant head,
The ftar, by whom the lights of heav'n are led:
Shakes from his rofy locks the pearly dews;
Difpels the darknefs, and the day renews.

DRYDEN.

* Arth, or Artho, the father of Cormac king of Ireland.

Son

Son of Conachar! he faid, is the king of Tura low? Why burfts thy figh in fecret? And why defcends the tear?---Comes the car-borne Torlath? Or the found of the red-haired Cairbar?——They come!---for I fee thy grief; and Tura's king is low!---Shall I not rufh to battle?---But I cannot lift the arms of my fa-thers!---O had mine arm the ftrength of Cu-chullin, foon would Cairbar fly; the fame of my fathers would be renewed; and the actions of other times!

He took his bow of yew. Tears flow from his fparkling eyes.---Grief faddens around: the bards bend forward from their harps. The blaft touches their ftrings, and the found of woe afcends.

A voice is heard at a diftance, as of one in grief; it was Carril of other times, who came from the dark Slimora*.---He told of the death of Cuchullin, and of his mighty deeds. The people were fcattered around his tomb: their arms lay on the ground. They had forgot the battle, for the found of his fhield had ceafed.

But who, faid the foft-voiced Carril, come like the bounding roes? their ftature is like the

* Slimora, a hill in Connaught, near which Cuchullin was kil'ed.

young

young trees of the plain, growing in a fhower:
---Soft and ruddy are their cheeks: but fearlefs
fouls look forth from their eyes?——Who but
the fons of Ufnoth, the car-borne chiefs of
Etha? The people rife on every fide, like the
ftrength of an half-extinguifhed fire, when the
winds come fuddenly from the defart, on their
ruftling wings.--- The found of Caithbat's
fhield was heard. The heroes faw Cuchullin *,
in the form of lovely Nathos. So rolled his
fparkling eyes, and fuch were his fteps on his
heath.——Pattles are fought at Lego: the fword
of Nathos prevails. Soon fhalt thou behold him
in thy halls, king of woody Temora!——

AND foon may I behold him, O Carril! replied the returning joy of Cormac. But my foul
is fad for Cuchullin; his voice was pleafant in
mine ear.——Often have we moved on Dora, at
the chace of the dark-brown hinds: his bow was
unerring on the mountains. --- He fpoke of
mighty men. He told of the deeds of my fathers; and I felt the joy of my breaft.——But fit
thou, at the feaft, O Carril; I have often heard
thy voice. Sing in thepraife of Cuchullin; and
of that mighty ftranger.

* That is, they faw a manifeft likenefs between the perfon of
Nathos and Cuchullin. .

S 3   DAY

DAY rofe on Temora, with all the beams of
the eaſt. Trathin came to the hall, the fon of
old Gellàma *.---I behold, he faid, a dark cloud
in the defart, king of Innis-fail! a cloud it
feemed at firſt, but now a crowd of men. One
ſtrides before them in his ſtrength ; and his red
hair flies in the wind. His ſhield glitters to the
beam of the eaſt. His ſpear is in his hand.

CALL him to the feaſt of Temora, replied the
king of Erin. My hall is the houfe of ſtrangers, fon of the generous Gellàma !---Perhaps it
is the chief of Etha, coming in the found of his
renown.---Hail, mighty ſtranger, art thou of
the friends of Cormac ?---But Carril, he is dark,
and unlovely ; and he draws his ſword. Is that
the fon of Ufnoth, bard of the times of old ?

IT is not the fon of Ufnoth, faid Carril, but
the chief of Atha.——Why comeſt thou in thy
arms to Temora, Cairbar of the gloomy brow ?
Let not thy ſword rife againſt Cormac ! Whither
doſt thou turn thy fpeed ?

HE paſſed on in his darknefs, and feized the
hand of the king. Cormac forefaw his death,
and the rage of his eyes arofe.---Retire, thou
gloomy chief of Atha : Nathos comes with battle.——Thou art bold in Cormac's hall, for his

* Geal-lamha, white-handed.

arm

arm is weak.---The fword entered Cormac's fide : he fell in the halls of his fathers. His fair hair is in the duft. His blood is fmoaking round.

And art thou fallen in thy halls, I faid *, O fon of noble Artho ? The fhield of Cuchullin was not near. Nor the fpear of thy father. Mournful are the mountains of Erin, for the chief of the people is low !——Bleft be thy foul, O Cormac ! thou art fnatched from the midft of thy courfe.

My words came to the ears of Cairbar, and he clofed us † in the midft of darknefs. He feared to ftretch his fword to the bards ‡ : though his foul was dark. Three days we pined alone : on the fourth, the noble Cathmor came.---He heard our voice from the cave ; he turned the eye of his wrath on Cairbar.

Chief of Atha ! he faid, how long wilt thou pain my foul ? Thy heart is like the rock of the defart ; and thy thoughts are dark.---But thou art the brother of Cathmor, and he will fight thy battles.——But Cathmor's foul is not like thine, thou feeble hand of war ! The light of

* Althan fpeaks.

† That is, himfelf and Carril, as it afterwards appears.

‡ The perfons of the bards were fo facred, that even he, who had juft murdered his fovereign, feared to kill them.

my

my bofom is ftained with thy deeds : the bards will not fing of my renown. They may fay, " Cathmor was brave, but he fought for " gloomy Cairbar." They will pafs over my tomb in filence, and my fame fhall not be heard.---Cairbar ! loofe the bards : they are the fons of other times. Their voice fhall be heard in other ages, when the kings of Temora have failed.

We came forth at the words of the chief. We faw him in his ftrength. He was like thy youth, O Fingal, when thou firft didft lift the fpear.---His face was like the funny field when it is bright : no darknefs moved over his brow. But he came with his thoufands to Ullin ; to aid the red-haired Cairbar : and now he comes to revenge his death, O king of woody Mor-ven.——

And let him come, replied the king ; I love a foe like Cathmor. His foul is great : his arm is ftrong, and his battles are full of fame.—— But the little foul is like a vapour that hovers round the marfhy lake : it never rifes on the green hill, left the winds meet it there : its dwelling is in the cave, and it fends forth the dart of death.

Usnoth ! thou haft heard the fame of Etha's car-borne chiefs.---Our young heroes, O war-

rior,

rior, are like the renown of our fathers.---
They fight in youth, and they fall: their names
are in the fong.---But we are old, O Ufnoth, let
us not fall like aged oaks ; which the blaft over-
turns in fecret. The hunter came paft, and
faw them lying gray acrofs a ftream. How have
thefe fallen, he faid, and whiftling paffed along.

RAISE the fong of joy, ye bards of Morven,
that our fouls may forget the paft.---The red
ftars look on us from the clouds, and filently defcend. Soon fhall the gray beam of the morning rife, and fhew us the foes of Cormac.——
Fillan! take the fpear of the king; go to Mora's
dark-brown fide. Let thine eyes travel over the
heath, like flames of fire. Obferve the foes of
Fingal, and the courfe of generous Cathmor.
I hear a diftant found, like the falling of rocks
in the defart.——But ftrike thou thy fhield, at
times, that they may not come through night,
and the fame of Morven ceafe.---I begin to be
alone, my fon, and I dread the fall of my renown.

THE voice of the bards arofe. The king
leaned on the fhield of Trenmor.---Sleep defcended on his eyes, and his future battles rofe
in his dreams. The hoft are fleeping around.
Dark-haired Fillan obferved the foe. His fteps
are

are on a diftant hill: we hear, at times, his
clanging fhicld.

_ One of the Fragments of Ancient Poetry lately publiflied,
gives a different account of the death of Of̄car, the fon of Of-
'fian. The tranflator, though he well knew the more probable
tradition concerning that hero, was unwilling to rejeſt a poem,
which, if not really of Offian's compofition, has much of his
manner, and concife turn of expreffion. A more correſt copy
of that fragment, which has fince come to the tranflator's hands,
has enabled him to correſt the miftake, into which a fimilari·y
of names had led thofe who handed down the poem by tradition.
—The heroes of the piece are Ofcar the fon of Caruth, and
Dermid the fon of Diaran. Offian, or perhaps his imitator,
opens the poem with a lamentation for Ofcar, and afterwards,
by an eafy tranfition, relates the ſtory of Ofcar the fon of Caruth, who feems to have bore the fame charaſter, as well as
name, with Ofcar the fon of Offian. Though the tranflator
thinks he has good reafon to rejeſt the fragment as the compofition of Offian; yet as it is, after all, ſtil fomewhat doubtful
whether it is or not, he has here fubjoined it.

'WHY openeſt thou afrefh the fpring of my grief, O fon of
Alpin, inquiring how Ofcar fell? My eyes are blind with
tears; but memory beams on my heart. How can I relate the
mournful death of the head of the people! Chief of the warriors,
Ofcar, my fon, fhall I fee thee no more!

He fell as the moon in a ftorm; as the fun from the midſt of
his courſe, when clouds rife from the watle of the waves, when
the blacknefs of the ftorm inwraps the rocks of Ardannider. I,
like an ancient oak on Morven, I moulder alone in my place.
The blaſt hath lopped my branches away; and I tremble at the
wings of the north. Chief of the warriors, Ofcar, my fon!
fhall I fee thee no more!

But, fon of Alpin, the hero fell not harmlefs as the grafs of
the field; the blood of the mighty was on his fword, and he
travelled with death through the ranks of their pride. But Ofcar, thou fon of Caruth, thou haſt fallen low! No enemy fell
by

by thy hand. Thy fpear was ftained with the blood of thy friend.

Dermid and Ofcar were one: They reaped the battle toge-ther. Their friendfhip was ftrong as their fteel; and death walked between them to the field. They came on the foe like two rocks falling from the brows of Ardven. Their fwords were ftained with the blood of the valiant: warriors fainted at their names. Who was equal to Ofcar, but Dermid? and who to Dermid, but Ofcar?

They killed mighty Dargo in the field; Dargo who never fled in war. His daughter was fair as the morn; mild as the beam of night. Her eyes, like two ftars in a fhower: her breath, the gale of fpring: her breafts, as the new-fallen fnow floating on the moving heath. The warriors faw her, and loved; their fouls were fixed on the maid. Each loved her as his fame; each muft poffefs her or die. But her foul was fixed on Ofcar; the fon of Caruth was the youth of her love. She forgot the blood of her father; and loved the hand that flew him.

Son of Caruth, faid Dermid, I love; O Ofcar, I love this maid. But her foul cleaveth unto thee; and nothing can heal Dermid. Here, pierce this bofom, Ofcar; relieve me, my friend, with thy fword.

My fword, fon of Diaran, fhall never be ftained with the blood of Dermid.

Who then is worthy to flay me, O Ofcar fon of Caruth? Let not my life pafs away unknown. Let none but Ofcar flay me. Send me with honour to the grave, and let my death be re-nowned.

Dermid, make ufe of thy fword; fon of Diaran, wield thy fteel. Would that I fell with thee! that my death came from the hand of Dermid!

They fought by the brook of the mountain, by the ftreams of Branno. Blood tinged the running water, and curdled round the moffy ftones. The ftately Dermid fell; he fell, and fmiled in death.

And falleft thou, fon of Diaran, falleft thou by Ofcar's hand! Dermid who never yielded in war, thus do I fee thee fall!——

He

He went, and returned to the maid of his love; he returned, but fhe perceived his grief.

Why that gloom, fon of Caruth? what fhades thy mighty foul?

Though once renowned for the bow, O maid, I have loft my fame. Fixed on a tree by the brook of the hill, is the fhield of the valiant Gormur, whom I flew in battle. I have wafted the day in vain, nor could my arrow pierce it.

Let me try, fon of Caruth, the fkill of Dargo's daughter. My hands were taught the bow : my father delighted in my fkill.

She went. He ftood behind the fhield. Her arrow flew, and pierced his breaft.

Bleffed be that hand of fnow; and bleffed that bow of yew! Who but the daughter of Dargo was worthy to flay the fon of Caruth ? Lay me in the earth, my fair one ; lay me by the fide of Dermid.

Ofcar! the maid replied, I have the foul of the mighty Dargo. Well pleafed I can meet death. My forrow I can end.——She pierced her white bofom with the fteel. She fell; fhe trembled ; and died.

By the brook of the hill their graves are laid ; a birch's un-equal fhade covers their tomb. Often on their green earthen tombs the branchy fons of the mountain feed, when mid-day is all in flames, and filence over all the hills.

C A R R I C-

CARRIC-THURA:

A POEM*.

H AST † thou left thy blue courfe in
heaven, golden-haired fon of the fky!
The weft has opened its gates; the bed of thy

* Fingal, returning from an expedition which he had made
into the Roman province, refolved to vifit Cathulla king of
Inis-tore, and brother to Comála, whofe ftory is related, at
large, in the dramatic poem, publifhed in this collection. Upon
his coming in fight of Carric-thura, the palace of Cathulla, he
obferved a flame on its top, which, in thofe days, was a fignal
of diftrefs. The wind drove him into a bay, at fome diftance
from Carric-thura, and he was obliged to pafs the night on the
fhore. Next day he attacked the army of Frothal king of Sora
who had befieged Cathulla in his palace of Carric-thura, and took
Frothal himfelf prifoner, after he had engaged him in a fingle
combat. The deliverance of Carric-thura is the fubject of the
poem, but feveral other epifodes are interwoven with it. It appears from tradition, that this poem was addreffed to a Culdee.
or one of the firft Chriftian miffionaries, and that the ftory of the
Spirit of Loda, fuppofed to be the ancient Odin of Scandinavia,
was introduced by Offian in oppofition to the Culdee's doctrine.
Be this as it will, it lets us into Offian's notions of a fuperior being; and fhews that he was not addicted to the fuperftition which
prevailed all the world over, before the introduction of Chriftianity.

† The fong of Ullin, with which the poem opens, is in a lyric
meafure. It was ufual with Fingal, when he returned from his
expeditions, to fend his bards finging before him. This fpecies
of triumph is called, by Offian, the *fong of victory*.

repofe

repofe is there. The waves come to behold thy
beauty : they lift their trembling heads: they fee
thee lovely in thy fleep; but they fhrink away
with fear. Reft, in thy fhadowy cave, O fun!
and let thy return be in joy.——But let a thoufand lights arife to the found of the harps of
Selma : let the beam fpread in the hall, the king
of fhells is returned ! The ftrife of Crona * is
paft, like founds that are no more : raife the
fong, O bards, the king is returned with his
fame!

SUCH was the fong of Ullin, when Fingal returned from battle: when he returned in the
fair bluſhing of youth; with all his heavy locks.
His blue arms were on the hero; like a gray
cloud on the fun, when he moves in his robes of
mift, and fhews but half his beams. His heroes
follow the king : the feaft of fhells is fpread.
Fingal turns to his bards, and bids the fong to
rife.

VOICES of echoing Cona! he faid, O bards of
other times! Ye, on whofe fouls the blue hofts
of our fathers rife! ftrike the harp in my hall;
and let Fingal hear the fong. Pleafant is the joy

* Offian has celebrated the *ftrife of Crona*, in a particular
poem. This poem is connected with it, but it was impoffible
for the tranflator to procure that part which relates to Crona,
with any degree of purity.

of

of grief! it is like the fhower of fpring, when it foftens the branch of the oak, and the young leaf lifts its green head. Sing on, O bards, to-morrow we lift the fail. My blue courfe is through the ocean, to Carric-thura's walls; the moffy walls of Sarno, where Comála dwelt. There the noble Cathulla fpreads the feaft of fhells. The boars of his woods are many, and the found of the chace fhall arife.

CRONNAN *, fon of fong! faid Ullin, Mi-nona, graceful at the harp! raife the fong of Shilric, to pleafe the king of Morven. Let Vinvela come in her beauty, like the fhowery bow, when its fhews its lovely head on the lake, and the fetting fun is bright. And fhe comes, O Fingal! her voice is foft but fad.

VINVELA.

My love is a fon of the hill. He purfues the flying deer. His gray dogs are panting around him; his bow-ftring founds in the wind. Doft thou reft by the fount of the rock, or by the noife of the mountain-ftream? the rufhes are

---

* One fhould think that the parts of Shilric and Vinvela were reprefented by Cronnan and Minona, whofe very names denote that they were fingers, who performed in public. Cron-nan fignifies *a mournful found*; Minona, or Mín-'ónn, *foft air*. All the dramatic poems of Offian appear to have been prefented before Fingal, upon folemn occafions.

nodding

nodding with the wind, the mift is flying over the hill. I will approach my love unperceived, and fee him from the rock. Lovely I faw thee firft by the aged oak of Branno * ; thou wert returning tall from the chace; the faireft among thy friends.

SHILRIC.

WHAT voice is that I hear? that voice like the fummer-wind.---I fit not by the nodding rufhes; I hear not the fount of the rock. Afar, Vinvela †, afar I go to the wars of Fingal. My dogs attend me no more. No more I tread the hill. No more from on high I fee thee, fair-moving by the ftream of the plain; bright as the bow of heaven; as the moon on the weftern wave.

VINVELA.

THEN thou art gone, O Shilric! and I am alone on the hill. The deer are feen on the brow; void of fear they graze along. No more

---

* Bran, or Branno, fignifies *a mountain-ftream:* it is here fome river known by that name, in the days of Offian. There are feveral fmall rivers in the north of Scotland ftill retaining the name of Bran ; in particular one which falls into the Tay at Dunkeld.

† Bhin-bheul, *a woman with a melodious voice. Bh* in the Galic Language has the fame found with the *v* in Englifh.

they

they dread the wind; no more the ruftling tree.
The hunter is far removed; he is in the field of
graves. Strangers! fons of the waves! fpare my
lovely Shilric.

SHILRIC.

IF fall I muft in the field, raife high my
grave, Vinvela. Gray ftones and heaped-up
earth, fhall mark me to future times. When the
hunter fhall fit by the mound, and produce his
food at noon, " Some warrior refts here," he
will fay; and my fame fhall live in his praife.
Remember me, Vinvela, when low on earth I
lie!

VINVELA.

YES!---I will remember thee---Indeed my
Shilric will fall. What fhall I do, my love!
when thou art gone for ever? Through thefe
hills I will go at noon: I will go through the
filent heath. There I will fee the place of thy
reft, returning from the chace. Indeed, my
Shilric will fall; but I will remember him.

AND I remember the chief, faid the king of
woody Morven; he confumed the battle in his
rage. But now my eyes behold him not. I
met him, one day, on the hill; his cheek was
pale; his brow was dark. The figh was frequent in his breaft: his fteps were towards the

T   defart.

defart. But now he is not in the crowd of my chiefs, when the founds of my fhields arife. Dwells he in the narrow houfe *, the chief of high Carmora ? †

CRONNAN! faid Ullin of other times, raife the fong of Shilric; when he returned to his hills, and Vinvela was no more. He leaned on her gray mofly ftone; he thought Vinvela lived. He faw her fair-moving ‡ on the plain : but the bright form lafted not : the fun-beam fled from the field, and fhe was feen no more. Hear the fong of Shilric, it is foft but fad.

I SIT by the mòffy fountain; on the top of the hill of winds. One tree is ruftling above me. Dark waves roll over the heath. The lake is troubled below. The deer defcend from the hill. No hunter at a diftance is feen ; no whift-ling cow-herd is nigh. It is mid-day : but all is filent. Sad are my thoughts alone. Didft thou but appear, O my love, a wanderer on the heath! thy hair floating on the wind behind thee; thy bofom heaving on the fight; thine

---

* The grave.

† Carn-mór, *high recky hill*.

‡ The diftinction, which the ancient Scots made between good and bad fpirits, was, that the former appeared fometimes in the day-time in lonely unfrequented places, but the latter fel-dom but by night, and always in a difmal gloomy fcene.

eyes

eyes full of tears for thy friends, whom the mift of the hill had concealed! Thee I would comfort, my love, and bring thee to thy father's houfe.

But is it fhe that there appears, like a beam of light on the heath? bright as the moon in autumn, as the fun in a fummer-ftorm, comeft thou, lovely maid, over rocks, over mountains to me?——She fpeaks: but how weak her voice! like the breeze in the reeds of the pool.

Returnest thou fafe from the war? Where are thy friends, my love? I heard of thy death on the hill; I heard and mourned thee, Shilric!

Yes, my fair, I return; but I alone of my race. Thou fhalt fee them no more: their graves I raifed on the plain. But why art thou on the defert hill? Why on the heath, alone?

Alone I am, O Shilric! alone in the winter-houfe. With grief for thee I expired. Shilric, I am pale in the tomb.

She fleets, fhe fails away; as gray mift before the wind!---and, wilt thou not ftay, my love? Stay and behold my tears? fair thou appeareft, Vinvela! fair thou waft, when alive!

By the moffy fountain I will fit; on the top of the hill of winds. When mid-day is filent around, converfe, O my love, with me! come

on

on the wings of the gale! on the blaſt of the mountain, come! Let me hear thy voice, as thou paſſeſt, when mid-day is ſilent around.

Such was the ſong of Cronnan, on the night of Selma's joy. But morning roſe in the eaſt; the blue waters rolled in light. Fingal bade his ſails to riſe, and the winds come ruſtling from their hills. Inis-tore roſe to ſight, and Carric-thura's moſſy towers. But the ſign of diſtreſs was on their top: the green flame edged with ſmoke. The king of Morven ſtruck his breaſt: he aſſumed, at once, his ſpear. His darkened brow bends forward to the coaſt: he looks back to the lagging winds. His hair is diſordered on his back. The ſilence of the king is terrible.

Night came down on the ſea; Rotha's bay received the ſhip. A rock bends along the coaſt with all its echoing wood. On the top is the circle * of Loda, and the moſſy ſtone of power. A narrow plain ſpreads beneath, co-vered with graſs and aged trees, which the mid-night winds, in their wrath, had torn from the ſhaggy rock. The blue courſe of a ſtream is there : and the lonely blaſt of ocean purſues the thiſtle's beard.

* The circle of Loda is ſuppoſed to be a place of worſhip among the Scandinavians, as the ſpirit of Loda is thought to be the ſame with their god Odin.

THE

THE flame of three oaks arofe: the feaft is fpread around: but the foul of the king is fad, for Carric-thura's battling chief. The wan, cold moon rofe, in the eaft. Sleep defcended on the youths: Their blue helmets glitter to the beam; the fading fire decays. But fleep did not reft on the king: he rofe in the midft cf his arms, and flowly afcended the hill to behold the flame of Sarno's tower.

THE flame was dim and diftant; the moon hid her red face in the eaft. A blaft came from the mountain, and bore, on its wings, the fpirit of Loda. He came to his place in his terrors*, and he fhook his dufky fpear.---His eyes appear like flames in his dark face; and his voice is like diftant thunder. Fingal advanced with the fpear of his ftrength, and raifed his voice on high.

SON of night, retire: call thy winds and fly! Why doft thou come to my prefence, with thy fhadowy arms? Do I fear thy gloomy form, difmal fpirit of Loda? Weak is thy fhield of clouds: feeble is that meteor, thy fword. The blaft rolls them together; and thou thyfelf doft vanifh. Fly from my prefence fon of night! call thy winds and fly!

* He is defcribed, in a fimile, in the poem concerning the death of Cuchullin.

T 3

Dost thou force me from my place, replied the hollow voice? The people bend before me. I turn the battle in the field of the valiant. I look on the nations and they vanish: my noſtrils pour the blaſt of death. I come * abroad on the winds: the tempeſts are before my face. But my dwelling is calm, above the clouds, the fields of my reſt are pleaſant.

Dwell then in thy calm field, ſaid Fingal, and let Comhal's ſon be forgot. Do my ſteps aſcend, from my hills, into thy peaceful plains? Do I meet thee, with a ſpear, on thy cloud, ſpirit of diſmal Loda? Why then doſt thou frown on Fingal? or ſhake thine airy ſpear? But thou frowneſt in vain: I never fled from mighty men. And ſhall the ſons of the wind frighten the king of Morven? No: he knows the weakneſs of their arms.

Fly to thy land, replied the form: receive the wind and fly. The blaſts are in the hollow of my hand: the courſe of the ſtorm is mine. The king of Sora is my ſon, he bends at the ſtone of my power. His battle is around Carric-thura; and he will prevail. Fly to thy land, ſon of Comhal, or feel my flaming wrath.

* There is a great reſemblance between the terrors of this mock divinity, and thoſe of the true God, as they are deſcribed in the 18th Pſalm.

HE

HE lifted high his fhadowy fpear; and bent forward his terrible height. But the king, advancing, drew his fword; the blade of dark-brown Luno *. The gleaming path of the fteel winds through the gloomy ghoft. The form fell fhapelefs into air, like a column of fmoke, which the ftaff of the boy difturbs, as it rifes from the half-extinguifhed furnace.

THE fpirit of Loda fhrieked, as, rolled into himfelf, he rofe on the wind. Iniftore fhook at the found. The waves heard it on the deep: they ftopped, in their courfe, with fear: the companions of Fingal ftarted, at once; and took their heavy fpears. They miffed the king: they rofe with rage; all their arms refound.

THE moon came forth in the eaft. The king returned in the gleam of his arms. The joy of his youths was great; their fouls fettled, as a fea from a ftorm. Ullin raifed the fong of gladnefs. The hills of Iniftore rejoiced. The flame of the oak arofe; and the tales of heroes are told.

BUT Frothal, Sora's battling king, fits in fadnefs beneath a tree. The hoft fpreads around Carric-thura. He looks towards the walls with

* The famous fword of Fingal, made by Lun, cr Luno, a fmith of Lochlin.

rage.   He longs for the blood of Cathulla, who, once, overcame the king in war.——When Annir reigned * in Sora, the father of car-borne Frothal, a blaft rofe on the fea, and carried Frothal to Iniftore.   Three days he feafted in Sarno's halls, and faw the flow rolling eyes of Comála.   He loved her, in the rage of youth, and rufhed to feize the white-armed maid.   Cathulla met the chief.   The gloomy battle rofe. Frothal is bound in the hall : three days he pined alone.   On the fourth, Sarno fent him to his fhip, and he returned to his land.   But wrath darkened in his foul againft the noble Cathulla.   When Annir's ftone † of fame arofe, Frothal came in his ftrength.   The battle burned round Carric-thura, and Sarno's mofly walls.

MORNING rofe on Iniftore.   Frothal ftruck his dark-brown fhield.   His chiefs ftarted at the found; they ftood, but their eyes were turned to the fea.   They faw Fingal coming in his ftrength ; and firft the noble Thubar fpoke.

WHO comes like the ftag of the mountain, with all his herd behind him ? Frothal, it is a

---

* Annir was alfo the father of Erragon, who was killed after the death of his brother Frothal.   The death of Erragon is the fubjeft of *the battle of Lora,* a poem in this collection.

† That is, after the death of Annir.   To erect the ftone of one's fame, was, in other words, to fay that the perfon was dead.

foe ;

foe; I fee his forward fpear. Perhaps it is the
king of Morven, Fingal the firft of men. His
actions are well known on Gormal; the blood
of his foes is in Starno's halls. Shall I afk the
peace * of kings? He is like the thunder of
heaven.

Son of the feeble hand, faid Frothal, fhall my
days begin in darknefs? Shall I yield before I
have conquered in battle, chief of ftreamy
Tora? The people would fay in Sora, Frothal
flew forth like a meteor; but the dark cloud
met it, and it is no more. No: Thubar, I will
never yield; my fame fhall furround me like
light. No: I will never yield, king of ftreamy
Tora.

He went forth with the ftream of his people,
but they met a rock: Fingal ftood unmoved,
broken they rolled back from his fide. Nor did
they roll in fafety; the fpear of the king purfued their flight. The field is covered with heroes. A rifing hill preferved the flying hoft.

Frothal faw their flight. The rage of his
bofom rofe. He bent his eyes to the ground,
and called the noble Thubar.——Thubar! my
people fled. My fame has ceafed to rife. I
will fight the king; I feel my burning foul.

* Honourable terms of peace.

Send a bard to demand the combat.   Speak not
againſt Frothal's words.---But, Thubar ! I love
a maid; ſhe dwells by Thano's ſtream, the
white-boſomed daughter of Herman, Utha with
the ſoftly-rolling eyes. She feared the daughter *
of Iniſtore, and her ſoft ſighs roſe, at my departure.   Tell to Utha that I am low ; but that
my ſoul delighted in her.

SUCH were his words, reſolved to fight. But
the ſoft ſigh of Utha was near.   She had followed
her hero over the ſea, in the armour of a man.
She rolled her eye on the youth, in ſecret, from
beneath a glittering helmet.   But now ſhe ſaw
the bard as he went, and the ſpear fell thrice
from her hand.   Her looſe hair flew on the
wind.   Her white breaſt roſe, with ſighs.   She
lifted up her eyes to the king; ſhe would ſpeak,
but thrice ſhe failed.

FINGAL heard the words of the bard; he
came in the ſtrength of ſteel.   They mixed their
deathful ſpears, and raiſed the gleam of their
ſwords.   But the ſteel of Fingal deſcended and
cut Frothal's ſhield in twain.   His fair ſide is
expoſed ; half bent he foreſees his death.

* By the daughter of Iriſtore, Frothal means Comála, of
whoſe death Utha probably had not heard ; conſequently ſhe
feared that the former paſſion of Frothal for Comála might
return.

DARKNESS gathered on Utha's foul. The tear rolled down her cheek. She rufhed to cover the chief with her fhield; but a fallen oak met her fteps. She fell on her arm of fnow; her fhield, her helmet flew wide. Her white bofom heaved to the fight; her dark-brown hair is fpread on earth.

FINGAL pitied the white-armed maid: he ftayed the uplifted fword. The tear was in the eye of the king, as, bending forward, he fpoke. King of ftreamy Sora! fear not the fword of Fingal. It was never ftained with the blood of the vanquifhed; it never pierced a fallen foe. Let thy people rejoice along the blue waters of Tora: let the maids of thy love be glad. Why fhouldeft thou fall in thy youth, king of ftreamy Sora?

FROTHAL heard the words of Fingal, and faw the rifing maid: they * ftood in filence, in their beauty: like two young trees of the plain, when the fhower of fpring is on their leaves, and the loud winds are laid.

DAUGHTER of Herman, faid Frothal, didft thou come from Tora's ftreams; didft thou come, in thy beauty, to behold thy warrior low? But he was low before the mighty, maid

---

* Frothal and Utha.

of the flow-rolling eye! The feeble did not overcome the fon of car-borne Annir. Terrible art thou, O king of Morven! in battles of the fpear. But, in peace, thou art like the fun, when he looks through a filent fhower: the flowers lift their fair heads before him ; and the gales fhake their ruftling wings. O that thou wert in Sora! that my feaft were fpread!---The future kings of Sora would fee thy arms and re-joice. They would rejoice at the fame of their fathers, who beheld the mighty Fingal.

Son of Annir, replied the king, the fame of Sora's race fhall be heard.---When chiefs are ftrong in battle, then does the fong arife! But if their fwords are ftretched over the feeble : if the blood of the weak has ftained their arms ; the bard fhall forget them in the fong, and their tombs fhall not be known. The ftranger fhall come and build there, and remove the heaped-up earth. An half-worn fword fhall rife before him ; and bending above it, he will fay, " Thefe " are the arms of chiefs of old, but their names " are not in fong."——Come thou, O Frothal, to the feaft of Iniftore ; let the maid of thy love be there; and our faces will brighten with joy.

Fingal took his fpear, moving in the fteps of his might. The gates of Carric-thura are opened.

opened. The feaft of fhells is fpread.---The voice of mufic arofe. Gladnefs brightened in the hall.——The voice of Ullin was heard; the harp of Selma was ftrung.---Utha rejoiced in his prefence, and demanded the fong of grief; the big tear hung in her eye, when the foft * Cri-mora fpoke. Crimora the daughter of Rinval, who dwelt at Lotha's † mighty ftream. The tale was long, but lovely; and pleafed the bluſhing maid of Tora.

Crimora ‡.

Who cometh from the hill, like a cloud tinged with the beam of the weft? Whofe voice is that, loud as the wind, but pleafant as the harp of Carril? § It is my love in the light of fteel; but fad is his darkened brow. Live the

* There is a propriety in introducing this epifode, as the fitua-tions of Crimora and Utha were fo fimilar.

† Lotha was the ancient name of one of the great rivers in the north of Scotland. The only one of them that ftill retains a name of a like found is Lochy, in Invernefsfhire; but whether it is the river mentioned here, the tranflator will not pretend to fay.

‡ Cri-móra, *a woman of a great foul.*

§ Perhaps the Carril mentioned here is the fame with Carril the fon of Kinfena, Cuchullin's bard. The name itfelf is pro-per to any bard, as it fignifies *a fprightly and harmonious found.*

mighty

4

mighty race of Fingal? or what difturbs my Connal?*

CONNAL.

THEY live. I faw them return from the chace, like a ftream of light. The fun was on their fhields. Like a ridge of fire they de-fcended the hill. Loud is the voice of the youth; the war, my love, is near. To-morrow the terrible Dargo comes to try the force of our race. The race of Fingal he defies; the race of battle and wounds.

CRIMORA.

CONNAL, I faw his fails like gray mift on the fable wave. They flowly came to land. Con-.ıal, many are the warriors of Dargo!

CONNAL.

BRING me thy father's fhield; the boffy, iron fhield of Rinval; that fhield like the full moon when it moves darkened through heaven.

* Connal, the fon of Diaran, was one of the moft famous heroes of Fingal; he was flain in a battle againft Dargo a Briton; but whether by the hand of the enemy, or that of his miftrefs, tradition does not determine.

CRIMORA.

CRIMORA.

THAT fhield I bring, O Connal; but it did not defend my father. By the fpear of Gormar he fell. Thou may'ft fall, O Connal!

CONNAL.

FALL indeed I may: But raife my tomb, Crimora. Gray ftones, a mound of earth, fhall keep my memory. Bend thy red eye over my tomb, and beat thy mournful heaving breaft. Though fair thou art, my love, as the light; more pleafant than the gale of the hill; yet I will not ftay. Raife my tomb, Crimora.

CRIMORA.

THEN give me thofe arms of light; that fword, and that fpear of fteel. I fhall meet Dargo with thee, and aid my lovely Connal. Farewel, ye rocks of Ardven! ye deer! and ye. ftreams of the hill!---We fhall return no more. Our tombs are diftant far.

AND did they return no more? faid Utha's burfting figh. Fell the mighty in battle, and did Crimora live?---Her fteps were lonely, and her foul was fad for Connal. Was he not young and lovely; like the beam of the fetting fun? Ullin faw the virgin's tear, and took the foftly-
trembling

trembling harp : the fong was lovely, but fad, and filence was in Carric-thura.

AUTUMN is dark on the mountains ; gray mift refts on the hills. The whirlwind is heard on the heath. Dark rolls the river through the narrow plain. A tree ftands alone on the hill, and marks the flumbering Connal. The leaves whirl round with the wind, and ftrew the grave of the dead. At times are feen here the ghofts of the deceafed, when the mufing hunter alone ftalks flowly over the heath.

WHO can reach the fource of thy race, O Connal ? and who recount thy fathers ? Thy family grew like an oak on the mountain, which meeteth the wind with its lofty head. But now it is torn from the earth. Who fhall fupply the place of Connal ?

HERE was the din of arms ; and here the groans of the dying. Bloody are the wars of Fingal ! O Connal ! it was here thou didft fall. Thine arm was like a ftorm ; thy fword a beam of the fky ; thy height, a rock on the plain ; thine eyes, a furnace of fire. Louder than a ftorm was thy voice, in the battles of thy fteel. Warriors fell by thy fword, as the thiftle by the ftaff of a boy.

DARGO the mighty came on, like a cloud of thunder. His brows were contracted and dark.

His

His eyes like two caves in a rock. Bright rofe their fwords on each fide; dire was the clang of their fteel.

THE daughter of Rinval was near; Crimora bright in the armour of man; her yellow hair is loofe behind, her bow is in her hand. She followed the youth to the war, Connal her much-beloved. She drew the ftring on Dargo; but erring pierced her Connal. He falls like an oak on the plain; like a rock from the fhaggy hill. What fhall fhe do, haplefs maid!---He bleeds; her Connal dies. All the night long fhe cries, and all the day, O Connal, my love, and my friend! With grief the fad mourner dies.

EARTH here inclofes the lovelieft pair on the hill. The grafs grows between the ftones of the tomb; I often fit in the mournful fhade. The wind fighs through the grafs; their memory rufhes on my mind. Undifturbed you now fleep together; in the tomb of the mountain you reft alone.

AND foft be your reft, faid Utha, children of ftreamy Lotha. I will remember you with tears, and my fecret fong fhall rife; when the wind is in the groves of Tora, and the ftream is roaring near. Then fhall ye come on my foul, with all your lovely grief.

U   THREE

THREE days feafted the kings : on the fourth
their white fails arofe.   The winds of the north
carry the fhip of Fingal to Morven's woody land.
——But the fpirit of Loda fat, in his cloud, behind the fhips of Frothal.   He hung forward
with all his blafts, and fpread the white-bofomed
fails.——The wounds of his form were not forgot ; he ftill feared * the hand of the king.

* The ftory of Fingal and the fpirit of Loda, fuppofed to be
the famous Odin, is the moft extravagant fiction in all Offian's
poems.   It is not, however, without precedents in the beft
poets ; and it muft be faid for Offian, that he fays nothing but
what perfectly agreed with the notions of the times, concerning
ghofts.   They thought the fouls of the dead were material, and
confequently fufceptible of pain.   Whether a proof could be
drawn from this paffage, that Offian had no notion of a divinity,
I fhall leave to others to determine : it appears, however, that he
was of opinion, that fuperior beings ought to take no notice of
what paffed among men.

THE

SONGS of SELMA*.

STAR of the defcending night! fair is thy
light in the weft! thou lifteft thy unfhorn
head from thy cloud : thy fteps are ftately on
thy hill. What doft thou behold in the plain ?
The ftormy winds are laid. The murmur of the
torrent comes from afar. Roaring waves climb
the diftant rock. The flies of evening are on

* This poem fixes the antiquity of a cuftom, which is well
known to have prevailed afterwards, in the north of Scotland,
and in Ireland. The bards, at an annual feaft, provided by the
king or chief, repeated their poems, and fuch of them as were
thought, by him, worthy of being preferved, were carefully
taught to their children, in order to have them tranfmitted to
pofterity.——It was one of thofe occafions that afforded the fubject of the prefent poem to Offian.—It is called in the original,
The Songs of Selma, which title it was thought proper to adcpt
in the tranflation.

The poem is entirely lyric, and has great variety of verfification. The addrefs to the evening ftar, with which it opens, has,
in the original, all the harmony that numbers could give it ;
flowing down with all that tranquillity and foftnefs, which the
fcene defcribed naturally infpires.—Three of the fongs which are
introduced in this piece, were publifhed among the fragments of
ancient poetry, printed laft year.

U 2   their

their feeble wings, and the hum of their courfe
is on the field. What doft thou behold, fair
light? But thou doft fmile and depart. The
waves come with joy around thee, and bathe thy
lovely hair. Farewel, thou filent beam!---Let
the light of Offian's foul arife.

AND it does arife in its ftrength! I behold my
departed friends. Their gathering is on Lora,
as in the days that are paft.——Fingal comes
like a watry column of mift; his heroes are
around. And fee the bards of the fong, gray-
haired Ullin; ftately Ryno; Alpin *, with the
tuneful voice, and the foft complaint of Minona!——How are ye changed, my friends,
fince the days of Selma's feaft! when we contended, like the gales of the fpring, that, flying over the hill, by turns bend the feebly-
whiftling grafs.

MINONA then came forth in her beauty;
with down-caft look and tearful eye; her hair
flew flowly on the blaft that rufhed unfrequent

---

* Alpin is from the fame root with Albion, or rather Albin,
the ancient name of Britain; Alp, *high* in *land*, or *coun.ry.*
The prefent name of our ifland has its origin in the Celtic
tongue; fo that thofe who derived it from any other, betrayed
their ignorance of the ancient language of our country.——
Britain comes from *Breac't in, variegated ifland,* fo called from
the face of the country, from the natives painting themfelves, or
from their party-coloured cloaths.

from

from the hill.——The fouls of the heroes were fad when fhe raifed the tuneful voice; for often had they feen the grave of Salgar *, and the dark dwelling of white-bofomed Colma †. Colma left alone on the hill, with all her voice of mufic! Salgar promifed to come: but the night defcended round.---Hear the voice of Colma, when fhe fat alone on the hill!

COLMA.

It is night;---I am alone, forlorn on the hill of ftorms. The wind is heard in the mountain. The torrent fhrieks down the rock. No hut receives me from the rain; forlorn on the hill of winds.

Rise, moon! from behind thy clouds; ftars of the night appear! Lead me, fome light, to the place where my love refts from the toil of the chace! his bow near him, unftrung; his dogs panting around him. But here I muft fit alone, by the rock of the moffy ftream. The ftream and the wind roar; nor can I hear the voice of my love.

Why delays my Salgar, why the fon of the hill, his promife? Here is the rock, and the tree; and here the roaring ftream. Thou didft

---

* Sealg-'er, *a hunter.*

† Cul-math, *a woman with fine hair.*

promife

promife with night to be here. Ah! whither is my Salgar gone? With thee I would fly, my father; with thee, my brother of pride. Our race have long been foes; but we are not foes, O Salgar!

CEASE a little while, O wind! ftream, be thou filent a while! let my voice be heard over the heath; let my wanderer hear me. Salgar! it is I who call. Here is the tree, and the rock. Salgar, my love! I am here. Why delayeft thou thy coming?

Lo! the moon appeareth. The flood is bright in the vale. The rocks are grey on the face of the hill. But I fee him not on the brow; his dogs before him tell not that he is coming. Here I muft fit alone.

BUT who are thefe that lie beyond me on the heath? Are they my love and my brother?--Speak to me, O my friends! they anfwer not. My foul is tormented with fears.——Ah! they are dead. Their fwords are red from the fight. O my brother! my brother! why haft thou flain my Salgar? why, O Salgar! haft thou flain my brother? Dear were ye both to me! what fhall I fay in your praife? Thou wert fair on the hill among thoufands; he was terrible in fight. Speak to me; hear my voice, fons of my love!

But

But alas! they are filent; filent for ever! Cold are their breafts of clay!

OH! from the rock of the hill; from the top of the windy mountain, fpeak ye ghofts of the dead! fpeak, I will not be afraid.---Whither are ye gone to reft? In what cave of the hill fhall I find you? No feeble voice is on the wind: no anfwer half-drownēd in the ftorms of the hill.

I SIT in my grief. I wait for morning in my tears. Rear the tomb, ye friends of the dead; but clofe it not till Colma come. My life flies away like a dream: why fhould I ftay behind? Here fhall I reft with my friends, by the ftream of the founding rock. When night comes on the hill; when the wind is on the heath; my ghoft fhall ftand in the wind, and mourn the death of my friends. The hunter fhall hear from his booth. He fhall fear but love my voice. For fweet fhall my voice be for my friends; for pleafant were they both to me.

SUCH was thy fong, Minona foftly-blufhing maid of Torman. Our tears defcended for Colma, and our fouls were fad.---Ullin came with the harp, and gave the fong of Alpin.--- The voice of Alpin was pleafant: the foul of Ryno was a beam of fire. But they had refted in the narrow houfe: and their voice was not

U 4

heard

heard in Selma.——Ullin had returned one day from the chace, before the heroes fell. He heard their ftrife on the hill; their fong was foft but fad. They mourned the fall of Morar, firft of mortal men. His foul was like the foul of Fingal; his fword like the fword of Ofcar.--- But he fell, and his father mourned: his fifter's eyes were full of tears.——Minona's eyes were full of tears, the fifter of car-borne Morar. She retired from the fong of Ullin, like the moon in the weft, when fhe forefees the fhower, and hides her fair head in a cloud.---I touched the harp, with Ullin; the fong of mourning rofe.

RYNO.

THE wind and the rain are over: calm is the noon of day. The clouds are divided in heaven. Over the green hills flies the inconftant fun. Red through the ftony vale comes down the ftream of the hill. Sweet are thy murmurs, O ftream! but more fweet is the voice I hear. It is the voice of Alpin, the fon of fong, mourning for the dead. Bent is his head of age, and red his tearful eye. Alpin, thou fon of fong, why alone on the filent hill? why complaineft thou, as a blaft in the wood; as a wave on the lonely fhore?

ALPIN,

ALPIN.

MY tears, O Ryno! are for the dead; my voice, for the inhabitants of the grave. Tall thou art on the hill; fair among the fons of the plain. But thou fhalt fall like Morar *; and the mourner fhall fit on thy tomb. The hills fhall know thee no more; thy bow fhall lie in the hall, unftrung.

THOU wert fwift, O Morar! as a rce on the hill; terrible as a meteor of fire. Thy wrath was as the ftorm. Thy fword in battle, as lightning in the field. Thy voice was like a ftream after rain; like thunder on diftant hills. Many fell by thy arm; they were confumed in the flames of thy wrath.

BUT when thou didft return from war, how peaceful was thy brow! Thy face was like the fun after rain; like the moon in the filence of night; calm as the breaft of the lake when the loud wind is laid.

NARROW is thy dwelling now; dark the place of thine abode. With three fteps I compafs thy grave, O thou who waft fo great before! Four ftones, with their heads of mofs, are the only memorial of thee. A tree with fcarce a leaf,

* Mór-ér, great man.

long

long grafs which whiftles in the wind, mark to the hunter's eye the grave of the mighty Morar. Morar! thou art low indeed. Thou haft no mother to mourn thee ; no maid with her tears of love. Dead is fhe that brought thee forth. Fallen is the daughter of Morglan.

WHO on his ftaff is this? who is this, whofe head is white with age, whofe eyes are red with tears, who quakes at every ftep.---It is thy father *, O Morar! the father of no fon but thee. He heard of thy fame in battle ; he heard of foes difperfed. He heard of Morar's fame ; why did he not hear of his wound? Weep, thou father of Morar! weep ; but thy fon heareth thee not. Deep is the fleep of the dead ; low their pillow of duft. No more fhall he hear thy voice ; no more fhall he awake at thy call. When fhall it be morn in the grave, to bid the flumberer awake?

FAREWEL, thou braveft of men! thou conqueror in the field! but the field fhall fee thee no more ; nor the dark wood be lightened with the fplendor of thy fteel. Thou haft left no fon. But the fong fhall preferve thy name. Future times fhall hear of thee ; they fhall hear of the fallen Morar.

---

* Torman, the fon of Carthul, lord of I-mora, one of the weftern ifles.

THE

The grief of all arofe, but moft the burfting figh of Armin *. He remembers the death of his fon, who fell in the days of his youth. Carmor † was near the hero, the chief of the echoing Galmal. Why burfts the figh of Armin, he faid? Is there a caufe to mourn? The fong comes, with its mufic, to melt and pleafe the foul. It is like foft mift, that, rifing from a lake, pours on the filent vale ; the green flowers are filled with dew, but the fun returns in his ftrength, and the mift is gone. Why art thou fad, O Armin, chief of fea-furrounded Gorma?

Sad! I am indeed: nor fmall my caufe of woe!---Carmor, thou haft loft no fon; thou haft loft no daughter of beauty. Colgar the valiant lives; and Annira faireft maid. The boughs of thy family flourifh, O Carmor! but Armin is the laft of his race. Dark is thy bed, O Daura! and deep thy fleep in the tomb.--- When fhalt thou awake with thy fongs? with all thy voice of mufic?

Rise, winds of autumn, rife ; blow upon the dark heath! ftreams of the mountains, roar! howl, ye tempefts, in the top of the oak! walk through broken clouds, O moon ! fhow by in-

* Armin, *a hero*. He was chief or petty king of Gorma, i. e. *the blue ifland*, fuppofed to be one of the Hebrides.

† Cear-mór, *a tall dark-complexioned man*.

tervals thy pale face! bring to my mind that fad night, when all my children fell; when Arindal the mighty fell; when Daura the lovely failed.

. DAURA, my daughter! thou wert fair; fair as the moon on the hills of Fura *; white as the driven fnow; fweet as the breathing gale. Arindal, thy bow was ftrong, thy fpear was fwift in the field: thy look was like mift on the wave; thy fhield, a red cloud in a ftorm. Armar, re-nowned in war, came, and fought Daura's love; he was not long denied; fair was the hope of their friends.

ERATH, fon of Odgal, repined; for his bro-ther was flain by Armar. He came difguifed like a fon of the fea: fair was his fkiff on the wave; white his locks of age; calm his ferious brow. Faireft of women, he faid, lovely daughter of Armin! a rock. not diftant in the fea, bears a tree on its fide; red fhines the fruit afar. There Armar waits for Daura. I came to carry his love along the rolling fea.

SHE went; and fhe called on Armar. Nought anfwered, but the fon † of the rock. Armar,

* Fuar-a, *cold ifland.*

† By *the fon of the rock* the poet means the echoing back of the human voice from a rock. The vulgar were of opinion, that this repetition of found was made by a fpirit within the rock; and they, on that account, called it *mac-talla; the fon who dwells in the rock.*

my

my love! my love! why tormenteſt thou me with fear? hear, ſon of Ardnart, hear: it is Daura who calleth thee! Erath the traitor fled laughing to the land. She lifted up her voice, and cried for her brother and her father. Arindal! Armin! none to relieve your Daura.

HER voice came over the ſea. Arindal my ſon deſcended from the hill; rough in the ſpoils of the chace. His arrows rattled by his ſide; his bow was in his hand: five dark gray dogs attended his ſteps. He ſaw fierce Erath on the ſhore: he ſeized and bound him to an oak. Thick bend the thongs * of the hide around his limbs; he loads the wind with his groans.

ARINDAL aſcends the wave in his boat, to bring Daura to land. Armar came in his wrath, and let fly the gray-feathered ſhaft. It ſung; it ſunk in thy heart, O Arindal my ſon! for Erath the traitor thou diedſt. The oar is ſtopped at once; he panted on the rock and expired. What is thy grief, O Daura, when round thy feet is poured thy brother's blood.

THE boat is broken in twain by the waves. Armar plunges into the ſea, to reſcue his Daura, or die. Sudden a blaſt from the hill comes over the waves. He ſunk, and he roſe no more.

* The poet here only means that Erath was bound with leathern thongs.

ALONE,

ALONE, on the fea-beat rock, my daughter
was heard to complain. Frequent and loud
were her cries; nor could her father relieve her.
All night I ftood on the fhore. I faw her by the
faint beam of the moon. All night I heard her
cries. Loud was the wind; and the rain beat
hard on the fide of the mountain. Before morning appeared, her voice was weak. It died
away, like the evening-breeze among the grafs
of the rocks. Spent with grief fhe expired.
And left thee Armin alone: gone is my ftrength
in the war, and fallen my pride among women.
WHEN the ftorms of the mountain come;
when the north lifts the waves on high; I fit by
the founding fhore, and look on the fatal rock.
Often by the fetting moon I fee the ghofts of my
children. Half-viewlefs, they walk in mournful
conference together. Will none of you fpeak in
pity? They do not regard their father. I am
fad, O Carmor, nor fmall my caufe of woe!

SUCH were the words of the bards in the days
of fong; when the king heard the mufic of harps,
and the tales of other times. The chiefs gathered from all their hills, and heard the lovely
found. They praifed the voice * of Cona! the
firft among a thoufand bards. But age is now

* Offian is fometimes poetically called *the voice of Cona.*

on my tongue; and my foul has failed. I hear,
fometimes, the ghofts of bards, and learn their
pleafant fong. But memory fails in my mind;
I hear the call of years. They fay, as they pafs
along, why does Offian fing? Soon fhall he lie
in the narrow houfe, and no bard fhall raife his
fame.

ROLL on, ye dark-brown years, for ye bring
no jóy on your courfe. Let the tomb open to
Offian, for his ftrength has failed. The fons of
fong are gone to reft: my voice remains, like a
blaft, that roars, lonely, on a' fea-furrounded
rock, after the winds are laid. The dark mofs
whiftles there, and the diftant mariner fees the
waving trees.

CALTHON and COLMAL:

A P O E M *.

PLEASANT is the voice of thy fong,
thou lonely dweller of the rock. It comes
on the found of the ftream, along the narrow

* This piece, as many more of Offian's compofitions, is addreffed to one of the firft Chriftian miffionaries.—The ftory of the
poem is handed down, by tradition, thus—In the country of
the Britons between the walls, two chiefs lived in the days of
Fingal, Dunthalmo, lord of Teutha, fuppofed to be the Tweed;
and Rathmor, who dwelt at Clutha, well known to be the river
Clyde.—— Rathmor was not more renowned for his generofity
and hofpitality, than Dunthalmo was infamous for his cruelty
and ambition.—Dunthalmo, through envy, or on account of
fome private feuds, which fubfifted between the families, murdered Rathmor at a feaft; but being afterwards touched with remorfe, he educated the two fons of Rathmor, Calthon and Colmar, in his own houfe.—They growing up to man's eftate,
dropped fome hints that they intended to revenge the death of
their father, upon which Dunthalmo fhut them up in two caves
on the banks of Teutha, intending to take them off privately.—
Colmal, the daughter of Dunthalmo, who was fecretly in love
with Calthon, helped him to make his efcape from prifon, and
fled with him to Fingal, difguifed in the habit of a young warrior, and implored his aid againft Dunthalmo.——Fingal fent
Offian with three hundred men, to Colmar's relief.—Dunthalmo
having previoufly murdered Colmar, came to a battle with Offian;
but he was killed by that hero, and his army totally defeated.

Calthon married Colmal, his deliverer; and Offian returned
to Morven.

rale.

vale. My foul awakes, O ftranger! in the midft of my hall. I ftretch my hand to the fpear, as in the days of other years.---I ftretch my hand, but it is feeble; and the figh of my bofom grows.---Wilt thou not liften, fon of the rock, to the fong of Offian? My foul is full of other times; the joy of my youth returns. Thus the fun * appears in the weft, after the fteps of his brightnefs have moved behind a ftorm; the green hills lift their dewy heads: the blue ftreams rejoice in the vale. The aged hero comes forth on his ftaff, and his grey hair glitters in the beam.

DOST thou not behold, fon of the rock, a fhield in Offian's hall? It is marked with the ftrokes of battle; and the brightnefs of its boffes has failed. That fhield the great Dunthalmo bore, the chief of ftreamy Teutha.———Dun-

---

* If chance the radiant fun with farewel fweet
Extend his evening beam, the fields revive,
The birds their notes renew, and bleating herds
Atteft their joy, that hill and valley rings. .

MILTON.

—The fair fun-fhine in fummer's day;
—When a dreadful ftorm away is flit
Through the broad world doth fpread his goodly ray;
At fight whereof each bird that fits on fpray,
And every beaft that to his den was fled,
Come forth afrefh out of their late difmay,
And to the light lift up their drooping head.

SPENCER.

thalmo

thalmo bore it in battle, before he fell by Offian's
fpear. Liften, fon of the rock, to the tale of
other years.---

RATHMOR was a chief of Clutha. The feeble
dwelt in his hall. The gates of Rathmor were
never clofed; his feaft was always fpread. The
fons of the ftranger came, and bleffed the generous chief of Clutha. Bards raifed the fong, and
touched the harp: and joy brightened on the
face of the mournful.---Dunthalmo came, in his
pride, and rufhed into the combat of Rathmor.
The chief of Clutha overcame: the rage of Dunthalmo rofe.---He came, by night, with his warriors; and the mighty Rathmor fell. He fell
in his halls, where his feaft was often fpread for
ftrangers.———

COLMAR and Calthon were young, the fons
of car-borne Rathmor. They came, in the joy
of youth, into their father's hall. They behold
him in his blood, and their burfting tears defcend.---The foul of Dunthalmo melted, when
he faw the children of youth ; he brought them
to Alteutha's * walls ; they grew in the houfe of

---

* Al-teutha, or rather Balteutha, *the town of Tweed*, the name
of Dunthalmo's feat. It is obfervable that all the names in this
poem, are derived from the Galic language ; which, as I have
remarked in a preceding note, is a proof that it was once the
univerfal language of the whole ifland.

their

their foe.---They bent the bow in his prefence; and came forth to his battles.

THEY faw the fallen walls of their fathers; they faw the green thorn in the hall. Their tears defcended in fecret; and, at times, their faces were mournful. Dunthalmo beheld their grief: his darkening foul defigned their death. He clofed them in two caves, on the echoing banks of Teutha. The fun did not come there with his beams; nor the moon of heaven by night. The fons of Rathmor remained in dark-nefs, and forefaw their death.

THE daughter of Dunthalmo wept in filence, the fair-haired, blue-eyed Colmal *. Her eye had rolled in fecret on Calthon; his lovelinefs fwelled in her foul. She trembled for her war-rior; but what could Colmal do? Her arm could not lift the fpear; nor was the fword formed for her fide. Her white breaft never rofe beneath a mail. Neither was her eye the terror of heroes. What canft thou do, O Colmal! for the falling chief?---Her fteps are unequal; her hair is loofe: her eye looks wildly through her

---

* Caol-mhal, *a woman with fmall eye brows*; fmall eye-brows were a diftinguifhing part of beauty in Offian's time: and he fel-dom fails to give them to the fine women of his poems.

tears.

tears.---She came, by night, to the hall *; and armed her lovely form in steel; the steel of a young warrior, who fell in the first of his battles.---She came to the cave of Calthon, and loosed the thong from his hands.

ARISE, son of Rathmor, she said, arise, the night is dark. Let us fly to the king of Selma †, chief of fallen Clutha! I am the son of Lamgal, who dwelt in thy father's hall. I heard of thy dark dwelling in the cave, and my soul arose. Arise, son of Rathmor, for the night is dark.——

BLEST voice! replied the chief, comest thou from the darkly-rolling clouds? for often the ghosts of his fathers descend to Calthon's dreams, since the sun has retired from his eyes, and darkness has dwelt around him. Or art thou the son of Lamgal, the chief I often saw in Clutha? But shall I fly to Fingal, and Colmar my brother low? Shall I fly to Morven, and the hero closed in night? No: give me that spear, son of Lamgal, Calthon will defend his brother.

---

* That is, the hall where the arms taken from enemies were hung up as trophies. Ossian is very careful to make his stories probable; for he makes Colmal put on the arms of a youth killed in his first battle, as more proper for a young woman, who cannot be supposed strong enough to carry the armour of a full-grown warrior.

† Fingal.

A THOUSAND warriors, replied the maid, ſtretch their ſpears round car-borne Colmar. What can Calthon do againſt a hoſt ſo great? Let us fly to the king of Morven, he will come with battle. His arm is ſtretched forth to the unhappy; the lightning of his ſword is round the weak.---Ariſe, thou ſon of Rathmor; the ſhades of night will fly away. Dunthalmo will behold thy ſteps on the field, and thou muſt fall in thy youth.

THE ſighing hero roſe; his tears deſcend for car-borne Colmar. He came with the maid to Selma's hall; but he knew not that it was Colmal. The helmet cover'd her lovely face; and her breaſt roſe beneath the ſteel. Fingal returned from the chace, and found the lovely ſtrangers. They were like two beams of light, in the midſt of the hall.

THE king heard the tale of grief; and turned his eyes around. A thouſand heroes half-roſe before him; claiming the war of Teutha.---I came with my ſpear from the hill, and the joy of battle roſe in my breaſt: for the king ſpoke to Oſſian in the midſt of the people.

SON of my ſtrength, he ſaid, take the ſpear of Fingal; go to Teutha's mighty ſtream, and ſave the car-borne Colmar.---Let thy fame return before thee like a pleaſant gale; that my

foul

foul may rejoice over my fon, who renews the renown of our fathers.---Offian ! be thou a ftorm in battle ; but mild when the foes are low!---It was thus my fame arofe, O my fon; and be thou like Selma's chief.---When the haughty come to my halls, my eyes behold them not. But my arm is ftretched forth to the unhappy. My fword defends the weak.

I REJOICED in the words of the king : and took my rattling arms.---Diaran * rofe at my fide, and Dargo † king of fpears.---Three hun-dred

---

* Diaran, father of that Connal who was unfortunately killed by Crimora, his miftrefs.

† Dargo, the fon of Collath, is celebrated in other poems by Offian. He is faid to have been killed by a boar at a hunting party. The lamentation of his miftrefs, or wife, Mingala, over his body, is extant ; but whether it is of Offian's compofition, I cannot determine. It is generally afcribed to him, and has much of his manner ; but fome traditions mention it as an imitation by fome later bard.——As it has fome poetical merit, I have fub-joined it.

THE fpoufe of Dargo came in tears : for Dargo was no more! The heroes figh over Lartho's chief: and what fhall fad Mingala do ? The dark foul vanifhed like morning mift, before the king of fpears : but the generous glowed in his prefence like the morning ftar.

Who was the faireft and moft lovely ? Who but Collath's ftately fon ? Who fat in the midft of the wife, but Dargo of the mighty deeds ?

Thy hand touched the trembling harp : Thy voice was foft as fummer-winds.---Ah me ! what fhall the heroes fay ? for Dargo fell before a boar. Pale is the lovely-cheek ; the look of which

was

A POEM. 311

dred youths followed our fteps: the lovely ftrangers were at my fide. Dunthalmo heard the found of our approach; he gathered the ftrength of Teutha.---He ftood on a hill with his hoft; they were like rocks broken with thunder, when their bent trees are finged and bare, and the ftreams of their chinks have failed.

THE ftream of Teutha rolled, in its pride, before the gloomy foe. I fent a bard to Dunthalmo, to offer the combat on the plain; but he fmiled in the darknefs of his pride.---His unfettled hoft moved on the hill; like the mountain-cloud, when the blaft has entered its womb, and fcatters the curling gloom on every fide.

THEY brought Colmar to Teutha's bank, bound with a thoufand thongs. The chief is

was firm in danger!—Why haft thou failed on our hills, thou fairer than the beams of the fun?

The daughter of Adonfion was lovely in the eyes of the valiant; fhe was lovely in their eyes, but fhe chofe to be the fpoufe of Dargo.

But thou art alone, Mingala! the night is coming with its clouds; where is the bed of thy repofe? Where but in the tomb of Dargo?

Why doft thou lift the ftone, O bard! why doft thou fhut the narrow houfe? Mingala's eyes are heavy, bard! She muft fleep with Dargo.

Laft night I heard the fong of joy in Lartho's lofty hall. But filence now dwells around my bed. Mingala refts with Dargo.

X 4   fad.

fad, but lovely, and his eye is on his friends; for we flood, in our arms, on the oppofite bank of Teutha. Dunthalmo came with his fpear, and pierced the hero's fide: he rolled on the bank in his blood, and we heard his broken fighs.

CALTHON rufhed into the ftream: I bounded forward on my fpear. Teutha's race fell before us. Night came rolling down. Dunthalmo refted on a rock, amidft an aged wood. The rage of his bofom burned againft the car-borne Calthon.---But Calthon ftood in his grief; he mourned the fallen Colmar; Colmar flain in youth, before his fame arofe.

I BADE the fong of woe to rife, to footh the mournful chief; but he ftood beneath a tree, and often threw his fpear on earth.---The humid eye of Colmal rolled near in a fecret tear: fhe forefaw the fall of Dunthalmo, or of Clutha's battling chief.

Now half the night had paffed away. Silence and darknefs were on the field; fleep refted on the eyes of the heroes: Calthon's fettling foul was ftill. His eyes were half-clofed; but the murmur of Teutha had not yet failed in his ear. ——Pale, and fhewing his wounds, the ghoft of Colmar came: he bended his head over the hero, and raifed his feeble voice.

SLEEPS the fon of Rathmor in his might, and his brother low ? Did we not rife to the chace together, and purfue the dark-brown hinds? Colmar was not forgot till he fell ; till death had blafted his youth. I lie pale beneath the rock of Lona. O let Calthon rife ! the morning comes with its beams ; and Dunthalmo will dif-honour the fallen.

HE paffed away in his blaft. The rifing Cal-thon faw the fteps of his departure.---He rufhed in the found of his fteel; and unhappy Colmal rofe. She followed her hero through night, and dragged her fpear behind.---But when Calthon came to Lona's rock, he found his fallen bro-ther---The rage of his bofom rofe, and he rufhed among the foe. The groans of death afcend. They clofe around the chief.---He is bound in the midft, and brought to gloomy Dunthalmo.---The fhout of joy arofe ; and the hills of night replied.---

I STARTED at the found: and took my fa-ther's fpear. Diaran rofe at my fide ; and the youthful ftrength of Dargo. We miffed the chief of Clutha, and our fouls were fad.---I dreaded the departure of my fame ; the pride of my valour rofe.

Sons of Morven, I faid, it is not thus our fa-thers fought. They refted not on the field of

ftrangers,

ſtrangers, when the foe did not fall before them.
——Their ſtrength was like the eagles of heaven; their renown is in the ſong. But our
people fall by degrees, and our fame begins to
depart.——What ſhall the king of Morven ſay,
if Oſſian conquers not at Teutha? Riſe in your
ſteel, ye warriors, and follow the ſound of
Oſſian's courſe. He will not return, but renowned, to the echoing walls of Selma.

MORNING roſe on the blue waters of Teutha;
Colmal ſtood before me in tears. She told of
the chief of Clutha: and thrice the ſpear fell
from her hand. My wrath turned againſt the
ſtranger; for my ſoul trembled for Calthon.

SON of the feeble hand, I ſaid, do Teutha's
warriors fight with tears? The battle is not won
with grief; nor dwells the ſigh in the ſoul of
war.——Go to the deer of Carmun, or the lowing herds of Teutha.---But leave theſe arms,
thou ſon of fear; a warrior may lift them in
battle.——

I TORE the mail from her ſhoulders. Her
ſnowy breaſt appeared. She bent her red face
to the ground.---I looked in ſilence to the
chiefs. The ſpear fell from my hand; and the
ſigh of my boſom roſe.——But when I heard the
name of the maid, my crowding tears deſcended.

I bleſſed

I bleſſed the lovely beam of youth, and bade the battle move.

WHY, ſon of the rock, ſhould Oſſian tell how Teutha's warriors died ? They are now forgot in their land ; and their tombs are not found on the heath,---Years came on with their tempeſts; and the green mounds mouldered away.---Scarce is the grave of Dunthalmo ſeen, or the place where he fell by the ſpear of Oſſian.---Some gray warrior, half blind with age, ſitting by night at the flaming oak of the hall, tells now my ac-tions to his ſons, and the fall of the dark Dun-thalmo. The faces of youth bend ſidelong to-wards his voice; ſurprize and joy burn in their eyes.---

I FOUND the ſon * of Rathmor bound to an oak ; my ſword cut the thongs from his hands. And I gave him the white-boſomed Colmal.--- They dwelt in the halls of Teutha ; and Oſſian returned to Selma.

* Calthon.

L A T H M O N:

L A T H M O N:

A P O E M*.

SELMA, thy halls are filent. There is no
found in the woods of Morven. The wave
tumbles alone on the coaft. The filent beam of
the fun is on the field. The daughters of Morven come forth, like the bow of the fhower;
they look towards green Ullin for the white fails
of the king. He had promifed to return, but
the winds of the north arofe.

WHO pours from the eaftern hill, like a ftream
of darknefs? It is the hoft of Lathmon. He

---

* Lathmon a Britifh prince, taking advantage of Fingal's abfence in Ireland, made a defcent on Morven, and advanced
within fight of Selma the royal palace. Fingal arrived in the
mean time, and Lathmon retreated to a hill, where his army
was furprifed by night, and himfelf taken prifoner by Offian and
Gaul the fon of Morni. This exploit of Gaul and Offian bears
a near refemblance to the beautiful epifode of Nifus and Euryalus
in Virgil's ninth Æneid. The poem opens, with the firft appearance of Fingal on the coaft of Morven, and ends, it may be
fuppofed, about noon the next day. The firft paragraph is in a
lyric meafure, and appears to have been fung, of old, to the
harp, as a prelude to the narrative part of the poem, which is
in heroic verfe.

has

has heard of the abfence of Fingal. He trufts in
the wind of the north. His foul brightens with
joy. Why doft thou come, Lathmon? The
mighty are not in Selma. Why comeft thou
with thy forward fpear? Will the daughters of
Morven fight? But ftop, O mighty ftream, in
thy courfe! Does not Lathmon behold thefe
fails? Why doft thou vanifh, Lathmon, like
the mift of the lake? But the fqually ftorm is
behind thee; Fingal purfues thy fteps!

THE king of Morven ftarted from fleep, as
we rolled on the dark-blue wave. He ftretched
his hand to his fpear, and his heroes rofe
around. We knew that he had feen his fathers,
for they often defcended to his dreams, when the
fword of the foe rofe over the land; and the
battle darkened before us.

WHITHER haft thou fled, O wind, faid the
king of Morven? Doft thou ruftle in the
chambers of the fouth, and purfue the fhower
in other lands? Why doft thou not come to my
fails? to the blue face of my feas? The foe is in
the land of Morven, and the king is abfent.
But let each bind on his mail, and each affume
his fhield. Stretch every fpear over the wave;
let every fword be unfheathed. Lathmon * is

* It is faid, by tradition, that it was the intelligence of
Lathmon's invafion, that occafioned Fingal's return from Ireland; though Offian, more poetically, afcribes the caufe of Fingal's knowledge to his dream.

before

before us with his hoft: he that fled * from Fingal on the plains of Lona. But he returns, like
a collected ftream, and his roar is between our
hills.

Such were the words of Fingal. We rufhed
into Carmona's bay. Offian afcended the hill;
and thrice ftruck his boffy fhield. The rock of
Morven replied; and the bounding rocs came
forth. The foes were troubled in my prefence:
and collected their darkened hoft; for I ftood,
like a cloud on the hill, rejoicing in the arms of
my youth.

Morni † fat beneath a tree, at the roaring
waters of Strumon ‡: his locks of age are gray:
he leans forward on his ftaff; young Gaul is
near the hero, hearing the battles of his youth.
Often did he rife, in the fire of his foul, at the
mighty deeds of Morni.

The aged heard the found of Offian's fhield:
he knew the fign of battle. He ftarted at once

* He alludes to a battle wherein Fingal had defeated Lathmon. The occafion of this firft war, between thofe heroes, is
told by Offian in another poem, which the tranflator has feen.

† Morni was chief of a numerous tribe, in the days of Fingal
and his father Comhal. The laft mentioned hero was killed in
battle againft Morni's tribe; but the valour and conduct of Fingal reduced them, at laft, to obedience. We find the two heroes perfectly reconciled in this poem.

‡ Stru'-moné, *ftream of the hill.* Here the proper name of
a rivulet in the neighbourhood of Selma.

from

from his place. His gray hair parted on his back. He remembers the actions of other years. My fon, he faid to fair-haired Gaul, I hear the found of battle. The king of Morven is returned, the fign of war is heard. Go to the halls of Strumon, and bring his arms to Morni. Bring the arms which my father wore in his age, for my arm begins to fail. Take thou thy armour, O Gaul; and rufh to the firft of thy battles. Let thine arm reach to the renown of thy fathers. Be thy courfe in the field, like the eagle's wing. Why fhouldft thou fear death, my fon! the valiant fall with fame; their fhields turn the dark ftream of danger away, and renown dwells on their gray hairs. Doft thou not fee, O Gaul, how the fteps of my age are honoured? Morni moves forth, and the young meet him, with reverence, and turn their eyes, with filent joy, on his courfe. But I never fled from danger, my fon! my fword lightened through the darknefs of battle. The ftranger melted before me; the mighty were blafted in my prefence.

GAUL brought the arms to Morni: the aged warrior covered himfelf with fteel. He took the fpear in his hand, which was often ftained with the blood of the valiant. He came towards Fingal, his fon attended his fteps. The

8

fon

fon of Comhal rejoiced over the warrior, when he came in the locks of his age.

KING of the roaring Strumon! faid the rifing joy of Fingal; do I behold thee in arms, after thy ftrength has failed? Often has Morni fhone in battles, like the beam of the rifing fun; when he difperfes the ftorms of the hill, and brings peace to the glittering fields. But why didft thou not reft in thine age? Thy renown is in the fong. The people behold thee, and blefs the departure of mighty Morni. Why didft thou not reft in thine age? For the foe will vanifh before Fingal.

SON of Comhal, replied the chief, the ftrength of Morni's arm has failed. I attempt to draw the fword of my youth, but it remains in its place. I throw the fpear, but it falls fhort of the mark; and I feel the weight of my fhield. We decay, like the grafs of the mountain, and our ftrength returns no more. I have a fon, O Fingal, his foul has delighted in the actions of Morni's youth; but his fword has not been lifted againft the foe, neither has his fame begun. I come with him to battle; to direct his arm. His renown will be a fun to my foul, in the dark hour of my departure. O that the name of Morni were forgot among the people!

that

that the heroes would only fay, " Behold the fa-
" ther of Gaul!"

KING of Strumon, Fingal replied, Gaul fhall
lift the fword in battle. But he fhall lift it before
Fingal; my arm fhall defend his youth. But
reft thou in the halls of Selma; and hear of our
renown. Bid the harp be ftrung; and the voice
of the bard arife, that thofe who fall may rejoice
in their fame; and the foul of Morni brighten
with gladnefs.——Offian! thou haft fought in
battles: the blood of ftrangers is on thy fpear :
let thy courfe be with Gaul in the ftrife; but depart not from the fide of Fingal; left the foe
find you alone ; and your fame fail at once.

I SAW * Gaul in his arms, and my foul was
mixed with his : for the fire of the battle was in
his eyes! he looked to the foe with joy. We
fpoke the words of friendfhip in fecret ; and the
lightning of our fwords poured together; for we
drew them behind the wood, and tried the
ftrength of our arms on the empty air.

NIGHT came down on Morven. Fingal fat
at the beam of the oak. Morni fat by his fide
with all his gray waving locks. Their difcourfe

* Offian fpeaks. The contraft between the old and young
heroes is ftrongly marked. The circumftance of the latter's
drawing their fwords is well imagined, and agrees with the impatience of young foldiers, juft entered upon action.

is of other times, and the actions of their fathers.
Three bards, at times, touched the harp; and
Ullin was near with his fong. He fung of the
mighty Comhal; but darknefs gathered * on
Morni's brow. He rolled his red eye on Ullin;
and the fong of the bard ceafed. Fingal obferved the aged hero, and he mildly fpoke.

CHIEF of Strumon, why that darknefs? Let
the days of other years be forgot. Our fathers
contended in battle; but we meet together, at
the feaft. Our fwords are turned on the foes,
and they melt before us on the field. Let the
days of our fathers be forgot, king of mofly
Strumon.

KING of Morven, replied the chief, I remember thy father with joy. He was terrible in
battle; the rage † of the chief was deadly. My
eyes were full of tears, when the king of heroes
fell. The valiant fall, O Fingal, and the feeble

---

* Ullin had chofen ill the fubject of his fong. The *darknef's*
which gathered on Morni's brow, did not proceed from any diflike
he had to Comhal's name, though they were foes, but from his
fear that the fong would awaken Fingal to remembrance of the
feuds which had fubfifted of old between the families. Fingal's
fpeech on this occafion abounds with generofity and good fenfe.

† This expreffion is ambiguous in the original. It either fignifies that Comhal killed many in battle, or that he was impla-
cable in his refentment. The tranflator has endeavoured to preferve the fame ambiguity in the verfion; as it was probably defigned by the poet.

remain

remain on the hills. How many heroes have paffed away, in the days of Morni! And I did not fhun the battle; neither did I fly from the ftrife of the valiant.

Now let the friends of Fingal reft; for the night is around; that they may rife, with ftrength, to battle againft car-borne Lathmon. I hear the found of his hoft, like thunder heard on a diftant heath. Offian! and fair-haired Gaul! ye are fwift in the race. Obferve the foes of Fingal from that woody hill. But approach them not, your fathers are not near to fhield you. Let not your fame fall at once. The valour of youth may fail.

We heard the words of the chief with joy, and moved in the clang of our arms. Our fteps are on the woody hill. Heaven burns with all its ftars. The meteors of death fly over the field. The diftant noife of the foe reached our ears. It was then Gaul fpoke, in his valour; his hand half-unfheathed the fword.

Son of Fingal, he faid, why burns the foul of Gaul? My heart beats high. My fteps are difordered; and my hand trembles on my fword. When I look towards the foe, my foul lightens before me, and I fee their fleeping hoft. Tremble thus the fouls of the valiant in battles of the fpear?——How would the foul of Morni

rife

rife if we fhould rufh on the foe! Our renown would grow in the fong; and our fteps be ftately in the eyes of the brave.

Son of Morni, I replied, my foul delights in battle. I delight to fhine in battle alone, and to give my name to the bards. But what if the foe fhould prevail; fhall I behold the eyes of the king? They are terrible in his difpleafure, and like the flames of death.---But I will not behold them in his wrath. Offian fhall prevail or fall. But fhall the fame of the vanquifhed rife?--- They pafs away like a fhadow. But the fame of Offian fhall rife. His deeds fhall be like his fathers. Let us rufh in our arms; fon of Morni, let us rufh to battle. Gaul! if thou fhalt return, go to Selma's lofty wall. Tell to Evirallin * that I fell with fame; carry this fword to Branno's daughter. Let her give it to Ofcar, when the years of his youth fhall arife.

Son of Fingal, Gaul replied with a figh; fhall I return after Offian is low!---What would my father fay, and Fingal king of men? The feeble would turn their eyes and fay, " Behold the " mighty Gaul who left his friend in his blood!"

* Offian had married her a little time before. The ftory of his courtfhip of this lady is introduced, as an epifode, in the fourth book of Fingal.

Ye

Ye fhall not behold me, ye feeble, but in the midft of my renown. Offian! I have heard from my father the mighty deeds of heroes; their mighty deeds when alone; for the foul in-creafes in danger.

Son of Morni, I replied and ftrode before him on the heath, our fathers fhall praife our valour, when they mourn our fall. A beam of glad-nefs fhall rife on their fouls, when their eyes are full of tears. They will fay, " Our fons have " not fallen like the grafs of the field, for they " fpread death around them."——But why fhould we think of the narrow houfe? The fword defends the valiant. But death purfues the flight of the feeble; and their renown is not heard.

We rufhed forward through night; and came to the roar of a ftream which bent its blue courfe round the foe, through trees that echoed to its noife; we came to the bank of the ftream, and faw the fleeping hoft. Their fires were de-cayed on the plain; and the lonely fteps of their fcouts were diftant far. I ftretched my fpear before me to fupport my fteps over the ftream. But Gaul took my hand, and fpoke the words of the valiant.

Shall

SHALL * the fon of Fingal rufh on a fleeping foe? Shall he come like a blaft by night when it overturns.the young trees in fecret? Fingal did not thus receive his fame, nor dwells renown on the gray hairs of Morni, for actions like thefe. Strike, Offian, ftrike the fhield of battle, and let their thoufands rife. Let them meet Gaul in his firft battle, that he may try the ftrength of his arm.

My foul rejoiced over the warrior, and my burfting tears defcended. And the foe fhall meet Gaul, I faid: the fame of Morni's fon fhall arife. But rufh not too far, my hero: let the gleam of thy fteel be near to Offian. Let our hands join in flaughter.——Gaul! doft thou not behold that rock? Its gray fide dimly gleams to the ftars. If the foe fhall prevail, let our back be towards the rock. Then fhall they fear to approach our fpears; for death is in our hands.

I STRUCK thrice my echoing fhield. The ftarting foe arofe. We rufhed on in the found

* This propofal of Gaul is much more noble, and more agreeable to true heroifm, than the behaviour of Ulyffes and Diomed in the Iliad, or that of Nifus and Euryalus in the Æneid. What his valour and generofity fuggefted became the foundation of his fuccefs. For the enemy being difmayed with the found of Offian's fhield, which was the common fignal of battle, thought that Fingal's whole army came to attack them; fo that they fly in reality from an army, not from two heroes; which reconciles the ftory to probability.

of

of our arms. Their crowded steps fly over the heath; for they thought that the mighty Fingal came; and the strength of their arms withered away. The sound of their flight was like that of flame, when it rushes through the blasted groves.

It was then the spear of Gaul flew in its strength: it was then his sword arose. Cremor fell; and mighty Leth. Dunthormo struggled in his blood. The steel rushed through Crotha's side, as bent, he rose on his spear; the black stream poured from the wound, and hissed on the half-extinguished oak. Cathmin saw the steps of the hero behind him, and ascended a blasted tree; but the spear pierced him from behind. Shrieking, panting, he fell; moss and withered branches pursue his fall, and strew the blue arms of Gaul.

Such were thy deeds, son of Morni, in the first of thy battles. Nor slept the sword by thy side, thou last of Fingal's race! Ossian rushed forward in his strength, and the people fell before him; as the grass by the staff of the boy, when he whistles along the field, and the gray beard of the thistle falls. But careless the youth moves on; his steps are towards the desart.

Gray morning rose around us, the winding streams are bright along the heath. The foe ga-

thered on a hill ; and the rage of Lathmon rofe.
He bent the red eye of his wrath : he is filent in
his rifing grief. He often ftruck his boffy
fhield ; and his fteps are unequal on the heath.
I faw the diftant darknefs of the hero, and I
fpoke to Morni's fon.

Car-borne * chief of Strumon, doft thou
behold the foe ? They gather on the hill in their
wrath. Let our fteps be towards the king †.
He fhall rife in his ftrength, and the hoft of
Lathmon vanifh. Our fame is around us, warrior, the eyes of the aged ‡ will rejoice. But
let us fly, fon of Morni, Lathmon defcends the
hill.

Then let our fteps § be flow, replied the
fair-haired Gaul ; left the foe fay, with a fmile,
" Behold the warriors of night, they are, like

* Car-borne is a title of honour beftowed, by Offian, indif-
criminately on every hero ; as every chief, in his time, kept a
chariot or litter by way of ftate.

† Fingal.

‡ Fingal and Morni.

§ The behaviour of Gaul, throughout this poem, is that of a
hero in the moft exalted fenfe. The modefty of Offian, concerning his own actions, is not lefs remarkable than his impartiality
with regard to Gaul, for it is well known that Gaul afterwards
rebelled againft Fingal, which might be fuppofed to have bred
prejudices againft him in the breaft of Offian. But as Gaul,
from an enemy, became Fingal's firmeft friend and greateft hero,
the poet paffes over one flip in his conduct, on account of his
many virtues.

" ghofts,

" ghofts, terrible in darknefs, but they melt
" away before the beam of the eaft." Offian,
take the fhield of Gormar who fell beneath thy
fpear, that the aged heroes may rejoice, when'
they fhall behold the actions of their fons.

Such were our words on the plain, when Sulmath * came to car-borne Lathmon : Sulmath
chief of Dutha at the dark-rolling ftream of
Duvranna †. Why doft thou not rufh, fon of
Nuäth, with a thoufand of thy heroes? Why
doft thou not defcend with thy hoft, before the
warriors fly? Their blue arms are beaming to
the rifing light, and their fteps are before us on
the heath.

Son of the feeble hand, faid Lathmon, fhall
my hoft defcend! They ‡ are but two, fon of
Dutha,

* Suil-mhath, *a man of good eye-fight.*

† Dubh-bhranna, *dark mountain-ftream.* What river went by
this name, in the days of Offian, is not eafily afcertained, at this
diftance of time. A river in Scotland, which falls into the fea
at Banff, ftill retains the name of Duvran. If that is meant, by
Offian, in this paffage, Lathmon muft have been a prince of the
Pictifh nation, or thofe Caledonians who inhabited of old the
eaftern coaft of Scotland.

‡ Offian feldom fails to give his heroes, though enemies, that
generofity of temper which, it appears from his poems, was a
confpicuous part of his own character. Thofe who too much
defpife their enemies do not reflect, that the more they take
from the valour of their foes, the lefs merit they have themfelves
in conquering them. The cuftom of depreciating enemies is not
altogether one of the refinements of modern heroifm. This
railing

Dutha, and fhall a thoufand lift their fteel! Nuäth would mourn, in his hall, for the departure of his fame. His eyes would turn from Lathmon, when the tread of his feet approached. ——Go thou to the heroes, chief of Dutha, for I behold the ftately fteps of Offian. His fame is worthy of my fteel; let him fight with Lathmon.

THE noble Sulmath came. I rejoiced in the words of the king. I raifed the fhield on my arm; and Gaul placed in my hand the fword of Morni. We returned to the murmuring ftream; . Lathmon came in his ftrength. His dark hoft rolled, like the clouds, behind him : but the fon of Nuäth was bright in his fteel.

Son of Fingal, faid the hero, thy fame has grown on our fall. How many lie. there of my people by thy hand, thou king of men! Lift now thy fpear againft Lathmon ; and lay the fon of Nuäth low. Lay him low among his people, or thou thyfelf muft fall. It fhall never be told in my halls that my warriors fell in my prefence ; that they fell in the prefence of Lathmon when

railing difpofition is one of the capital faults in Homer's characters, which, by the bye, cannot be imputed to the poet, who kept to the manners of the times of which he wrote. Milton has followed Homer in this refpect ; but railing is lefs fhocking in infernal fpirits, who are the objects of horror, than in heroes, who are fet up as patterns of imitation.

his

his fword refted by his fide: the blue eyes of Cutha * would roll in tears, and her fteps be lonely in the vales of Dunlathmon.

NEITHER fhall it be told, I replied, that the fon of Fingal fled. Were his fteps covered with darknefs, yet would not Offian fly; his foul would meet him and fay, " Does the bard of " Selma fear the foe?" No: he does not fear the foe. His joy is in the midft of battle.

LATHMON came on with his fpear, and pierced the fhield of Offian. I felt the cold fteel at my fide; and drew the fword of Morni: I cut the fpear in twain; the bright point fell glittering on the ground. The fon of Nuäth burnt in his wrath, and lifted high his founding fhield. His dark eyes rolled above it, as bending forward, it fhone like a gate of brafs. But Offian's fpear pierced the brightnefs of its boffes, and funk in a tree that rofe behind. The fhield hung on the quivering lance! but Lathmon ftill advanced. Gaul forefaw the fall of the chief, and ftretched his buckler before my fword; when it defcended, in a ftream of light over the king of Dunlathmon.

LATHMON beheld the fon of Morni, and the tear ftarted from his eye. He threw the fword

---

* Cutha appears to have been Lathmon's wife or miftrefs.

of

of his fathers on the ground, and fpoke the
words of the valiant. Why fhould Lathmon
fight againft the firft of mortal men ? Your fouls
are beams from heaven ; your fwords the flames
of death. Who can equal the renown of the
heroes, whofe actions are fo great in youth! O
that ye were in the halls of Nuäth, in the green
dwelling of Lathmon ! then would my father
fay, that his fon did not yield to the feeble.---
But who comes, a mighty ftream, along the
echoing heath ? the little hills are troubled before
him, and a thoufand fpirits are on the beams of
his fteel; the fpirits * of thofe who are to fall by
the arm of the king of refounding Morven.---
Happy art thou, O Fingal, thy fons fhall fight
thy battles ; they go forth before thee ; and they
return with the fteps of renown.

Fingal came, in his mildnefs, rejoicing in
fecret over the actions of his fon. Morni's face
brightened with gladnefs, and his aged eyes
looked faintly through the tears of joy. We
came to the halls of Selma, and fat round the
feaft of fhells. The maids of the fong came into
our prefence, and the mildly blufhing Evirallin.
Her dark hair fpread on her neck of fnow, her

---

* It was thought, in Offian's time, that each perfon had his
attending fpirit. The traditions concerning this opinion are dark
and unfatisfactory.

eye

eye rolled in fecret on Offian; fhe touched the harp of mufic, and we bleffed the daughter of Branno.

FINGAL rofe in his place, and fpoke to Dunlathmon's battling king. The fword of Trenmor trembled by his fide, as he lifted up his mighty arm. Son of Nuäth, he faid, why doft thou fearch for fame in Morven? We are not of the race of the feeble; nor do our fwords gleam over the weak. When did we come to Dunlathmon, with the found of war? Fingal does not delight in battle, though his arm is ftrong. My renown grows on the fall of the haughty. The lightning of my fteel pours on the proud in arms. The battle comes; and the tombs of the valiant rife; the tombs of my people rife, O my fathers! and I at laft muft remain alone. But I will remain renowned, and the departure of my foul fhall be one ftream of light. Lathmon! retire to thy place. Turn thy battles to other lands. The race of Morven are renowned, and their foes are the fons of the unhappy.

O I T H Ó N A:

A P O E M *.

D ARKNESS dwells around Dunlathmon,
though the moon shews half her face on
the hill. The daughter of night turns her eyes
away; for she beholds the grief that is coming.---
The

---

* Gaul, the son of Morni, attended Lathmon into his own
country, after his being defeated in Morven, as related in the
preceding poem. He was kindly entertained by Nuäth, the father of Lathmon, and fell in love with his daughter Oithóna.
——The lady was no lefs enamoured of Gaul, and a day was
fixed for their marriage. In the mean time Fingal, preparing
for an expedition into the country of the Britons, fent for Gaul.
He obeyed, and went; but not without promifing to Oithóna to
return, if he furvived the war, by a certain day.—Lathmon too
was obliged to attend his father Nuäth in his wars, and Oithóna
was left alone at Dunlathmon, the feat of the family.—Dunrommath, lord of Uthal, fuppofed to be one of the Orkneys,
taking advantage of the abfence of her friends, came and carried
off, by force, Oithóna, who had formerly rejected his love, into
Tromáthon, a defart ifland, where he concealed her in a cave.

Gaul returned on the day appointed; heard of the rape, and
failed to Tromáthon, to revenge himfelf on Dunrommath.
When he landed, he found Oithóna difconfolate, and refolved
not to furvive the lofs of her honour.—She told him the ftory of
her misfortunes, and she fcarce ended, when Dunrommath,
with

The fon of Morni is on the plain; but there is no found in the hall. No long-ftreaming * beam of light comes trembling through the gloom. The voice of Oithóna † is not heard amidft the noife of the ftreams of Duvranna.——

WHITHER art thou gone in thy beauty, dark-haired daughter of Nuäth? Lathmon is in the field of the valiant, but thou didft promife to remain in the hall; thou didft promife to re-main in the hall till the fon of Morni returned. Till he returned from Strumon, to the maid of his love. The tear was on thy cheek at his de-parture: the figh rofe in fecret in thy breaft. But thou doft not come to meet him, with fongs, with the lightly-trembling found of the harp.——

with his followers, appeared at the further end of the ifland. Gaul prepared to attack him, recommending to Oithóna to re-tire, till the battle was over.—She feemingly obeyed; but fhe fecretly armed herfelf, rufhed into the thickeft of the battle, and was mortally wounded.—Gaul purfuing the flying enemy, found her juft expiring on the field: he mourned over her, raifed her tomb, and returned to Morven.——Thus is the ftory handed down by tradition; nor is it given with any material difference in the poem, which opens with Gaul's return to Dunlathmon, after the rape of Oithóna.

* Some gentle taper
——vifit us
With thy long levelled rule of ftreaming light.

MILTON.

† Oi-thóna, *the virgin of the wave.*

SUCH

SUCH were the words of Gaul, when he came to Dunlathmon's towers. The gates were open and dark. The winds were bluftering in the hall. The trees ftrowed the threfhold with leaves; and the murmur of night was abroad. ---Sad and filent, at a rock, the fon of Morni fat : his foul trembled for the maid; but he knew not whither to turn his courfe. The fon * of Leth ftood at a diftance, and heard the winds in his bufhy hair. But he did not raife his voice, for he faw the forrow of Gaul.

SLEEP defcended on the heroes. The vifions of night arofe. Oithóna ftood in a dream, before the eyes of Morni's fon. Her dark hair was loofe and difordered : her lovely eye rolled in tears. Blood ftained her fnowy arm. The robe half hid the wound of her breaft. She ftood over the chief, and her voice was heard.

SLEEPS the fon of Morni, he that was lovely in the eyes of Oithóna? Sleeps Gaul at the diftant rock, and the daughter of Nuäth low? The fea rolls round the dark ifle of Tromáthon; I fit in my tears in the cave. Nor do I fit alone, O Gaul, the dark chief of Cuthal is there. He is

---

* Morlo. the fon of Leth, is one of Fingal's moft famous heroes. He and three other men attended Gaul on his expedition to Tromáthon.

there

there in the rage of his love.---And what can Oithóna do?

A ROUGHER blaft rufhed through the oak. The dream of night departed. Gaul took his afpen fpear; he ftood in the rage of wrath. Often did his eyes turn to the eaft, and accufe the lagging light.---At length the morning came forth. The hero lifted up the fail. The winds came ruftling from the hill; and he bounded on the waves of the deep.---On the third day arofe Tromathon *, like a blue fhield in the midft of the fea. The white wave roared againft its rocks; fad Oithóna fat on the coaft. She looked on the rolling waters, and her tears defcend. ------But when fhe faw Gaul in his arms, fhe ftarted and turned her eyes away. Her lovely cheek is bent and red; her white arm trembles by her fide.---Thrice fhe ftrove to fly from his prefence; but her fteps failed her as fhe went.

---

* ἐφάνη ὄρεα σκιόεντα
Γαίης Φαιήκων,——
——ὡς ὅτε ξίνον ἐν ηεροειδεῖ πόντῳ.

HOM. Od. v. 280.

Then fwell'd to fight Phæacia's dufky coaft,
And woody mountains half in vapours loft;
That lay before him indiftinct and vaft,
Like a broad fhield amid the watry wafte.

Tróm-thón, *heavy or deep-founding wave.*

Z   DAUGHTER

DAUGHTER of Nuäth, faid the hero, why doft thou fly from Gaul? Do my eyes fend forth the flame of death? Or darkens hatred in my foul? Thou art to me the beam of the eaft rifing in a land unknown. But thou covereft thy face with fadnefs, daughter of high Dunlathmon! Is the foe of Oithóna near? My foul burns to meet him in battle. The fword trembles on the fide of Gaul, and longs to glitter in his hand. ——Speak, daughter of Nuäth, doft thou not behold my tears?

CAR-BORNE chief of Strumon, replied the fighing maid, why comeft thou over the dark-blue wave to Nuäth's mournful daughter? Why did I not pafs away in fecret, like the flower-of the rock, that lifts its fair head unfeen, and throws its withered leaves on the blaft? Why didft thou come, O Gaul, to hear my departing figh? I pafs away in my youth; and my name fhall not be heard. Or it will be heard with forrow, and the tears of Nuäth will fall. Thou wilt be fad, fon of Morni, for the fallen fame of Oithóna. But fhe fhall fleep in the narrow tomb, far from the voice of the mourner.——Why didft thou come, chief of Strumon, to the fea-beat rocks of Tromathon.

I CAME to meet thy foes, daughter of car-borne Nuäth! the death of Cuthal's chief dar-

kens

kens before me; or Morni's fon fhall fall.---
Oithóna! when Gaul is low, raife my tomb on
that oozy rock; and when the dark-bounding
fhip fhall pafs, call the fons of the fea; call
them, and give this fword, that they may carry
it to Morni's hall; that the grey-haired hero
may ceafe to look towards the defart for the return of his fon.

AND fhall the daughter of Nuäth live, fhe replied with a burfting figh? Shall I live in Tromáthon, and the fon of Morni low? My heart
is not of that rock; nor my foul carelefs as that
fea, which lifts its blue waves to every wind, and
rolls beneath the ftorm. The blaft which fhall
lay thee low, fhall fpread the branches of Oithóna on earth. We fhall wither together, fon
of car-borne Morni!——The narrow houfe is
pleafant to me, and the gray ftone of the dead:
for never more will I leave thy rocks, fea-furrounded Tromáthon!---Night * came on with
her clouds, after the departure of Lathmon,
when he went to the wars of his fathers, to the
mofs-covered rock of Duthórmoth; night came
on, and I fat in the hall, at the beam of the
oak. The wind was abroad in the trees. I
heard the found of arms. Joy rofe in my face;

* Oithóna relates how fhe was carried away by Dunrommath.

for I thought of thy return. It was the chief of Cuthal, the red-haired ſtrength of Dunrommath. His eyes rolled in fire: the blood of my people was on his ſword. They who defended Oithóna fell by the gloomy chief.——What could I do? My arm was weak; it could not lift the ſpear. He took me in my grief, amidſt my tears he raiſed the ſail. He feared the returning ſtrength of Lathmon, the brother of unhappy Oithóna. ——But behold, he comes with his people! the dark wave is divided before him!---Whither wilt thou turn thy ſteps, ſon of Morni? Many are the warriors of Dunrommath!

MY ſteps never turned from battle, replied the hero, as he unſheathed his ſword; and ſhall I begin to fear, Oithóna, when thy foes are near? Go to thy cave, daughter of Nuäth, till our battle ceaſe. Son of Leth, bring the bows of our fathers; and the ſounding quiver of Morni. Let our three warriors bend the yew. Ourſelves will lift the ſpear. They are an hoſt on the rock; but our ſouls are ſtrong.

THE daughter of Nuäth went to the cave: a troubled joy roſe on her mind, like the red path of the lightning on a ſtormy cloud.---Her ſoul was reſolved, and the tear was dried from her wildly-looking eye.---Dunrommath ſlowly ap-proached; for he ſaw the ſon of Morni. Con-

tempt

tempt contracted his face, a fmile is on his dark-brown cheek; his red eye rolled, half-conceal'd, beneath his fhaggy brows.

WHENCE are the fons of the fea, begun the gloomy chief? Have the winds driven you to the rocks of Tromáthon? Or come you in fearch of the white-handed daughter of Nuäth? The fons of the unhappy, ye feeble men, come to the hand of Dunrommath. His eyes fpares not the weak; and he delights in the blood of ftrangers. Oithóna is a beam of light, and the chief of Cuthal enjoys it in fecret; would thou come on its lovelinefs like a cloud, fon of the feeble hand!---Thou mayft come, but fhalt thou return to the halls of thy fathers?

DOST thou not know me, faid Gaul, red-haired chief of Cuthal? Thy feet were fwift on the heath, in the battle of car-borne Lathmon; when the fword of Morni's fon purfued his hoft, in Morven's woody land. Dunrommath! thy words are mighty, for thy warriors gather behind thee. But do I fear them, fon of pride? I am not of the race of the feeble.

GAUL advanced in his arms; Dunrommath fhrunk behind his people. But the fpear of Gaul pierced the gloomy chief, and his fword lopped off his head, as it bended in death.——— The fon of Morni fhook it thrice by the lock;

the

the warriors of Dunrommath fled. The arrows of Morven purfued them: ten fell on the moffy rocks. The reft lift the founding fail, and bound on the echoing deep.

GAUL advanced towards the cave of Oithóna. He beheld a youth leaning againft a rock. An arrow had pierced his fide; and his eye rolled faintly beneath his helmet.---The foul of Morni's fon is fad, he came and fpoke the words of peace.

CAN the hand of Gaul heal thee, youth of the mournful brow? I have fearched for the herbs of the mountains; I have gathered them on the fecret banks of their ftreams. My hand has clofed the wound of the valiant, and their eyes have bleffed the fon of Morni. Where dwelt thy fathers, warrior? Were they of the fons of the mighty? Sadnefs fhall come, like night, on thy native ftreams; for thou art fallen in thy youth.———

MY fathers, replied the ftranger, were of the fons of the mighty; but they fhall not be fad; for my fame is departed like morning mift. High walls rife on the banks of Duvranna; and fee their moffy towers in the ftream; a rock af-cends behind them with its bending firs. Thou mayft behold it far diftant. There my brother dwells.

dwells. He is renowned in battle: give him this glittering helmet.

THE helmet fell from the hand of Gaul; for it was the wounded Oithóna. She had armed herself in the cave, and came in search of death. Her heavy eyes are half closed; the blood pours from her side.——

SON of Morni, she said, prepare the narrow tomb. Sleep comes, like a cloud, on my soul. The eyes of Oithóna are dim. O had I dwelt at Duvranna, in the bright beam of my fame! then had my years come on with joy; and the virgins would bless my steps. But I fall in youth, son of Morni, and my father shall blush in his hall.——

SHE fell pale on the rock of Tromáthon. The mournful hero raised her tomb.——He came to Morven; but we saw the darkness of his soul. Ossian took the harp in the praise of Oithóna. The brightness of the face of Gaul returned. But his sigh rose, at times, in the midst of his friends, like blasts that shake their unfrequent wings, after the stormy winds are laid.

C R O M A:

A P O E M*.

IT was the voice of my love! few are his
vifits to the dreams of Malvina! Open your
airy halls, ye fathers of mighty Tofcar. Un-
fold the gates of your clouds; the fteps of Mal-

---

* Malvina the daughter of Tofcar is overheard by Offian la-
menting the death of Ofcar her lover. Offian, to divert her
grief, relates his own actions in an expedition which he under-
took, at Fingal's command, to aid Crothar the petty king of
Croma, a country in Ireland, againft Rothmar who invaded his
dominions. The ftory is delivered down thus, in tradition.
Crothar king of Croma being blind with age, and his fon too
young for the field, Rothmar the chief of Tromlo refolved to
avail himfelf of the opportunity offered of annexing the dominions of Crothar to his own. He accordingly marched into the
country fubject to Crothar, but which he held of Aith or Artho,
who was, at the time, fupreme king of Ireland.

Crothar being, on account of his age and blindnefs, unfit for
action, fent for aid to Fingal king of Scotland; who ordered his
fon Offian to the relief of Crothar. But before his arrival Fovar-
gormo, the fon of Crothar, attacking Rothmar, was flain himfelf, and his forces totally defeated. Offian renewed the war;
came to battle, killed Rothmar, and routed his army. Croma
being thus delivered of its enemies, Offian returned to Scotland.

vina's

vina's departure are near. I have heard a voice in my dream. I feel the fluttering of my foul. Why didft thou come, O blaft, from the dark-rolling of the lake? Thy ruftling wing was in the trees, the dream of Malvina departed. But fhe beheld her love, when his robe of mift flew on the wind; the beam of the fun was on his fkirts, they glittered like the gold of the ftranger. It was the voice of my love! few are his vifits to my dreams!

But thou dwelleft in the foul of Malvina, fon of mighty Offian. My fighs arife with the beam of the caft; my tears defcend with the drops of night. I was a lovely tree, in thy prefence, Ofcar, with all my branches round me; but thy death came like a blaft from the defart, and laid my green head low; the fpring returned with its fhowers, but no leaf of mine arofe. The virgins faw me filent in the hall, and they touched the harp of joy. The tear was on the cheek of Malvina: the virgins beheld me in my grief. Why art thou fad, they faid; thou firft of the maids of Lutha? Was he lovely as the beam of the morning, and ftately in thy fight?

Pleasant is thy fong in Offian's ear, daughter of ftreamy Lutha! Thou haft heard the mufic of departed bards in the dream of thy reft,

when

when sleep fell on thine eyes, at the murmur of Moruth *. When thou didst return from the chace, in the day of the sun, thou hast heard the music of the bards, and thy song is lovely. It is lovely, O Malvina, but it melts the soul. There is a joy in grief when peace dwells in the breast of the sad. But sorrow wastes the mournful, O daughter of Toscar, and their days are few. They fall away, like the flower on which the sun looks in his strength after the mildew has passed over it, and its head is heavy with the drops of night. Attend to the tale of Ossian, O maid; he remembers the days of his youth.

THE king commanded; I raised my sails, and rushed into the bay of Croma; into Croma's sounding bay in lovely Innis-fail †. High on the coast arose the towers of Crothar king of spears; Crothar renowned in the battles of his youth; but age dwelt then around the chief. Rothmar raised the sword against the hero; and the wrath of Fingal burned. He sent Ossian to meet Rothmar in battle, for the chief of Croma was the companion of his youth.

I SENT the bard before me with songs; I came into the hall of Crothar. There sat the hero

---

* Mor'-ruth, *great stream.*

† *Innis-fail,* one of the ancient names of Ireland.

amidst

amidft the arms of his fathers, but his eyes had
failed. His gray locks waved around a ftaff, on
which the warrior leaned. He hummed the
fong of other times, when the found of our arms
reached his ears. Crothar rofe, ftretched his
aged hand, and bleffed the fon of Fingal.

OSSIAN! faid the hero, the ftrength of Crothar's arm has failed. O could I lift the fword,
as on the day that Fingal fought at Strutha! He
was the firft of mortal men; but Crothar had
alfo his fame. The king of Morven praifed
me, and he placed on my arm the boffy fhield of
Calthar, whom the hero had flain in war. Doft
thou not behold it on the wall, for Crothar's
eyes have failed? Is thy ftrength, like thy fathers, Offian? let the aged feel thine arm.

I GAVE my arm to the king; he feels it with
his aged hands. The figh rofe in his breaft, and
his tears defcended. Thou art ftrong, my fon,
he faid, but not like the king of Morven. But
who is like that hero among the mighty in war!
Let the feaft of my halls be fpread; and let my
bards raife the fong. Great is he that is within
my walls, fons of echoing Croma!

THE feaft is fpread. The harp is heard; and
joy is in the hall. But it was joy covering a
figh, that darkly dwelt in every breaft. It was
like the faint beam of the moon fpread on a
cloud

cloud in heaven. At length the mufic ceafed, and the aged king of Croma fpoke; he fpoke without a tear, but the figh fwelled in the midft of his voice.

'Son of Fingal! doft thou not behold the darknefs of Crothar's hall of fhells? My foul was not dark at the feaft, when my people lived. I rejoiced in the prefence of ftrangers, when my fon fhone in the hall. But, Offian, he is a beam that is departed, and left no ftreak of light behind. He is fallen, fon of Fingal, in the battles of his father.——Rothmar the chief of graffy Tromlo heard that my eyes had failed; he heard that my arms were fixed in the hall, and the pride of his foul arofe. He came towards Croma; my people fell before him. I took my arms in the hall, but what could fight-lefs Crothar do? My fteps were unequal; my grief was great. I wifhed for the days that were paft. Days! wherein I fought; and conquered in the field of blood. My fon returned from the chace; the fair-haired Fovar-gormo *. He had not lifted his fword in battle, for his arm was young. But the foul of the youth was great; the fire of valour burnt in his eyes. He faw the difordered fteps of his father, and his figh arofe.

* Faobhar-gorm, *the blue point of fteel.*

King of Croma, he faid, is it becaufe thou haft
no fon ; is it for the weaknefs of Fovar-gorma's
arm that thy fighs arife? I begin, my father,
to feel the ftrength of my arm ; I have drawn
the fword of my youth ; and I have bent the
bow. Let me meet this Rothmar, with the
youths of Croma : let me meet him, O my father ; for I feel my burning foul.

AND thou fhalt meet him, I faid, fon of the
fightlefs Crothar ! But let others advance before
thee, that I may hear the tread of thy feet at
thy return ; for my eyes behold thee not, fair-
haired Fovar-gormo !——He went, he met the
foe ; he fell. The foe advances towards Croma.
He who flew my fon is near, with all his pointed
fpears.

IT is not time to fill the fhell, I replied, and
took my fpear. My people faw the fire of my
eyes, and they rofe around. All night we ftrode
along the heath. Gray morning rofe in the eaft.
A green narrow vale appeared before us ; nor
did it want its blue ftream. The dark hoft of
Rothmar are on its banks, with all their glittering arms. We fought along the vale ; they fled ;
Rothmar funk beneath my fword. Day had
not defcended in the weft when I brought his
arms to Crothar. The aged hero felt them with
his hands ; and joy brightened in his foul.

THE

THE people gather to the hall ; the found of
the fhells is heard. Ten harps are ftrung ; five
bards advance, and fing, by turns *, the praife
of

* Thofe extempore compofitions were in great repute among
fucceeding bards. The pieces extant of that kind fhew more of
the good ear, than of the poetical genius of their authors. The
tranflator has only met with one poem of this fort, which he
thinks worthy of being pieferved. It is a thoufand years later
than Offian, but the authors feem to have obferved his manner,
and adopted fome of his exprcffions. The ftory of it is this.
Five bards, paffing the night in the houfe of a chief, who was a
poet himfelf, went feverally to make their obfervations on, and
returned with an extempore defcription of, night. The night
happened to be one in October, as appears from the poem; and
in the north of Scotland, it has all that variety which the bards
afcribe to it, in their defcriptions.

FIRST BARD.

NIGHT is dull and dark. The clouds reft on the hills. No
ftar with green trembling beam ; no moon looks from the
fky. I hear the blaft in the wood; but I hear it diftant far.
The ftream of the valley muimurs ; but its murmur is fullen and
fad. From the tree at the grave of the dead the long-howling
owl is heard. I fee a dim form on the plain !—It is a ghoft !—
it fades—it flies. Some funeral fhall pafs this way : the meteor
marks the path.

The diftant dog is howling from the hut of the hill. The
ftag lies on the mountain mofs : the hind is at his fide. She
hears the wind in his branchy horns. She ftarts, but lies again.

The roe is in the cleft of the rock ; the heath-cocks head is
beneath his wing. No beaft, no bird is abroad, but the owl
and the howling fox. She on a leaflefs tree : he in a cloud on
the hill.

Dark, panting, trembling, fad the traveller has loft his way.
Through fhrubs, through thorns, he goes, along the gurgling
rill.

of Offian; they poured forth their burning fouls, and the harp anfwered to their voice. The joy of Croma was great: for peace returned to the land. The night came on with filence,

rill. He fears the rock and the fen. He fears the ghoft of night. The old tree groans to the blaft; the falling branch refounds. The wind drives the withered burs, clung together, along the grafs. It is the light tread of a ghoft!—He trembles amidft the night.

Dark, dufky, howling is night, cloudy, windy, and full of ghofts! The dead are abroad! my friends, receive me from the night.

SECOND BARD.

The wind is up. The fhower defcends. The fpirit of the mountain fhrieks. Woods fall from high. Windows flap. The growing river roars. The traveller attempts the ford. Hark that fhriek! he dies:—The ftorm drives the horfe from the hill, the goat, the lowing cow. They tremble as drives the fhower, befide the mouldering bank.

The hunter ftarts from fleep, in his lonely hut; he wakes the fire decayed. His wet dogs fmoke around him. He fills the chinks with heath. Loud roar two mountain ftreams which meet befide his booth.

Sad on the fide of a hill the wandering fhepherd fits. The tree refounds above him. The ftream roars down the rock. He waits for the rifing moon to guide him to his home.

Ghofts ride on the ftorm to-night. Sweet is their voice between the fqualls of wind. Their fongs are of other worlds.

The rain is paft. The dry wind blows. Streams roar, and windows flap. Cold drops fall from the roof. I fee the ftarry fky. But the fhower gathers again. The weft is gloomy and dark. Night is ftormy and difmal; receive me, my friends, from night.

THIRD

filence, and the morning returned with joy: No foe came in darknefs, with his glittering fpear. The joy of Croma was great; for the gloomy Rothmar was fallen.

I RAISED

THIRD BARD.

The wind ſtill ſounds between the hills: and whiſtles through the graſs of the rock. The firs fall from their place. The turfy hut is torn. The clouds, divided, fly over the ſky, and ſhew the burning ſtars. The meteor, token of death! flies ſparkling through the gloom. It reſts on the hill. I ſee the withered fern, the dark-browed rock, the fallen oak. Who is that in his ſhrowd beneath the tree, by the ſtream?

The waves dark-tumble on the lake, and laſh its rocky ſides. The boat is brimful in the cove; the oars on the rocking tide. A maid fits ſad beſide the rock, and eyes the rolling ſtream. Her lover promiſed to come. She ſaw his boat, when yet it was light, on the lake. Is this his broken boat on the ſhore? Are theſe his groans on the wind?

Hark! the hail rattles around. The flaky ſnow deſcends. The tops of the hills are white. The ſtormy winds abate. Various is the night and cold; receive me, my friends, from night.

FOURTH BARD.

Night is calm and fair; blue, ſtarry, ſettled is night. The winds, with the clouds, are gone. They ſink behind the hill. The moon is up on the mountain. Trees glitter: ſtreams ſhine on the rock. Bright rolls the ſettled lake; bright the ſtream of the vale.

I ſee the trees overturned; the ſhocks of corn on the plain. The wakeful hind rebuilds the ſhocks, and whiſtles on the diſtant field.

Calm, ſettled, fair is night!—Who comes from the place of the dead? That form with the robe of ſnow; white arms and dark-brown hair! It is the daughter of the chief of the people;

ſhe

I RAISED my voice for Fovar-gormo, when they laid the chief in earth. The aged Crothar was there, but his figh was not heard. He

searched

fhe that lately fell! Come, let us view thee, O maid! thou that haft been the delight of heroes! The blaft drives the phantom away; white, without form, it afcends the hill.

The breezes drive the blue mift, flowly over the narrow vale. It rifes on the hill, and joins its head to heaven.—Night is fettled, calm, blue, ftarry, bright with the moon. Receive me not, my friends, for lovely is the night.

FIFTH BARD.

Night is calm, but dreary. The moon is in a cloud in the weft. Slow moves that pale beam along the fhaded hill. The diftant wave is heard. The torrent murmurs on the rock. The cock is heard from the booth. More than half the night is paft. The houfe-wife, groping in the gloom, rekindles the fettled fire. The hunter thinks that day approaches, and calls his bounding dogs. He afcends the hill and whiftles on his way. A blaft removes the cloud. He fees the ftarry plough of the north. Much of the night is to pafs. He nods by the mofiy rock.

Hark! the whirlwind is in the wood! A low murmur in the vale! It is the mighty army of the dead returning from the air.

The moon refts behind the hill. The beam is ftill on that lofty rock. Long are the fhadows of the trees. Now it is dark over all. Night is dreary, filent, and dark; receive me, my friends, from night.

The CHIEF.

Let clouds reft on the hills: fpirits fly and travellers fear. Let the winds of the woods arife, the founding ftorms defcend. Roar ftreams and windows flap, and green winged meteors fly; rife the pale moon from behind her hills, or inclofe her head in

A a

clouds:

searched for the wound of his son, and found it in his breast. Joy rose in the face of the aged. He came and spoke to Offian.

KING. of spears! he said, my son has not fallen without his fame. The young warrior did not fly ; but met death; as he went forward in his strength. Happy are they who die in youth, when their renown is heard! The feeble will not. behold them in the hall ; or smile at their trembling hands. Their memory shall be honoured in the song; the young tear of the virgin falls. But the aged wither away, by degrees, and the fame of their youth begins to be forgot. They fall in secret; the sigh of their

clouds ; night is alike to me, blue, stormy, or gloomy the sky. Night flies before the beam, when it is poured on the hill. The young day returns from his clouds, but we return no more.

Where are our chiefs of old ? Where our kings of mighty name ? The fields of their battles are silent. Scarce their mossy tombs remain. We shall also be forgot. This lofty house shall fall. Our sons shall not behold the ruins in grass. They shall ask of the aged, " Where stood the walls of our fathers ?"

Raise the song, and strike the harp ; send round the shells of joy. Suspend a hundred tapers on high. Youth and maids begin the dance. Let some gray bard be near me to tell the deeds of other times; of kings renowned in our land, of chiefs we behold no more. Thus let the night pass until morning shall appear in our halls. Then let the bow be at hand, the dogs, the youths of the chace. We shall ascend the hill with day ; and awake the deer.

son

fon is not heard. Joy is around their tomb;
and the ftone of their fame is placed without a
tear. Happy are they who die in youth, when
their renown is around them !

B E R R A T H O N:

A   P O E M*.

BEND thy blue courfe, O ftream, round
the narrow plain of Lutha †. Let the
green woods hang over it from their mountains:
and the fun look on it at noon. The thiftle is
there

of

there on its rock, and shakes its beard to the
wind. The flower hangs its heavy head, waving,
at times, to the gale. Why doft thou awake
me, O gale, it seems to say, I am covered with
the drops of heaven ? The time of my fading is
near, and the blaft that fhall fcatter my leaves.
To-morrow fhall the traveller come, he that faw
me in my beauty fhall come ; his eyes will
fearch the field, but they will not find me ?---
So fhall they fearch in vain, for the voice of

of Berrathon. She was relieved by Offian, who, in company
with Tofcar, landing on Berrathon, defeated the forces of
Uthal, and killed him in a fingle combat. Nina-thoma, whofe
love not all the bad behaviour of Uthal could erafe, hearing of
his death, died of grief. In the mean time Larthmor is reftored,
and Offian and Tofcar returned in triumph to Fingal.

The prefent poem opens with an elegy on the death of Malvina the daughter of Tofcar, and clofes with prefages of the
poet's death. It is almoft altogether in a lyric meafure, and has
that melancholy air which diftinguifhes the remains of the works
of Offian. If ever he compofed any thing of a merry turn it is
long fince loft. The ferious and melancholy make the moft lafting impreffions on the human mind, and bid faireft for being
tranfmitted from generation to generation by tradition. Nor is
it probable that Offian dealt much in chearful compofition. Melancholy is fo much the companion of a great genius, that it is
difficult to feparate the idea of levity from chearfulnefs, which is
fometimes the mark of an amiable difpofition, but never the cha-
racteriftic of elevated parts.

† Lutha, *fwift ftream*. It is impoffible, at this diftance of
time, to afcertain where the fcene here defcribed lies. Tradition
is filent on that head, and there is nothing in the poem from
which a conjecture can be drawn.

Cona, after it has failed in the field. The hunter shall come forth in the morning, and the voice of my harp shall not be heard. " Where " is the son of car-borne Fingal?" The tear will be on his cheek.

THEN come thou, O Malvina *, with all thy music, come ; lay Ossian in the plain of Lutha : let his tomb rise in the lovely field.---Malvina ! where art thou, with thy songs : with the soft found of thy steps?---Son † of Alpin art thou near ? where is the daughter of Tofcar ?

I PASSED, O son of Fingal, by Tar-lutha's mossy walls. The smoke of the hall was ceased : silence was among the trees of the hill. The voice of the chace was over. I saw the daughters of the bow. I asked about Malvina, but they answered not. They turned their faces away : thin darkness covered their beauty. They were like stars, on a rainy hill, by night, each looking faintly through her mist.

PLEASANT ‡ be thy rest, O lovely beam! soon hast thou set on our hills ! The steps of thy

---

* Mal-mhina, *soft or lovely brow*. *Mh* in the Galic language has the same found with *v* in English.

† Tradition has not handed down the name of this son of Alpin. His father was one of Fingal's principal bards, and he appears himself to have had a poetical genius.

‡ Ossian speaks. He calls Malvina a beam of light, and continues the metaphor throughout the paragraph.

departure

departure were ſtately, like the moon ꞏon the
blue, trembling wave. ꞏ But thou haſt left us in
darkneſs, firſt of the maids of Lutha! We ſit, at
the rock, and there is no voice; no light but
the meteor of fire! Soon haſt thou ſet, Malvina,
daughter of generous Toſcar!

But thou riſeſt like the beam of the eaſt,
among the ſpirits of thy friends, where they ſit
in their ſtormy halls, ꞏ the chambers of the thun-
ꞏder.——A cloud hovers over Cona: its blue
curling ſides are high. ꞏ The winds are beneath
it, with their wings; within it is the dwelling *
of Fingal. ꞏ There the hero ſits in darkneſs; his
ꞏairy ſpear is in his hand. His ſhield half covered
with clouds, is like the darkened moon; when
one half ſtill remains in the wave, and the other
looks ſickly on the field.

His friends ſit around the king, on miſt; and
ꞏ hear the ſongs of Ullin: he ſtrikes the half-
ꞏviewleſs harp; and raiſes the feeble voice. ꞏ The
ꞏ leſſer heroes, with a thouſand meteors, light the
airy hall. Malvina riſes, in the midſt; a bluſh

---

* The deſcription of this ideal palace of Fingal is very poetical, and agreeable to the notions of thoſe times, concerning
the ſtate of the deceaſed, who were ſuppoſed to purſue, after
death, the pleaſures and employments of their former life. The
ſituation of Oſſian's heroes, in their ſeparate ſtate, if not entirely
happy, is more agreeable, than the notions of the ancient
Greeks concerning their departed heroes. See Hom. Odyſſ l. 11.

is on her cheek. She beholds the unknown
faces of her fathers, and turns afide her humid
eyes.

ART thou come fo foon, faid Fingal, daughter of generous Tofcar? Sadnefs dwells in the
halls of Lutha. My aged fon * is fad. I hear
the breeze of Cona, that was wont to lift thy
heavy locks. It comes to the hall, but thou art
not there; its voice is mournful among the
arms of thy fathers. Go with thy ruftling wing,
O breeze! and figh on Malvina's tomb. It
rifes yonder beneath the rock, at the blue
ftream of Lutha. The maids † are departed
to their place; and thou alone, O breeze,
mourneft there.

BUT who comes from the dufky weft, fupported on a cloud? A fmile is on his gray, watry face; his locks of mift fly on the wind: he
bends forward on his airy fpear: it is thy father, Malvina! Why fhineft thou, fo foon, on
our clouds, he fays, O lovely light of Lutha!
---But thou wert fad, my daughter, for thy
friends were paffed away. The fons of little

---

* Offian; who had a great friendfhip for Malvina, both on
account of her love for his fon Ofcar, and her attention to his
own poems.

† That is, the young virgins who fung the funeral elegy over
her tomb.

men

men * were in the hall; and none remained of the heroes, but Offian king of fpears.

And doft thou remember Offian, car-borne Tofcar † fon of Conloch? The battles of our youth were many; our fwords went together to the field. They faw us coming like two falling rocks; and the fons of the ftranger fled. There come the warriors of Cona, they faid; their fteps are in the paths of the vanquifhed.

Draw near, fon of Alpin, to the fong of the aged. The actions of other times are in my foul : my memory beams on the days that are paft. On the days of the mighty Tofcar, when our path was in the deep. Draw near, fon of Alpin, to the laft found ‡ of the voice of Cona.

The king of Morven commanded, and I raifed my fails to the wind. Tofcar chief of

---

* Offian, by way of diirefpect, calls thofe, who fucceeded the heroes whofe actions he celebrates, *the fons of little men.* Tradition is entirely filent concerning what paffed in the north, immediately after the death of Fingal and all his heroes ; but it appears from that term of ignominy juft mentioned, that the actions of their fucceffors were not to be compared to thofe of the renowned Fingalians.

† Tofcar was the fon of that Conloch, who was alfo father to the lady, whofe unfortunate death is related in the laft epifode of the fecond book of Fingal.

‡ Offian feems to intimate by this expreffion, that this poem was the laft of his compofition ; fo that there is fome foundation for the traditional title of *the laft hymn of Offian.*

Lutha

Lutha flood at my fide, as I rofe on the dark-
blue wave. Our courfe was to fea-furrounded
Berrathon *, the ifle of many florms. There
dwelt, with his locks of age, the ftately ftrength
of Larthmor. Larthmor who fpread the feaft
of fhells to Comhal's mighty fon, when he went
to Starno's halls, in the days of Agandecca.
But when the chief was old, the pride of his fon
arofe, the pride of fair-haired Uthal, the love of
a thoufand maids. He bound the aged Larthmor, and dwelt in his founding halls.

LONG pined the king in his cave, befide his
rolling fea. Morning did not come to his
dwelling; nor the burning oak by night. But
the wind of ocean was there, and the parting
beam of the moon. The red ftar looked on the
king, when it trembled on the weftern wave.
Snitho came to Selma's hall: Snitho companion
of Larthmor's youth. He told of the king of
Berrathon : the wrath of Fingal rofe. Thrice
he affumed the fpear, refolved to ftretch his
hand to Uthal. But the memory † of his ac-

---

* Barrathón, *a promontory in the midft of waves.* The poet
gives it the epithet of fea-furrounded, to prevent its being taken
for a peninfula in the literal fenfe.

† The meaning of the poet is, that Fingal remembered his
own great actions, and confequently would not fully them by engaging in a petty war againft Uthal, who was fo far his inferior
in valour and power.

tions

tions rofe before the king, and he fent his
fon and Tofcar.   Our joy was great on the rolling fea; and we often half unfheathed our
fwords *.   For never before had we fought alone,
in the battles of the fpear.   Night came down
on the ocean; the winds departed on their wings.
Cold and pale is the moon.   The red ftars lift
their heads.   Our courfe is flow along the coaft
of Berrathon; the white waves tumble on the
rocks.

WHAT voice is that, faid Tofcar, which
comes between the founds of the waves? It is
foft but mournful, like the voice of departed
bards.   But I behold the maid †, fhe fits on the
rock alone.   Her head bends on her arm of
fnow: her dark hair is in the wind.   Hear, fon
of Fingal, her fong, it is fmooth as the gliding
waters of Lavath.---We came to the filent bay,
and heard the maid of night.

* The impatience of young warriors, going on their firft expedition, is well marked by their half-drawing their fwords.
The modefty of Offian, in his narration of a ftory which does
him fo much honour, is remarkable; and his humanity to Nina-
thoma would grace a hero of our own polifhed age.   Though
Offian paffes over his own actions in filence, or flightly mentions them; tradition has done ample juftice to his martial fame,
and perhaps has exaggerated the actions of the poet beyond the
bounds of credibility.

† Nina-thoma the daughter of Torthóma, who had been confined to a defart ifland by her lover Uthal.

How long will ye roll around me, blue-tum-
bling waters of ocean? My dwelling was not
always in caves, nor beneath the whiftling tree.
The feaft was fpread in Torthóma's hall; my
father delighted in my voice. The youths beheld me in the fteps of my lovelinefs, and they
bleffed the dark-haired Nina-thoma. It was
then thou didft come, O Uthal! like the fun of
heaven. The fouls of the virgins are thine, fon
of generous Larthmor! But why doft thou
leave me alone in the midft of roaring waters.
Was my foul dark with thy death? Did my
white hand lift the fword? Why then haft thou
left me alone, king of high Finthormo! *

THE tear ftarted from my eye, when I heard
the voice of the maid. I ftood before her in
my arms, and fpoke the words of peace.——
Lovely dweller of the cave, what figh is in that
breaft? Shall Offian lift his fword in thy prefence, the deftruction of thy foes?---Daughter of
Torthóma, rife, I have heard the words of thy
grief. The race of Morven are around thee,
who never injured the weak. Come to our dark-
bofomed fhip, thou brighter than that fetting
moon. Our courfe is to the rocky Berrathon,

* Finthormo, the palace of Uthal. The names in this epifode
are not of a Celtic original; which makes it probable that Offian
founds his poem on a true ftory.

to the echoing walls of Finthormo.——She came in her beauty, fhe came with all her lovely fteps. Silent joy brightened in her face, as when the fhadows fly from the field of fpring; the blue-ftream is rolling in brightnefs, and the green bufh bends over its courfe.

THE morning rofe with its beams. We came to Rothma's bay. A boar rufhed from the wood; my fpear pierced his fide. I rejoiced over the blood *, and forefaw my growing fame. ——But now the found of Uthal's train came from the high Finthormo; they fpread over the heath to the chace of the boar. Himfelf comes flowly on, in the pride of his ftrength. He lifts two pointed fpears. On his fide is the hero's fword. Three youths carry his polifhed bows: the bounding of five dogs is before him. His warriors move on, at a diftance, admiring the fteps of the king. Stately was the fon of Larthmor! but his foul was dark. Dark as the troubled face of the moon, when it foretels the ftorms.

WE rofe on the heath before the king; he ftopt in the midft of his courfe. His warriors

---

* Offian thought that his killing the boar, on his firft landing in Berrathon, was a good omen of his future fuccefs in that ifland. The prefent highlanders look, with a degree of fuper-ftition, upon the fuccefs of their firft action, after they have en-gaged in any defperate undertaking.

gathered

gathered around, and a gray-haired bard advanced. Whence are the fons of the ftrangers? begun the bard. The children of the unhappy come to Berrathon; to the fword of car-borne Uthal. He fpreads no feaft in his hall: the blood of ftrangers is on his ftreams. If from Selma's walls ye come, from the moffy walls of Fingal, chufe three youths to go to your king to tell of the fall of his people. Perhaps the hero may come and pour his blood on Uthal's fword; fo fhall the fame of Finthormo arife, like the growing tree of the vale.

NEVER will it rife, O bard, I faid in the pride of my wrath. He would fhrink in the prefence of Fingal, whofe eyes are the flames of death. The fon of Comhal comes, and the kings vanifh in his prefence; they are rolled together, like mift, by the breath of his rage. Shall three tell to Fingal, that his people fell? Yes!---they may tell it, bard! but his people fhall fall with fame.

I STOOD in the darknefs of my ftrength; Tofcar drew his fword at my fide. The foe came on like a ftream: the mingled found of death arofe. Man took man, fhield met fhield; fteel mixed its beams with fteel.---Darts hifs through air; fpears ring on mails; and fwords on broken bucklers bound. As the noife of an

aged

aged grove beneath the roaring wind, when a thoufand ghofts break the trees by night, fuch was the din of arms.——But Uthal fell beneath· my fword; and the fons of Berrathon fled.---It was then I faw him in his beauty, and the tear hung in my eye. Thou art fallen.*, young tree, I faid, with all thy beauty round thee. Thou art fallen on thy plains, and the field is bare. The winds come from the defart, and there is no found in thy leaves! Lovely art thou in death, fon of car-borne Larthmor.

NINA-THOMA fat on the fhore, and heard the found of battle. She turned her red eyes on Lethmal the gray-haired bard of Selma, for he had remained on the coaft, with the daughter of Torthóma. Son of the times of old! fhe faid, I. hear the noife of death. Thy friends have met with Uthal and the chief is low! O that I had.

---

*. To mourn over the fall of their enemies was a practice univerfal among Offian's heroes. This is more agreeable to humanity, than the fhameful infulting of the dead, fo common in Homer, and after him, fervilely copied by all his imitators, the humane Virgil not excepted, who have been more fuccefsful in borrowing the imperfections of that great poet than in their imitations of his beauties. Homer, it is probable, gave the manners of the times in which he wrote, not his own fentiments: Offian alfo feems to keep to the fentiment of his heroes. The reverence, which the moft barbarous highlanders have ftill for the remains of the deceafed, feems to have defcended to them from their moft remote anceftors.

remained

remained on the rock, inclofed with the tumbling waves! Then would my foul be fad, but
his death would not reach my ear. Art thou
fallen on thy heath, O fon of high Finthormo!
thou didft leave me on a rock, but my foul was
full of thee. Son of high Finthormo! art thou
fallen on thy heath?

SHE rofe pale in her tears, and faw the bloody
fhield of Uthal; fhe faw it in Offian's hand; her
fteps were diftracted on the heath. She flew;
fhe found him; fhe fell. Her foul came forth
in a figh. Her hair is fpread on his face. My
burfting tears defcend. A tomb arofe on the
unhappy; and my fong was heard.

REST, haplefs children of youth! at the
noife of that mofly ftream. The virgins will fee
your tomb, at the chace, and turn away their
weeping eyes. Your fame will be in the fong;
the voice of the harp will be heard in your
praife. The daughters of Selma fhall hear it;
and your renown fhall be in other lands.---Reft,
children of youth, at the noife of the mofly
ftream.

TWO days we remained on the coaft. The
heroes of Berrathon convened. We brought
Larthmor to his halls; the feaft of fhells was
fpread.---The joy of the aged was great; he
looked to the arms of his fathers; the arms
which

which he left in his hall, when the pride of Uthal arofe.——We were renowned before Larthmor, and he bleffed the chiefs of Morven; but he knew not that his fon was low, the ftately ftrength of Uthal. They had told, that he had retired to the woods, with the tears of grief; they had told it, but he was filent in the tomb of Rothma's heath.

On the fourth day we raifed our fails to the roar of the northern wind. Larthmor came to the coaft, and his bards raifed the fong. The joy of the king was great, he looked to Rothma's gloomy heath; he faw the tomb of his fon; and the memory of Uthal rofe.——Who of my heroes, he faid, lies there: he feems to have been of the kings of fpears? Was he renowned in my halls, before the pride of Uthal rofe?

Ye are filent, ye fons of Berrathon, is the king of heroes low?---My heart melts for thee, O Uthal; though thy hand was againft thy father.——O that I had remained in the cave! that my fon had dwelt in Finthormo!——I might have heard the tread of his feet, when he went to the chace of the boar.---I might have heard his voice on the blaft of my cave. Then would my foul be glad : but now darknefs dwells in my halls.

B b

Such

SUCH were my deeds, fon of Alpin, when the
arm of my youth was ftrong ; fuch were * the
actions of Tofcar, the car-borne fon of Conloch. But Tofcar is on his flying cloud; and I
am alone at Lutha : my voice is like the laft
found of the wind, when it forfakes the woods.
But Offian fhall not be long alone, he fees the
mift that fhall receive his ghoft. He beholds
the mift that fhall form his robe, when he appears on his hills. The fons of little men fhall
behold me, and admire the ftature of the chiefs
of old. They fhall creep to their caves, and
look to the fky with fear ; for my fteps fhall be
in the clouds, and darknefs fhall roll on my
fide.

LEAD, fon of Alpin, lead the aged to his
woods. The winds begin to rife. The dark
wave of the lake refounds. Bends there not a
tree from Mora with its branches bare? It bends,
fon of Alpin, in the ruftling blaft. My harp
hangs on a blafted branch. The found of its
ftrings is mournful.——Does the wind touch
thee, O harp, or is it fome paffing ghoft !——
It is the hand of Malvina! but bring me the
harp, fon of Alpin; another fong fhall rife.
My foul fhall depart in the found; my fathers

* Offian fpeaks.

fhall

fhall hear it in their airy hall.---Their dim faces
fhall hang, with joy, from their clouds; and
their hands receive their fon.

    * The aged oak bends over the ftream. It
fighs with all its mofs. The withered fern
whiftles near, and mixes, as it waves, with
Offian's hair.——Strike the harp and raife the
fong: be near, with all your wings, ye winds.
Bear the mournful found away to Fingal's airy
hall. Bear it to Fingal's hall, that he may hear
the voice of his fon; the voice of him that
praifed the mighty.---The blaft of the north
opens thy gates, O king, and I behold thee fitting on mift, dimly gleaming in all thine arms.
Thy form now is not the terror of the valiant:
but like a watery cloud; when we fee the ftars
behind it with their weeping eyes. Thy fhield is
like the aged moon: thy fword a vapour half-
kindled with fire. Dim and feeble is the chief,
who travelled in brightnefs before.---

    But thy fteps † are on the winds of the de-
fart, and the ftorms darken in thy hand. Thou
takeft

---

* Here begins the lyric piece, with which, tradition fays,
Offian concluded his poems.—It is fet to mufic, and ftill fung in
the north, with a great deal of wild fimplicity, but little variety
of found.

† This magnificent defcription of the power of Fingal over
the winds and ftorms, and the image of his taking the fun, and

hiding

takeft the fun in thy wrath, and hideft him in
thy clouds. The fons of little men are afraid;
and a thoufand fhowers defcend.---

But when thou comeft forth in thy mildnefs;
the gale of the morning is near thy courfe. The
fun laughs in his blue fields; and the gray
ftream winds in its valley.——The bufhes fhake
their green heads in the wind. The roes bound
towards the defart.

But there is a murmur in the heath! the
ftormy winds abate! I hear the voice of Fingal.
Long has it been abfent from mine ear!——
Come, Offian, come away, he fays: Fingal has
received his fame. We paffed away, like flames
that had fhone for a feafon, our departure was
in renown. Though the plains of our battles

hiding him in the clouds, do not correfpond with the preceding
paragraph, where he is reprefented as a feeble ghoft, and no
more the TERROR OF THE VALIANT; but it agrees with the
notion of the times concerning the fouls of the deceafed, who, it
was fuppofed, had the command of the winds and ftorms, but in
combat were not a match for valiant men.

It was the immoderate praife beftowed by the poets on their
departed friends, that gave the firft hint to fuperftition to deify
the deceafed heroes; and thofe new divinities owed all their attributes to the fancy of the bard who fung their elegies.

We do not find, that the praifes of Fingal had this effect upon
his countrymen; but that is to be imputed to the idea they had
of power, which they always connected with bodily ftrength and
perfonal valour, both which were diffolved by death.

are

are dark and filent; our fame is in the four gray
ftones. The voice of Offian has been heard;
and the harp was ftrung in Selma. --- Come
Offian, come away, he fays, and fly with thy
fathers on clouds.

AND come I will, thou king of men! the
life of Offian fails. I begin to vanifh on Cona;
and my fteps are not feen in Selma. Befide the
ftone of Mora I fhall fall afleep. The winds
whiftling in my grey hair fhall not waken me.
——Depart on thy wings, O wind: thou canft
not difturb the reft of the bard. The night is
long, but his eyes are heavy; depart, thou ruftling blaft.

BUT why art thou fad, fon of Fingal? Why
grows the cloud of thy foul? The chiefs of other
times are departed; they have gone without
their fame. The fons of future years fhall pafs
away; and another race arife. The people are
like the waves of ocean: like the leaves * of
woody

---

* The fame thought may be found almoft in the fame words,
in Homer, vi. 46.

Οἵη περφύλλων γενεὴ, τοιήδε καὶ ἀνδρῶν.
Φύλλα ταμίν τ᾽ ἄνεμος χαμάδις χέει, ἄλλα δὲ δ᾽ ὕγη
Τηλεθόωσα φύει ἔαρος δ᾽ ἐπιγίγνεται ὥρη.

Mr. Pope falls fhort of his original; in particular he has
omitted altogether the beautiful image of the wind ftrewing the
withered leaves on the ground.

woody Morven, they pafs away in the ruftling
blaft, and other leaves lift their green heads.---
D I D thy beauty laft, O Ryno *? Stood the
ftrength of car-borne Ofcar? Fingal himfelf
paffed

> Like leaves on trees the race of men are found,
> Now green in youth, now with'ring on the ground;
> Another race the following fpring fupplies;
> They fall fucceffive, and fucceffive rife.
>
> POPE.

* Ryno, the fon of Fingal, who was killed in Ireland, in the
war againft Swaran, [Fing. b. 5.] was remarkable for the beauty
of his perfon, his fwiftnefs and great exploits. Minvane, the
daughter of Morni, and fifter to Gaul fo often mentioned in
Offian's compofitions, was in love with Ryno.—Her lamentation
over her lover is introduced as an epifode in one of Offian's
great poems. The lamentation is the only part of the poem
now extant, and as it has fome poetical merit, I have fubjoined
it to this note. The poet reprefents Minvane as feeing, from
one of the rocks of Morven, the fleet of Fingal returning from
Ireland.

S H E blufhing fad, from Morven's rocks, bends over the
darkly-rolling fea. She faw the youths in all their arms.—
Where, Ryno, where art thou?

Our dark looks told that he was low!—That pale the hero
flew on clouds! That in the grafs of Morven's hills, his feeble
voice was heard in wind!

And is the fon of Fingal fallen, on Ullin's moffy plains?
Strong was the arm that conquered him!—Ah me! I am alone.

Alone I will not be, ye winds! that lift my dark-brown hair.
My fighs will not long mix with your ftream; for I muft fleep
with Ryno.

I fee thee not with beauty's fteps returning from the chace.—
The night is round Minvane's love; and filence dwells with Ryno.

9   Where

paſſed away ; and the halls of his fathers forgot his ſteps.——And ſhalt thou remain, aged bard! when the mighty have failed?——But my fame ſhall remain, and grow like the oak of Morven; which lifts its broad head to the ſtorm, and re-joices in the courſe of the wind.

Where are thy dogs, and where thy bow? Thy ſhield that was ſo ſtrong? Thy ſword like heaven's deſcending fire? The bloody ſpear of Ryno.

I ſee them mixed in thy ſhip; I ſee them ſtained with blood-—No arms are in thy narrow hall, O darkly-dwelling Ryno!

When will the morning come, and ſay, ariſe, thou king of ſpears! ariſe, the hunters are abroad. The hinds are near thee, Ryno!

Away, thou fair-haired morning, away! the ſlumbering king hears thee not! The hinds bound over his narrow tomb; for death dwells round-young Ryno.

But I will tread ſoftly, my king! and ſteal to the bed of thy repoſe. Minvane will lie in ſilence, near her ſlumbering Ryno.

The maids ſhall ſeek me; but they ſhall not find me : they ſhall follow my departure with ſongs. But I will not hear you, O maids : I ſleep with fair-haired Ryno.

F I N I S.

Advertifement.

SINCE the printing of the fecond Edition, Doctor
Warner publifhed a pamphlet, entitled, *Remarks on
the Hiftory of Fingal and other Poems of Offian.* The
Doctor, it appears, is compiling a general hiftory of
Ireland, and is of opinion that Offian, and the heroes he
celebrates, were natives of that country. As he has advanced no argument to fupport fo fingular an opinion, I fhould
have paffed over his pamphlet in filence, had he not too
precipitately accufed me of a falfe quotation from O'Flaherty. I had faid, in a note, on one of the leffer poems
of Offian, that *Fingal is celebrated by the Irifh hiftorians, for
his wifdom in making laws, his poetical genius, and his foreknowledge of events, and that O'Flaherty goes fo far as to fay,
that Fingal's laws were extant, when he (O'Flaherty) wrote
his Ogygia.* The Doctor denies that there is any fuch
thing in O'Flaherty ; and modeftly quotes a paffage from
the fame Author, which he fuppofes, I have mifrepre-
fented. I fhall here give the whole paragraph, and the
world will judge whether the Doctor has not been too
hafty in his affertions. *Finnius ex Morniâ filia Thaddæi,
filius Cuballi, jurifprudentia, fuper quâ fcripta ejus hac-
tenus extant, carminibus patriis, & ut quidam ferunt pro-
phetiis celeberrimus, qui ob egregia fua, & militiæ fuæ, faci-
nora uberrimam vulgo, & poetis comminifcendi materiem re-
linquens, a nulla ætate reticebitur.* Ogyg. p. 338.

As the Doctor founds his claim of Offian and his heroes,
on the authority of fome obfcure paffages in Keating and
O'Flaherty, what he fays on the fubject ftands felf-confuted.
Thefe writers neither meet with, nor deferve credit. Credu-
lous and partial, they have altogether difgraced the antiquities they meant to eftablifh. Without producing records, or even following the ancient traditions of their
country, they formed an ideal fyftem of antiquity, from
legends

ADVERTISEMENT.

legends of modern invention. Sir James Ware, who was
indefatigable in his refearches, after the monuments of the
Irifh hiftory, and had collected all the real, and pretendedly
ancient manufcripts, concerning the antiquity of his nation,
rejects as mere fiction and romance, all that is faid concerning the times before Saint Patrick, and the reign of
Leogaire, in the fifth century. I fhall tranfcribe the paffage, for the benefit of thofe who are compiling the hiftory
of Ireland from the *earlieft ages*, and at the fame time,
caution them, not to look upon the antiquities of that country, through the falfe mediums of Keating and O'Flaherty,
Per exiguam fupereffe notitiam rerum in Hybernia geftarum
ante exortam ibi evangelii auroram liquido conftat. Neque
me latet a viris nonnullis doctis plæraque quæ de antiquoribus
illis temporibus ante S. Patricii in Hyberniam adventum tra-
duntur, tanquam figmenta effe explofa. Notandum quidem de-
fcriptiones fere omnium quæ de illis temporibus (antiquioribus
dico) extant, opera effe pofteriorum feculorum.
Waræus de antiq. Præf. p. 1.

I muft obferve that the Doctor's claiming Offian's
poems (p. 8.) *in forma pauperis*, not only invalidates his
caufe, but is alfo no very genteel compliment to the Irifh
nation. I am far from being of his opinion, that that nation can produce no monument of genius, but the works of
Offian, fhould thefe be tacitly ceded to them. On the
contrary, I am convinced that Ireland has produced men
of great and diftinguifhed abilities, which, notwithftanding
the Doctor's prefent opinion, I hope, will appear from his
own hiftory, even though he, confeffedly, does not under-
ftand the language, or ancient records of that country.

www.ingramcontent.com/pod-product-compliance
Lightning Source LLC
Chambersburg PA
CBHW032338280326
41935CB00008B/367